CHRISTIANS
AND MUSLIMS

CHRISTIANS AND MUSLIMS

From double standards to mutual understanding

Hugh Goddard

Lecturer in Islamic Theology
University of Nottingham

CURZON PRESS

First published in 1995
by Curzon Press
St John's Studios, Church Road, Richmond
Surrey, TW9 2QA

Typeset in Times by LaserScript, Mitcham, Surrey
Printed in Great Britain by
TJ Press (Padstow) Ltd, Padstow, Cornwall

British Library Cataloguing in Publication Data
A catalogue record for this book is available from the British Library

Library of Congress in Publication Data
A catalog record for this book has been requested

ISBN 0–7007–0364–0 (Pbk)
ISBN 0–7007–0363–2 (Hbk)

To
Bethany
[whose coming made a big difference]

CONTENTS

Preface and acknowledgements ix
Abbreviations and technicalities xi

Introduction 1
The problem 1
A possible solution: the approach which will be adopted 9

1 Origins 17
Introduction 17
Christian origins 17
The establishment of the Muslim community 24
Some similarities 27
Conclusion 29

2 Scriptures 33
Introduction 33
Contents and form 33
Compilation and editing 36
Later developments in the understanding of "scripture" 40
Conclusion 43

3 The development of religious thought 49
Introduction 49
Early Christian thought a) Internal 49
b) External 54
Early Muslim thought a) Internal 56
b) External 60
Conclusion 62

4 Law and ethics 67
Introduction 67
Islamic law 67
Christian ethics 71

A case-study: Christian and Muslim thinking on the position of women in society 74
Conclusion 78

5 Worship and spirituality 83
Introduction 83
Christian worship 83
Muslim worship 87
Christian and Muslim spirituality a) Mysticism 90
b) Sacrifice 92
c) Letters from prison 95
Conclusion 98

6 Unity and diversity 103
Introduction 103
The Islamic community 103
The Christian community 109
Ecumenism 117
Some similarities . . . .? 119
Conclusion 120

7 Spread and history 125
Introduction 125
The spread of Islam in history 126
The spread of Christianity in history 131
The treatment of subject peoples and minorities 139
Conclusion 142

8 Modern developments 147
Introduction 147
The phenomenon of modernity 147
One reaction - "fundamentalism" 154
Another reaction - liberalism 159
Tolerance and dissent 161
Conclusion 163

Conclusion 167
Introduction 167
Conversion between the two traditions 167
How to picture the relationship between the two traditions 169

Bibliography 177
Index 185

PREFACE AND ACKNOWLEDGEMENTS

I am grateful to a great many different people for the stimulus and encouragement to undertake a project such as this. In particular I would like to mention colleagues and friends in the following institutions, in all of which earlier drafts and outlines of this book have been presented and commented on: the Department of Theology in the University of Nottingham, the Centre for the Study of Islam and Christian-Muslim relations in Selly Oak in Birmingham, the 1993 conference of the British Association for the Study of Religion, held in Newcastle-upon-Tyne, the Department of Religious Studies in the University of Ibadan, Nigeria, and the International Islamic University in Kuala Lumpur, Malaysia. I am also grateful to my editors at Curzon Press, not least for their patience and forbearance when a rather dramatic change to my family circumstances resulted in some delay in the submission of the script. I alone, however, am responsible for any errors remaining in the text.

ABBREVIATIONS AND TECHNICALITIES

Biblical quotations

Quotations from the Bible have generally been taken from the *Common Bible*, an ecumenical edition of the texts originally prepared by the Division of Christian Education of the National Council of the Churches of Christ in the USA. This translation is based upon the Revised Standard Version, and is widely-used by English-speaking members of all Christian churches, Protestant, Roman Catholic and Orthodox.

Qur'ānic quotations

These are usually taken from M.M. Pickthall *The meaning of the glorious Koran*, published in many different editions. I have used the undated edition published as a Mentor paperback.

Dates

In giving the dates of events prior to the establishment of the Muslim community, I have used the system of BCE (before common era) and CE (common era), rather than the more traditional (and confessionally-based) BC and AD. For events subsequent to the establishment of the Muslim community I have given two dates, the first CE and the second AH (literally Anno Hegirae), which commences with Muḥammad's Hijra (migration) from Mecca to Medina in 622CE.

Transliteration of Arabic terms

I have generally used the system of the Encyclopaedia of Islam (2nd edition, Brill, Leiden, 1960ff.), with two alterations which are widely-used in the English-speaking world, namely q for the Arabic letter qāf and j for the Arabic letter jīm.

INTRODUCTION

The problem

In the world of today Christians and Muslims together make up something between a third and a half of the world's population of six billion (six thousand million) people. So-called global statistics are never much more than estimates, but serious attempts to calculate the figures generally result in a figure of between eight hundred million and one thousand two hundred million for the Muslim community and a figure of between one thousand two hundred million and one thousand eight hundred million for the Christian community.

The level of mutual understanding between these two communities, however, is often very low; indeed it could be said that mutual ignorance is far more widespread than mutual understanding. For example, a British-based Muslim who was born and educated in South Asia told the story of his Christian (Jesuit) school teacher who surprised him one day by asking him why Muslims worshipped pigs. It has to be said that an absolutely basic understanding of Islam should be enough to make it clear that, whatever else Muslims do, they certainly do not worship pigs, since Islam is an insistently monotheistic faith. Further conversation between teacher and pupil revealed that what lay behind the former's question was this: he had observed that in South Asian society members of the Hindu community do not eat beef, and he had gathered that the reason for this was that cows were considered to be in some sense sacred animals and so their meat was not to be eaten. He had also observed that members of the Muslim community did not eat pork, and he simply assumed that what lay behind this was a similar belief, that pigs were considered sacred and worshipped. The question therefore did have a certain logic to it, but it cannot be denied that it was based on ignorance.[1]

A kind of mirror-image of this ignorance is the widespread conviction among Muslims that Christians worship three gods. It has to be admitted that this view is of a rather different order from the supposition that Muslims worship pigs, since it is a view which is at least suggested in the Muslim scripture, the Qur'ān, which in a number of places (for example Chapter Four, verse 171 and Chapter Five, verses 71 and 72) seems to accuse Christians of believing in three deities, but it is a view which the overwhelming majority of Christians utterly reject, and so as a comment on what Christians actually believe, it has to be said that this view is based on ignorance.

Mutual ignorance, then, is one obstacle in the way of mutual understanding between Christians and Muslims. There is also, however, a more subtle and a difficult problem which needs to be confronted, for in the long, often acrimonious history of relationships between Christians and Muslims, one of the major problems has been, and still is, the application of what in almost any other walk of life would be called double standards. Christians and Muslims, in other words, each apply one set of standards or criteria to their own faith and a completely different set of standards to the faith of the other.

It has to be said that this is not a new perception; it was Karl Marx who first drew attention to theologians who insisted that their own faith was from God while insisting that the faith of everyone else was a human construct, in his *The Poverty of Philosophy* (1847).[2] But the consequences of this attitude are perhaps particularly dangerous in the twentieth/fourteenth century, when Christians and Muslims find themselves living in close proximity to each other, and therefore needing, for better for worse, to co-exist rather more peaceably than may often have been the case in the past.

Let me therefore give one or two examples, at different levels, of how double standards are applied by members of the two communities. Firstly there is the case of those evangelical Christians in Britain who protest vociferously about the missionary activities of Muslim organizations in the West; "there should be a law against it", the cry goes up. Yet these same evangelical Christians are those who are the keenest supporters of Christian missionary activities, sometimes of an extremely insensitive kind, in Islamic societies, and who see any Muslim opposition to these Christian missionary activities as proof of Islam's innate hostility not only to Christianity but also to any idea of religious freedom or tolerance! The link between these two views is obviously not clear to those who hold it.

Secondly, among Muslims, there are often vehement protests against the support, both in finance and in other ways, which is given to, for example, the ancient Christian churches of the Middle East, by Christians in the West. The protest goes up that this is external interference, even a modern kind of religious imperialism. It has to be said, of course, that there is a considerable element of truth in the charge with reference to, for example, nineteenth/thirteenth century history, for in that period the various Christian churches of the Middle East were indeed used by the rival powers of Europe as a way of extending their influence; thus the French developed links with the Catholics, the Russians with the Orthodox, and the British with whoever was left, since the Protestants were relatively few in number, and this therefore meant other minority communities such as the Jews, and the Druzes in the Lebanon. There is therefore some justification for Muslim resentment of these external influences. But if we move into the twentieth/fourteenth century and look at the situation of the Muslim community in, for example, Britain, we find that a remarkably similar process seems to be developing in reverse, namely that the various rival powers in Islamic societies are all seeking to further their influence among Muslim minorities such as those in Britain and Europe. Thus considerable efforts are made, through the provision of personnel and finance, to ensure that it is Sa'udi, or Iranian, or Libyan, or Egyptian, or Pakistani, or Iraqi or whatever interpretations of Islam that gain the upper hand. But most Muslims in Britain see any resentment of this process not as a mirror image of their own resentment of earlier foreign influence in Islamic societies but rather as a clear demonstration of British prejudice and discrimination against Muslims.[3]

In the aftermath of the Gulf Crisis, a number of incidents serve as mirror-images to each other in demonstrating a more contemporary aspect to these resentments. At the time of the Suez Campaign in 1956/1376, when Britain, France and Israel joined together in using military force in order to recover control of the Suez Canal from President Gamal 'Abd al-Nāṣir of Egypt, among those who were unwitting victims of the campaign were a considerable number of Egyptian Copts, whose churches were burnt down by furious Muslims; and now, in 1990/1411, we have reports of attempts by right-wing elements in British society to burn down the Saddam Hussain mosque in the West Midlands.[4] Incidents such as these, regrettable as they are, do at least perhaps serve to show the urgency of the task of clarifying the many influences at work on relationships between Christians and Muslims, and of high-lighting double standards where they are at work; and, of course, they also show clearly how the migrations of large numbers of people since the end of World War II has brought about a kind of reciprocity between the treatment of Christian minorities in Islamic societies and the treatment of Muslim minorities in the West.

On an international level too double standards are sometimes evident today. The crisis in Bosnia is well-known and highly-publicised. Here we have a fierce conflict between the Bosnian government, most of whose members are Muslim, and Bosnian Serbs and Croats, almost all of whom are respectively Orthodox and Roman Catholic Christians, and this conflict is widely understood in the Muslim world as being the result of an anti-Islamic conspiracy on the part of Western powers, who are accused of conspicuous reluctance to become involved in the defence of justice and a legitimate government, especially as compared with their eagerness to resort to military action in the case of defending Kuwait a short time ago. In Africa, however, in the Sudan, a not dissimilar situation exists. Here southern, mainly black, Christians, are attempting to secure a greater measure of political independence from the northern, mainly Arabic-speaking Muslim, government, which has been accused of implementing some fairly savage measures against Christians in order to crush the movement for more independence. Any criticism of such government actions on the part of western Christians, however, is seen by many Muslims as an unjustified interference in the internal affairs of the country.

As a balance to this, it is also true that many Christians dismiss the suggestion that there is any Christian involvement in the Bosnian crisis by simply asserting that it is nothing to do with religion, or at least with "true Christianity". The same was often said about the conflicts in Northern Ireland or in South Africa, about which it was also often asserted that they were nothing to do with true religion, despite the frequent use of religious vocabulary and rhetoric for the legitimation of their positions by many of those most intimately involved in the conflicts. Such Christians are very insistent, however, that the conflict in the Sudan, or the First Gulf War between Iraq and Iran, are essentially and indeed primarily religious, so that any attempt to point to other factors, political, social, economic and cultural, which are involved in the conflict, is determinedly resisted and presented as an attempt to evade or provide a distraction from the religious dimension of the struggle. Double standards are thus applied in both communities, especially in the sense that both Christians and Muslims sometimes use narrow definitions (i.e. only a few people are "really" Christian or Muslim) with reference to their own community while using broad definitions (i.e. everyone who has any connection, however tenuous, with the Christian or Muslim faiths, should be described as Christian or Muslim) with reference to the other community.[5]

Something similar also happens in the discussion of historical events so that, for example, the interpretation of the expulsion of the Muslims from Spain after the Reconquista at the end of the fifteenth/ninth century is presented by some Muslim writers as an example of Christian prejudice against and intolerance of Muslims. One recent discussion, by a Western convert to Islam, of these events is entitled "Blood on the cross".[6] Any attempt by a Western scholar to provide any justification or explanation for the Spanish decision to proceed in this way, because of suspicion that Muslims might act as a kind of fifth column within the Spanish state, is dismissed.[7] A similar sequence of events in the life of Muḥammad, however, namely the expulsion and then massacre of the Jewish tribes in Medina, is presented as a quite justifiable act on the basis of the risk of subversion to the Muslim state by the members of those tribes. Conversely Christian writers over the centuries have not hesitated to argue that Muḥammad's treatment of the Jews is clear evidence that his claim to prophethood should not be taken seriously, while the actions of the Spanish monarchs should be seen as perfectly legitimate defences of the interests of the state. Similar historical events are therefore interpreted completely differently, and in the process double standards are clearly employed.[8]

The interpretation of current events also serves as an example of double standards, especially with reference to such things as natural disasters. Thus when floods affect, for example, affect the United States of America, magazines in some parts of the Muslim world pronounce confidently that the floods are the judgement of God upon a wicked and sinful nation. A different tone, however, is adopted when a third of Pakistan disappears under the flood waters of the River Indus a few months later. Equally when floods affect a part of the Muslim world, such as Pakistan, some Christian magazines confidently assert that they are a divine judgement upon Islam, but a different interpretation is presented when hurricanes lash the coast of Florida. The readiness of such magazines to exult at the execution of God's judgement, always, of course, on someone else, displays an interesting religious understanding of God's involvement in the current affairs of the world, but it also displays a certain inconsistency, at the very least.[9]

Different perspectives are also sometimes evident in the interpretations put upon incidents in which large numbers of people, as a result of the influence of a religious teacher, perform actions which have disastrous consequences: examples of this are the mass suicide of a Christian community at Jonestown in Central America in 1978/1398 or the more recent destruction of a Christian community at Waco in Texas in 1993/1413 in a Christian context, and the incident in Pakistan in 1983/1403 where, at the bidding of a female Shīʿī teacher, a number of Pakistani Shīʿīs walked into the sea off Karachi, having been told that they would walk through the sea to the Shīʿī shrines in Iraq, and drowned. It is important, however, that these events are interpreted on the basis of the same criteria and according to similar standards.[10]

Another area in which double standards are sometimes applied is over the whole question of unity and diversity within the two traditions. What tends to happen here is that Christians and Muslims each insist that the manifold divisions within their own community are not on matters of fundamental importance, and so Christians and Muslims "really" agree with all other members of their own community, whereas the equally manifold (and manifest) divisions of the other are presented as inherent to the fissiparous nature of the other's community, and thus demonstrate the lack of stability and cohesion in the other's faith. Muslim writers thus insist that the Christological controversies of the fourth and fifth centuries CE are clear proof of the incoherence of Christian theology, while arguing that the differences between the various schools of thought which evolved in India in the nineteenth/thirteenth century by no means discredit the claim of Muslims to be a united community. And Christians sometimes point with glee to the current rivalries between Sunnī and Shīʿī Muslims as clear evidence of the fragmentation of the Muslim community while conveniently forgetting the Wars of Religion in Western Europe in the sixteenth/tenth and seventeenth/eleventh centuries, which left half the population of some parts of Germany, for example, dead.[11]

There is a contemporary aspect to this issue too because of the emergence in both traditions, in the nineteenth/thirteenth and twentieth/fourteenth centuries particularly, of movements which are claimed by their adherents to be renewal movements and yet which are seen by the majority in each tradition as being suspect, or even non-Christian or non-Muslim. Sometimes here too double standards are applied: how many Christians see Muslim harassment of the Aḥmadiyya in the Indian Sub-Continent, or of the Bahāʾīs in Iran as proof of the intolerance and inflexibility of Islam, while themselves seeking to restrict the activities and freedom of the so-called "new religious movements" in Christian societies which in their origins have some kind of link with the Christian tradition yet which have also evolved in their own rather distinctive way? And how many Muslims argue that the emergence of the Unitarian Church in Europe, for example, or the Mormon Church or the Jehovah's Witnesses and other American "sects" in the nineteenth/thirteenth century, was a sign of the re-emergence of original and authentic Christianity, while arguing that the Aḥmadiyya and the Bahā'is are no more than apostates, who therefore deserve a harsh punishment?[12]

Yet another area of difficulty concerns the approach used to the study of the two faiths. Here the problem is simply that the number of people who have roughly equal expertise in the studies of the two faiths can more or less be counted on two hands. What happens, therefore, is that some figures who are extremely learned in one tradition are crassly ignorant in the other. This can be illustrated by the experience of the twentieth/fourteenth century Christian theologian Paul Tillich, who pronounced on Buddhism on one occasion but included in his pronouncement an error for which he was criticised in the Harvard University student paper by an undergraduate, who was thus able to point out the ignorance of the eminent theologian with respect to the religious traditions of Asia.[13] Ironically, it is not always the faith of the other that people are ignorant of, for one of the interesting things about modern interaction between Christians and Muslims is the extent to which some in each tradition are formidably learned in the tradition of the other but apparently rather ignorant of their own. Examples of this might be the contemporary Muslim writer Shabbir Akhtar, who sometimes seems more at home with the detail of modern Western religious thought than its Islamic equivalent, or the nineteenth/thirteenth century Protestant missionary to Muslims K.F. Pfander, who was rare in those days in that he had undertaken serious study of Islam, but on the other hand was rather unfamiliar with the intra-Christian debates of his own day. This had some unforeseen consequences when he was presented with the latest Biblical criticism in a public debate in Agra in North India in 1854/1270 and was unable to respond effectively to his Muslim protagonists who were familiar with it.[14]

What is at stake here, therefore, is essentially the use of "critical" or "radical" scholarship, and particularly the tendency of some Christians and some Muslims to make good use of the findings and arguments of critical scholars with reference to the tradition of the other while unquestioningly prohibiting, or vetoing them with reference to their own tradition. Thus *The Myth of God Incarnate*, edited by John Hick,[15] was rapidly taken up and translated into Arabic in Cairo because it was seen to support the traditional Islamic view that the Christian language about Jesus is not true. John Hick was even the first Christian theologian to receive an official invitation to lecture at an Islamic University in Sa'udi Arabia on the strength of the book (which he declined). *Hagarism*, by Patricia Crone and Michael Cook, however, with its attempt to reconstruct the emergence of the Islamic community by the use of sources other than Islamic ones, with some rather radical results, was excoriated by the same Muslims in Cairo,[16] and John Wansbrough the author of *Qur'anic Studies*,[17] again a "radical" attempt to reconstruct the processes by which the Qur'ān was assembled and interpreted is reported as having received a death threat for his efforts, as a result of which he moved his field of research back to the comparatively tranquil pastures of the treaties worked out between Crusaders and Muslims in the Middle East in the twelfth/sixth and thirteenth/seventh centuries! Some Christians, however, lapped up the conclusions of Crone and Cook and of Wansbrough as proof of the fraudulent nature of Islam's claims for its origins and its scripture, while claiming that "The Myth" was an unacceptable travesty of the development of early Christian thought.[18]

Another comparison of this kind might be between the so-called *Gospel of Barnabas*, almost certainly written by a sixteenth/tenth century Spanish Jew who had been forcibly converted to Christianity by the Inquisition in Venice and who then converted to Islam in order to get his own back, yet widely-accepted by modern Muslims as being the original authentic and uncorrupted account of Jesus' life and work, and the incident of "The Satanic Verses", made widely-known by the novel of the same name by Salman Rushdie, which has been taken up and used by many Christians as being evidence from within the Muslim tradition for the existence of error within the text of the Qur'ān, which is then taken as disproving any claim to divine authorship.[19]

Perhaps the most fundamental area in which double standards are applied, however, is in Christians' and Muslims' assessment of each other's faith. In particular, what is involved here is the recurring tendency in both communities to compare the *ideals* of their own faith with the *realities* of the other. Christians, in other words, are adept at comparing the wonderful ideals of the Christian faith with the painful realities of Islamic societies, and Muslims are equally expert at highlighting the obvious problems in societies influenced by the Christian faith while pointing to never-implemented Islamic ideals as the solution to these problems. Thus Christians point to the conflicts and violence evident in different parts of the Middle East and attribute these things to Islam, while insisting that Christianity is a religion of peace and the problems of Northern Ireland or South Africa are nothing at all to do with Christianity; and Muslims say that Islam is a religion of peace and tolerance, so the problems of the Middle East are nothing to do with Islam since "those involved are not true Muslims" – that great ideal excuse which is used so often in both communities! And then the same

Muslims go on to suggest that Western societies are riddled with problems of sexual promiscuity, drug abuse and economic inequality, and these things are all the direct result of Christianity.[20]

The two communities, of course, bitterly resent the other's caricature of themselves, but only rarely does this affect their continuing love of their own caricature of the other, which they love because it makes them feel good – and superior.

A possible solution: the approach which will be adopted

This, then, is the background and context in which I wonder if there is not a place, or even a rather urgent need, for this kind of book, namely a study of Christianity and Islam that approaches the two traditions, as far as is possible, in the same way, using the same criteria.

Is this possible? In an ultimate sense, the answer has to be "probably not", yet the attempt is, as I have already suggested, a matter of some urgency. I am bold enough to suggest that my own background may be helpful to such a first shot, or if that metaphor is inappropriate in the light or earlier history, such a first attempt, for my formal academic qualifications do not include a degree in Christian theology, in other words in the elaboration of my own tradition, but they do include a degree in Islamic History, which involved investigation of the tradition of "the other", as well as a Ph.D. in the interaction of the two traditions, under the overall title of Theology. Two useful features may result from this apparent paradox; firstly an awareness of the *different levels* at which both faiths work – the Islam (or Christianity) of the theologians may work somewhat differently from the Islam (or Christianity) of the humble believer – the faith as lived, in other words. And secondly an awareness of *the tension that exists between the view of the insider and the view of the outsider*, as exemplified by the conviction of many believers, both Christian and Muslim, that phenomenological studies of their faith miss out on certain vital aspects of their faith. The attempt will thus be made to outline the meaning as well as the form of the various elements of the two faiths.[21]

All this is not to underestimate the difficulty of the task, but it does, I hope, highlight the one vital principle which must serve as the basis of the attempt, and that is that no criterion of judgement can be applied to the faith of the other that has not already been applied to one's own faith. There must, in other words, be no double standards.

In particular, what is not permissible is the pattern outlined above whereby "critical" standards are applied to the faith of the other but not permitted with reference to one's own faith. Either critical standards must be applied equally to both, or else they must be applied to neither. And just to make it absolutely clear, my view-point is that they must be applied to both! "Critical", however, does not mean "negative" so much as "analytical", and so the approach may perhaps also be described as being that of "critical sympathy", since there is no intention to be pejorative or dismissive.[22]

How then might this approach work out in practice? Fundamentally, it must clearly involve some kind of parallelism, some kind of comparative approach, for if both Islam and Christianity are religious systems, and if they are both multi-dimensional phenomena, then many of the same elements will be present in both traditions. They will probably be put together in different ways, of course, and different priorities will be given to different features in the two traditions, but there will be some commonality.[23]

Additionally, the approach will then be historical, seeing both Christianity and Islam as faiths which have developed over the centuries and which have evolved in a wide variety of contexts, both geographical and cultural, and phenomenological, in the sense of attempting, insofar as is possible, to outline the two traditions accurately from a neutral and independent standpoint. This does not mean, however, that the two faiths will simply be described with respect to their outward forms; an attempt will also be made to give some insight into their inner meaning and the effects that they have in the lives of their adherents.[24]

On this basis eight themes will therefore be investigated in the chapters which follow. Each chapter investigates a different aspect of the two traditions, and I have tried to vary the diet so that some chapters begin with the Christian tradition and then move to the Islamic tradition before drawing out some comparisons, highlighting areas of similarity and of difference (Chapters One, Three and Five), other chapters reverse the order, investigating the Muslim tradition first and then moving to the Christian tradition (Chapters Four, Six and Seven), and two chapters (Two and Eight) are organised on a more comparative basis throughout.

The whole approach adopted in this book obviously carries a number of risks, not least the danger of superficiality, since entire undergraduate textbooks are written on subjects which will be treated here in half of a chapter![25] But given the problems of ignorance and of double standards which have been outlined earlier it does seem important to produce a book which will give an overview of both traditions despite the risk of generalisation, and my hope is that at least the generalisations will be equally sweeping about both traditions!

Given that the book is being written in English I have usually referred to other material in English in references and in the Bibliography, since it is this material which will be most easily available to English-speakers.[26] Inevitably this means that important discussions in other languages concerning both traditions have been omitted, but while English is clearly the original language of neither the Christian nor Muslim communities, it is certainly one of the most widely-used languages in the Christian world today and is also perhaps the second most-widely used language of the Muslim world.

The hope of the author is therefore that this may be a book about both Christianity and Islam which will be useful to both Christians and Muslims, and that it may contribute to the development of authentic mutual understanding between the two communities. The recent work of Edward Said, entitled *Orientalism*,[27] which suggests that for all the so-called objectivity and impartiality of early modern Western studies of the Orient, the picture presented of it was in fact vitiated by suspect pre-suppositions if not downright prejudice, so that the works of Orientalists reveal as much if not more about them than about their supposed subject-matter, makes the difficulty of this task abundantly clear, especially since there is also a kind of "Occidentalism", a mirror-image of Orientalism in which certain descriptions of the West appear again and again in Muslim writings and perhaps reveal as much about those who make them as about the reality of the West itself. But a verse from the Qur'ān (49:13) suggests both that the task is important and that the aim is not unattainable:

wa ja'alnākum shu'ūban wa qabā'ila li-ta'ārafū

We (i.e. God) have made you peoples and tribes so that you can get to know each other.

Notes

1 Today's Jesuits are considerably better-informed and educated concerning other religious traditions.

2 See D. McLellan *Karl Marx: selected writings*, Oxford U.P., 1977, p 209.

3 One of the interesting features of *The Muslim Manifesto*, produced by the Muslim Institute in London and its director, Dr Kalim Siddiqui, in 1990, is its explicit suggestion that the nineteenth/thirteenth century development of links between Middle Eastern Christians and different European powers should be taken as a model by Muslim minorities in Europe today, who should actively seek Middle Eastern "protectors". See p 22 of the "Manifesto".

4 See the report in "The Times" on 18th September 1990.

5 Thus some Christians unhesitatingly describe Saddam Hussain as a devout Muslim because he has been seen speaking to an Imam, while Radovan Karadzic is, in their view, not a "true" Christian despite the fact that he is seen talking to a Serbian Orthodox priest (and vice versa). Another example of different conflicts being judged by different standards is the fact that during the last two years two capital cities in different parts of the world have been subjected to siege, Sarajevo (the Bosnian capital) and Kabul (the Afghan capital); it seems likely that more people have been killed in the latter (12,000 as opposed to 10,000 for Sarajevo), but because the quarrel around Kabul is an intra-Muslim one it has sometimes been interpreted in a different way from the Bosnian dispute.

6 A. Thompson *Blood on the cross*, Ta-Ha, 1989.

7 See, for example, John Edwards "Mission and inquisition among conversos and Moriscos in Spain, 1250–1550" in W.J. Shiels (ed.) *Persecution and toleration* (Studies in Church History, 21), Blackwell, 1984, pp 139–151.

8 There has been a considerable amount of recent scholarly discussion concerning Muḥammad's treatment of the Jews, and especially concerning the historicity or otherwise of the massacre of the Banū Qurayza. See W.N. Arafat "New light on the story of Banū Qurayza and the Jews of Medina" in *Journal of the Royal Asiatic Society*, 1976, pp 100–107, B. Ahmad *Muhammad and the Jews*, Vikas, New Delhi, 1979, and M.J. Kister "The massacre of the Banū Qurayza" in *Jerusalem studies in Arabic and Islam*, 6 (1986), pp 61–96.

9 An example of this in Christian literature may be seen in the magazine *Prophecy today*, which displays a rather gloating tone in its commentary on events in the Muslim world on pages 26–27 of its March/April 1992 number (Volume 8, number 2): "Late last year yet another disaster hit the Muslim world. On 14 December, in one of the world's worst shipping accidents in recent years, 476 passengers and crew drowned when the Egyptian ferry Salem Express returning from Jeddah struck a coral reef ten miles off the port of Safaga, on Egypt's east coast. It had been in regular use between Safaga and Jeddah, in Sa'udi Arabia. According to press reports, nearly 300 of the 678 people aboard were Muslim pilgrims returning from a visit to Mecca, Islam's most holy shrine. In Prophecy Today for September/October we published a list of accidents and misfortunes that have befallen Islam in recent years. They included most recently the crash with the loss of all 261 lives of a DC-8 airliner at Jeddah, returning to Nigeria after last year's Hajj celebrations, and the stampede by pilgrims in a tunnel during the 1990/1410 Hajj in which 1,426 were crushed to death." Conversely, from within the Muslim community Colonel Gaddafi announced that the earthquake which devastated the town of Kobe in Japan in 1995/1415 was divine punishment for Japan's links with the United States.

10 On Jonestown, see T. Robbins "Religious mass suicide before Jonestown: the Russian old believers" (which draws some interesting parallels with earlier examples of Christian mass suicide) in *Sociological analysis*, 47 (1986), pp 1–20, and on the Pakistani incident see A.S. Ahmed "Death in Islam: the Hawkes Bay case" in *Man*, 21 (1986), pp 120–135.

11 A small practical illustration of this may be seen in the reaction of some

Christians when they hear that Muslims in Britain do not always celebrate the main festivals of the Muslim calendar on the same date. This is because the festival at the end of Ramaḍān, the month of fasting, in particular, is dependant on the new moon being seen (which indicates the start of the next month), but some British Muslims follow Mecca, some follow the practice of their ancestral home-country, and some follow Morocco (the nearest Muslim majority society to Britain). The 'Īd may therefore be celebrated on different days by different parts of the Muslim community, and this is sometimes greeted with incredulity by Christians who forget that Christians too use different calendars, with Eastern and Western Christians mostly celebrating Christmas on December 25th and January 6th respectively, and sometimes celebrating Easter on dates which may be as much as five weeks apart. See further Chapter Five below on this.

12 Something similar also sometimes occurs with reference to the earlier history of the two communities, especially on the question of change. Is change seen as development, in other words a perfectly legitimate change within the acceptable boundaries of a religious tradition, or is it rather seen as corruption, or deviation from the authentic foundations of the tradition? Some writers, both Christian and Muslim, identify change in their own community as development but change in the other community as corruption. See Chapter Three below for further elaboration of this point.

13 See J. Hick and B. Hebblethwaite (eds.) *Christianity and other religions*, Fount, 1980, p 91.

14 For Akhtar's work see especially *Light in the Enlightenment: Christianity and the secular heritage*, Grey Seal, 1990. On Pfander see A.A. Powell *Muslims and missionaries in pre-Mutiny India*, Curzon Press, 1993, especially Chapters Five and Eight.

15 SCM, 1976.

16 An *Open Letter to the Pope*, produced in Egypt in 1978, specifically asked His Holiness to put a stop to this kind of thing!

17 Oxford U.P., 1977.

18 It has to be admitted that these two works may not be altogether comparable, since Hick's discussion of the Incarnation is that of an "insider" to the Christian community, whereas the opinions of Cook and Crone are those of "outsiders" to the Muslim community, but the question of the differing uses to which the arguments of radical critical scholarship are put is still a legitimate one. See Chapter Eight below for further discussion of this point.

19 On the (so-called) Gospel of Barnabas, see J. Slomp "The Gospel in dispute" in *Islamochristiana*, 4 (1978), pp 67–112, and for a convenient summary of the incident of the "Satanic verses" see W.M. Watt *Muhammad: prophet and statesman*, Oxford U.P., 1961, pp 60–65.

20 Thus according to a Christian view of this kind Christians love one another and pray for those who persecute them, while Muslims are violent in their use of terrorism, oppressive in their attitudes towards women, and totalitarian in their attitude towards dissent, and according to a Muslim view, all Muslims are members of one community which is completely unanimous over every detail of belief and practice and is completely devoid of any element of disagreement, while Christians are godless immoral imperialists,

disseminating drug-abuse, sexual immorality and HIV across the whole globe.

21 The difficulty of interpreting a faith other than one's own is clearly outlined by Michael Pye in his "Religion: shape and shadow" in *Numen*, 41 (1994), pp 51–75, where he indicates how easy it is to read other religious systems in the light of the assumptions of another religious system, thus producing a picture which is not recognised by the members of the tradition which is under examination.

22 Kenneth Cragg, in his recent book *To meet and to greet*, Epworth, 1992, has a pleasing way of describing the attitude which should be avoided. He writes: "If we are to meet, we must come out of Adamant Square and leave Cavil Row behind" (p 26), these places being the abodes of the habits of "impregnable hardness" and "finding fault unfairly" respectively.

23 The approach here builds on the work of two important figures within the general field of Religious Studies, John Bowker and Ninian Smart. The former is significant for his analysis of religion and of religious traditions as systems, using the analogy of information systems, originally in the 1981 report of the Doctrine Commission of the Church of England, *Believing in the Church* (SPCK, 1981), and later reprinted as an Appendix in his *Licensed Insanities* (Darton, Longman and Todd, 1987). This can sometimes make it seem as if God is the great computer, or perhaps the great database, in the sky, but it does have many strengths. And the latter is significant for his scheme of the different dimensions of religion, a scheme which is now known throughout the world of religious education, right down to primary schools. Originally, as in *The Religious Experience of Mankind* (Collins, 1971), there were six dimensions, the ritual, the mythological, the doctrinal, the ethical, the social and the experiential, though it is interesting to note that in Smart's latest volume, the lavishly illustrated *The World's Religions* (Cambridge U.P., 1989), the number of dimensions has increased to seven, via the addition of the iconographical.

24 Two influential pioneers of this kind of approach are Wilfred Cantwell Smith and Clifford Geertz. The former, in his *The meaning and end of religion*, Macmillan, 1962, outlines the view that religious traditions consist of two elements, that of faith, which is an existential attitude of trust and which broadly speaking is not dissimilar in different religious traditions or in different times and places, and that of what Smith calls the "cumulative tradition", the various expressions of faith which are worked out in terms of both beliefs and practices and which do vary between traditions and develop over the course of time. The latter, working as an anthropologist, analyses cultures as language-systems, which make perfect sense to those who know and make use of them but are opaque and even incomprehensible to those who do not know them until they have made some effort to learn the language and make some effort to interpret what they observe. For a general outline of this view see his "Religion as a cultural system" in *The interpretation of cultures*, Basic Books, New York, 1973, and for an example of his work on Islam in particular see *Islam observed*, University of Chicago Press, 1968. A Christian theologian who has made use of this insight in seeking to examine the relationship between the Christian faith and other faiths is George Lindbeck; see his *The nature of doctrine: religion*

and theology in a postliberal age, SPCK, 1984. One of the great strengths of this whole approach is that it permits a clear analysis of the means by which religious traditions change and develop, and thus of how they sift their resources in order to re-formulate themselves. With reference to the Christian tradition this is clearly acknowledged in T.S. Eliot's famous remark: "Christianity is always changing into something that can be believed". For an interesting study of how Christianity has evolved over the course of the centuries see D.E. Nineham *Christianity mediaeval and modern: a study in religious change*, SCM, 1993.

25 The reaction of many colleagues at the seminars at which I presented an outline of the book was "how many volumes are you thinking of?" Encouragement was provided, however, by the recent publication of a number of books attempting a similar comparison of different traditions in the series "Themes in Comparative Religion". See, for example J. Brockington *Hinduism and Christianity*, Macmillan, 1992 and J. Ching *Chinese religions*, Macmillan, 1993, which despite the lack of any reference to Christianity in the title, does contain comparative discussions, which are more fully developed in her *Christianity and Chinese religions*, written jointly with Hans Küng, and published by SCM in 1994.

26 For the same reason books referred to in foot-notes and the Bibliography are, unless otherwise stated, published in London.

27 Routledge and Kegan Paul, 1978.

1

ORIGINS

Introduction

Jesus was a Jew who lived in the Roman-occupied province of Palestine. Muḥammad was an Arab who lived in the tribal feud-ridden area of Arabia. These simple facts go a considerable way to explaining both the different natures of the early communities which were influenced by the two figures and also the different messages which Jesus and Muḥammad proclaimed.

Christian origins

Because of his Jewish background Jesus was the heir to a long well-established tradition of both monotheism and the idea of religious guidance through law and prophecy. More concretely, in the Jewish community of his day there already existed a community which had been broadly monotheistic for over a millennium, worshipping the one God in either Temple or synagogue depending on political circumstance and geographical location, and which was also well accustomed to the idea of receiving guidance from God through individual charismatic figures, whose words had later come to be written down as scriptures and then collected together with the words of other similar figures in a kind of compendium of messages, or words, from God.

As a result of these facts there seems to have been no great stress on monotheism in the message proclaimed by Jesus; rather it was simply assumed. And on the basis of already-existing scriptures Jesus was able to appeal to a wide range of earlier precedents and paradigms in support of his teaching.

There were, however, particular issues facing the Jewish community of his day which gave a special focus and form to the message of Jesus, and many of these related to the fact that Palestine was then under Roman occupation.[1] Rome, the greatest political power of the day, had occupied Palestine in 63 BCE, and the province had been incorporated into the Empire, even if a kind of indirect rule preserved an appearance of independence. Real power lay with the Roman governor, and partly because of this the Jewish community of the day was deeply divided over a number of questions.

Firstly, opinion varied over the attitude which it was proper for Jews to hold towards the Romans: should their rule be tolerated or actively opposed? Two groups were especially important here: the Pharisees opposed Roman rule, while the Sadducees were prepared to tolerate it. These groups did not simply differ over this political question, however. They also differed over religious and theological questions. Two issues in particular were actively debated: firstly the question of whether or not human beings would be resurrected after death, to which the Pharisees replied affirmatively and the Sadducees negatively, and secondly the question of the "over-ruling" of God, in other words predestination, which the Pharisees accepted but the Sadducees rejected. Additionally, the Sadducees were essentially the priestly party, dominating the affairs of the Jewish Temple, the main place of Jewish worship, while the Pharisees were the party of the Law, seeking to promote strict observance of the Torah and of later regulations. In an Islamic context they might have been known as the Sharī'a party.

Other groups also existed which were more extreme than either of these two groups. On the one hand there were the Zealots, militants who sought to promote and organise armed rebellion against Rome. Antecedents to this group can be seen in the Maccabees, who fought against an earlier occupying power in Palestine, the Hellenistic Seleucid dynasty in 166–163BCE. And then on the other hand there were the Essenes, who adopted a directly opposite approach to that of the Zealots, preferring a quietist approach, withdrawing to the desert to lead a separate community life, almost monastic in style and comparable in style to some groups of Sufi Muslims.

Palestine, then, in the time of Jesus, was a seething mass of disagreement, on both political and religious questions, and the struggle between the different groups in the Jewish community for power and influence was often harsh. Additional urgency was given to these struggles by the prominence in Jewish thought of the idea of a Messiah, a deliverer, who would arise and deliver Jews from oppression, and then establish a reign of justice. Like King David in an earlier period of Jewish history the Messiah, the Anointed One, would set up the kingdom of righteousness.

There was therefore a great sense of expectation and waiting in the Jewish community at large.

It was into this situation, then, that Jesus was born, in Bethlehem, probably in either 4 or 6 BCE.[2] Little is known about his early years, with Christian records pointing only to one incident of real significance, namely an event which took place when Jesus travelled with his parents to the Temple in Jerusalem (Luke 2:41–52). On their return journey, and they had travelled in a large group, his parents discovered that Jesus was not with them. Enquiries elsewhere in the group did not result in his being found, so his parents returned to Jerusalem and found Jesus in the Temple, discussing with Jewish teachers there, listening and asking questions, and, according to Luke, "all who heard him were amazed at his understanding and his answers" (Luke 2:47).

Silence then descends on Jesus' career for another 18 years or so until the start of his public ministry when he was aged around 30. This began with baptism at the hands of John the Baptist, baptism being a sign of repentance, consisting of immersion in the river Jordan to symbolize a change of life springing from repentance. After his baptism Jesus' ministry then focused on two main elements. Firstly there was his teaching and preaching, sometimes in the context of small groups of disciples and sometimes in the context of huge crowds, and at the heart of Jesus' teaching lay the idea of the kingdom of God, the place where God rules, a place of harmony, perfection and justice. This utopian vision proved very attractive to many, and some began to ask whether he might be the awaited Messiah. Secondly, alongside the words were actions, and these involved miracles and acts of healing, some of which, as recorded in the Christian sources, were truly remarkable: the blind, the lame, the diseased, even the dead, were healed and resurrected. Demons and evil spirits were also driven out, exorcised, and people were made whole, and all of these acts, according to Jesus, were parables or signs of the kingdom of God.

There was also, according to the early Christian accounts, an apocalyptic dimension to the teaching of Jesus: the end was near, so that judgement and destruction were imminent. The message "Repent for the kingdom of God is at hand" was not new to Jesus, since John the Baptist had also proclaimed it, but Jesus' teaching seems to have developed it and taken it further.

What was the reaction to all of this? How was it received? Some of Jesus' contemporaries responded warmly and enthusiastically, finding his message music to their ears: they became his disciples, and of them an inner group of 12 disciples enjoyed special intimacy with Jesus, accompanying him throughout much of his travelling. Not particularly intellectual, they were very much ordinary Jews from Palestine, many of them having originally been fishermen. Many others, including many women, also became followers of Jesus, even if they were more like occasional visitors than permanent followers. It is clear, therefore, that Jesus' message proved very attractive to many people in the Palestine of his day.

This was not the case for all, however, since for a number of reasons Jesus' teaching and actions managed to alienate and anger most of the existing schools of thought in the Jewish community at the time. The Zealots, with their wish to overthrow Roman rule by violence, were alienated by Jesus' teaching "my kingdom is not of this world"; for them this was far too spiritual, since they wanted liberation and they wanted it immediately. The Pharisees, who stressed rigorous practice of the Law, were alienated by a number of incidents where Jesus apparently sat rather lightly to the requirements of the law: for example, he healed on the Sabbath, which was meant to be a day of rest since according to tradition on the Sabbath God had rested from the work of creation, but Jesus' response was to argue that the Sabbath was made for man and not man for the Sabbath, so that it was permissible to sit rather loose to the detail of the law, especially since meeting human need was more significant than punctilious observance of the law. (See Luke 13:10–17 and 14:1–6).

The Sadducees, the priestly party, Jesus offended by not only implying but also publicly protesting that the administration of the Temple was corrupt, so that instead of being a place of worship it had become a den of thieves, who were more interested in money-making than in true religion. And with respect to the Essenes, despite some considerable commonality between their views and the views of Jesus, recently brought out more clearly by some of the discoveries in the Dead Sea Scrolls, it seems that Jesus did not accept their suggested solution to the problems and issues of the day, namely withdrawal to a life of contemplation, preferring rather a more active involvement in attempts to face up to and confront the difficulties.

Conflict, then, between Jesus on the one hand and the different religious parties of the day, therefore grew. A number of attempts were made to arrest Jesus, but these failed, partly because of his popularity with the crowds. In addition a number of attempts were made to catch Jesus out. Sometimes these attempts involved asking him awkward questions about Roman rule, which was a significant area given the realities of Roman control in Palestine and the desire of the Romans not to have to deal with unrest. The Pharisees on one occasion put a hard question to him, (Matthew 22:15–22): "Is it lawful to pay taxes to Caesar (i.e. to Rome)?" If Jesus answered "No" he could then have been presented as being a Zealot, a subversive, whom the Romans would have felt it necessary to deal with; if, on the other hand he answered "Yes", he could have been presented as a Collaborator, someone who did not take observance of the Jewish law or membership of the Jewish community sufficiently seriously. Jesus' answer was to ask for a coin to be brought to him. On one side of the coin was an image, the head of the Roman Emperor of the day. "Whose image is found on this coin?" Jesus asked. "Caesar's" came the reply. "Render (or give) to Caesar what is Caesar's", Jesus said, "and to God what is God's". This masterly answer avoided both of the traps which he could have fallen into, but it did nothing to endear him to the Pharisees who had asked the question.

In another incident a woman who had been caught in the act of adultery was brought to Jesus, again by the Pharisees, in order to test him. Their challenge was that in the law of Moses it was clearly stated that a woman caught in the act of adultery should be stoned to death. "What do you say?" they asked, thus testing Jesus' attitude towards the Jewish law – did he respect it and take it seriously, or rather set it aside and reject it? Jesus bent over and wrote on the ground. Then he stood up and said: "let he who is innocent cast the first stone". The challenge, in other words, was thrown back. The law was not specifically rejected, but anyone who regarded themselves as innocent was invited to throw the first stone. No-one could, and the crowd slunk away until Jesus was left alone with the woman, whom he told to go and not sin again. (See John 8:1–11)

Jesus' teaching and actions, therefore, proved deeply challenging to the various schools of thought existing at the time in the Jewish community, and in particular it was his insistence on the necessity of going beyond simple outward observance to the question of inner thoughts and motivations which provoked much controversy. (cf Matthew 5: 21–22 and 27–28)

Tension between Jesus and the Jewish leadership therefore intensified until Jesus was eventually arrested and brought to trial before the Jewish Supreme Council, the Sanhedrin (Matthew 26:47–67; Mark 14:43–65; Luke 22:47–71; John 18:1–24) by an alliance between the Sadducees and the Pharisees, who managed to agree on virtually nothing except the fact that they wished to be rid of Jesus. The question which was put to Jesus was a simple one concerning whether or not he was the Messiah: an affirmative answer would have made it possible for him to be handed over to the Romans as a subversive. According to the Christian sources, Jesus refused to answer the question, but witnesses were produced to testify that he had claimed to be the Messiah, and so he was duly handed over to the Roman authorities for trial. The Roman governor, Pontius Pilate, at first found Jesus innocent, and sent him away, but he was brought back and on the next day, encouraged by a crowd outside the balcony of his home calling for Jesus to be killed, Pilate found Jesus guilty and sentenced him to execution. According to the Roman custom, this took the form of crucifixion, a long and painful death, and Jesus was crucified on the next day.[3]

The movement of Jesus' followers, however, did not come to an end at this point. Not surprisingly the disciples of Jesus were initially demoralised and disorientated, since their high hopes and expectations appeared to have been shattered. Indeed only perhaps three or four of his disciples seem to have remained with Jesus until his crucifixion. But gradually the whole situation was transformed by the realisation on the part of the disciples that Jesus' death did not mean the end of Jesus: rather it was simply the precursor of some kind of resurrection, whereby Jesus was raised from the dead on the third day after his crucifixion, and thus he conquered death rather than being conquered by death. There is some difference among Christians as to the interpretation and understanding of Jesus' resurrection, and especially over whether the idea of resurrection should be understood as historical fact or as some kind of myth or metaphor.[4] But what is not disputed is the dramatic effect that the idea of resurrection, however it is understood, had on Jesus' disciples. From being demoralised and disenchanted they were transformed into a dynamic renewed movement, convinced that Jesus' death was not the end but rather the beginning, and determined therefore to make known the significance of Jesus' life and death as widely as possible. They began to teach widely about Jesus' death and resurrection, and even, in some cases according to the Christian sources, to heal.

The Jesus movement, therefore, did not die. Rather it continued and grew, originally in Jerusalem and Palestine, among Jews, since all of Jesus' earliest disciples were themselves Jewish, but it was not long before the movement began to spread more widely too, including among non-Jews. The key personality here was Paul. Paul was not one of Jesus' original disciples; rather, after Jesus' death, he had been one of the leading Jewish opponents of the Jesus movement. As a Pharisee, concerned for the Jewish law, he had persecuted and harassed the followers of Jesus, actually hoping to eradicate the movement completely. Some time around ten years after the crucifixion of Jesus, however, Paul seems to have had some kind of dramatic conversion experience (Acts 9:1–19, and also 22:6–16 and 26:12–18). From being someone harassing the followers of Jesus he was transformed into someone who joined the movement, and indeed did so with enthusiasm.

Significantly, Paul was an educated Jew, unlike most of Jesus' earliest disciples, and he came originally not from Palestine but from Tarsus (which is now in Turkey). He also had the unusual combination of talents of being a visionary and an organiser. He is thus responsible for two major developments in the Christian movement.[5] First of all, Paul real- ised that the significance of Jesus was not simply for Jews; rather it was of universal significance, and so he determined to carry the message of Jesus also to non-Jews. This decision was the cause of perhaps the first major disagreement among the followers of Jesus, as to whether or not he was right, but at the Council of Jerusalem, whose deliberations are recorded in Acts 15, the leaders of the Christian movement agreed that Paul was right, so the Christian movement thus began the process of its transformation from a group with its roots very definitely within Judaism to a group with a universal message.

Secondly, Paul undertook a number of missionary journeys way beyond the area of Jerusalem and Palestine, travelling widely throughout the eastern Mediterranean and even getting as far as Rome itself. Wherever he travelled he brought the message of the significance of Jesus, and, in most cases, he succeeded in establishing small communities, or churches, made up of those who came to accept the message. News of Jesus was therefore carried over a far wider geographical area than had been the case during his lifetime, and small congregations of Jesus-followers were established in many important cities of the Roman empire.

With respect to Christian origins, then, what we have is a faith which has its roots in the long-established monotheistic tradition of Judaism and which, in the context of the Roman occupation of Palestine, is based on the life and teaching of a figure who managed to alienate all of the different schools of Jewish thought which existed at the time, to the extent of being crucified. Rather than representing the end of the Jesus movement, however, in time this crucifixion came to be understood rather as the climax of Jesus' life, as the message of the resurrected Jesus came to be spread abroad by his disciples, even, at the hands of Paul, coming to be understood as a message of universal significance.

The establishment of the Muslim community

The Arabia in which Muḥammad was born, probably in the year 570 or 571 of the Common Era, was essentially a tribal and a polytheistic society. It was politically independent, since its geographical features, especially its desert, contrived to frustrate any attempt by an external power to subject the area. Thus a Roman army, for example, under Aelius Gallus in 24BCE marched into Arabia but was completely lost, its members being presumed to have died of thirst. But any gain resulting from independence from foreign powers was effectively vitiated by the feuds and disputes which frequently arose between the many tribes of the different regions of Arabia.

Religiously most of Arabia before the time of Muḥammad remained in what might be called an animistic phase of development. A number of gods and goddesses, in other words, existed and served as objects of worship, some animate and some inanimate. Thus the sun and moon, stones, trees, and other physical objects were sometimes worshipped, as were more personalised deities, sometimes associated with particular shrines, such as Allāt, Manāt, and al-'Uzzā. In general terms, different tribes had their own deities, who served to promote the interests of the tribe where possible.

On this foundation, however, by the 6th century CE, a number of new developments were beginning to take place. Firstly, as a result of migration and trade and other contact with surrounding areas, newer religious communities had become established in Arabia, and in some cases their ideas were beginning to become diffused into Arabian society. Thus some towns, including the important town of Yathrib in the Hijaz, the western part of Arabia, had a Jewish presence within them, in some cases going back to the destruction of the temple in Jerusalem by the Romans in 70CE, while others had a more recent Christian presence of one kind or another, which had usually become established as a result of trade with a neighbouring Christian state. The town of Najrān in south Arabia is reported by both Christian and Muslim sources as containing a substantial Christian community.

Partly as a result of influence from these monotheistic communities, and partly as a result of its own internal religious evolution and development, by the time of Muḥammad certain trends towards monotheism seem to have already been emerging within Arabian religion. This can be seen, for example, in the individuals known as *ḥanīfs*, a term which is difficult to translate precisely into English, but which is usually taken to mean Arab monotheists. The *ḥanīfs*, in other words, had not become

Jews or Christians; rather they had remained adherents of a broadly Arabian religion, but in their minds it had become a monotheistic Arabian religion. So Allāh, an Arabic word which had a long ancestry and which originally meant the supreme or high god (with a small g), in the minds of the *ḥanifs* came to be understood as the only God (with a capital g).

Neither the Jews and the Christians nor the *ḥanīfs*, however, had become anything more than minority groups in Arabia as a whole prior to the time of Muḥammad. Most regions, and most tribes, remained polytheistic, and this was almost certainly the case in the town of Mecca, in western Arabia, where Muḥammad was born. In particular the Meccans seem to have had a special affection for the goddesses Allāt, Manāt and al-'Uzzā.

Little is known about the early career of Muḥammad beyond the fact that he was an orphan, his father having died before he was born and his mother then dying when he was aged around six. Only one incident of any note is referred to in the Muslim sources for his life as having taken place during his first thirty years, and that is an incident which demonstrates a first involvement in the public affairs of his home town of Mecca. There, somewhere around the year 595CE, a dispute had arisen between some of the leading clans of the city concerning the Ka'ba, the main shrine of Mecca. In one corner of the Ka'ba there was a kind of niche or alcove, in which a black stone, possibly originally a meteorite and certainly a focus of some devotion, had sat. The stone, however, had fallen out of its base, and given its religious significance, whoever replaced it might be able to lay claim to some pre-eminence in the life of the town. This was the cause of the argument between the different clans; each wished to perform the task of replacing the stone itself, and none was willing to see another clan do so. Eventually a way out of the impasse was agreed, in that whoever entered the open area around the Ka'ba would be asked to mediate between the clans and reach a possible solution. That person turned out to be Muḥammad, and his masterly solution to the problem was that the stone should be placed on a blanket, each of whose corners would then be picked up by a representative of each of the four clans and carried to the Ka'ba, and he, Muḥammad, would then replace the stone in its niche. His solution proved acceptable to all, and for the ingenuity of his solution Muḥammad was given the title "al-amīn", the trustworthy.

The climactic event of Muḥammad's career came in the year 610 CE when during a visit to a cave on Mount Ḥirā, just outside Mecca, for the purpose of meditation, Muḥammad had some kind of vision, or heard a voice speaking to him, an experience which he eventually became convinced was a call, a commissioning, from Allāh, God, to be a prophet. This involved proclaiming a message of monotheism, that there is only one God, and the ethical consequences of monotheism, in terms of social justice and care for the vulnerable members of society. All of this was backed up by the confident assertion of imminent judgement by God, and so the Meccans were called upon to repent.

Muḥammad's message should be seen, therefore, as a classic "prophetic message", involving both a passionate call to belief in one God and an equally passionate call for just and compassionate behaviour towards other members of society. A Christian scholar, indeed, R.C. Zaehner, went so far as to describe the Qur'ān, the written distillation of the message of Muḥammad, as the "quintessence of prophecy".[6]

While some people in Mecca responded warmly to Muḥammad's message and joined the community of Muslims, of those who had obeyed the call to submit to Allāh (which is what the word Muslim literally means), others were not so enthusiastic. In particular some of the rich merchants of the town did not respond positively to Muḥammad's assertions that they were pursuing wealth and personal gain regardless of the cost to others and that they were neglecting their traditional responsibilities to the weak and vulnerable, and the guardians of the traditional religion of the city, especially those responsible for the upkeep of the Ka'ba, the shrine of Mecca, did not take kindly to the statement that the many gods and goddesses who were worshipped there were of little value since there is only one true God. Opposition to Muḥammad therefore developed.

At first this resulted in minor inconveniences such as heckling and interruption at Muḥammad's meetings, but over the years it became more serious as an economic boycott of Muḥammad's clan was arranged and more serious attempts at harassment were undertaken. In 622CE, therefore, responding to an invitation from the neighbouring town of Yathrib to come and mediate in some serious inter-tribal disputes which were disrupting the life of the town, Muḥammad took the opportunity to move away from Mecca and establish his base more securely. This was the event which came to be known as the Hijra, or migration, which later came to serve as the starting-point of the Muslim calendar.[7]

In Yathrib, because of the invitation issued to him to mediate in the town's disputes, Muḥammad was immediately a figure of some influence, and over the course of the next few years he succeeded in strengthening his position further. This involved dealing, in some cases forcefully, with internal opposition from some of the tribes, especially

Jewish ones, in Yathrib, and also resisting the efforts of the Meccans to crush the Muslim community. Muḥammad therefore became involved in military skirmishes, and also in diplomatic activity to pre-empt Meccan attempts to create an alliance against him involving tribes in other parts of Arabia. In both of these activities Muḥammad proved highly successful, and as a result of this by 630CE/8AH not only had the Meccans submitted and recognised his authority, but much of the rest of Arabia had also done so. By the time of his death in 632CE/10AH, therefore, Muḥammad had succeeded in establishing a Muslim community whose monotheistic message and whose political control had been accepted more or less throughout Arabia. The previously polytheistic and tribal feud-ridden society was thus united under one God and the prophet Muḥammad.[8]

This achievement was consolidated by Muḥammad's first successors as leaders of the Muslim community, Abū Bakr (632–634CE/11–13AH), 'Umar ibn al-Khaṭṭāb (634–644CE/13–23AH), and 'Uthmān (644–656CE/23–35AH), who together resisted any attempt by Arabian tribes to throw off the rule of the Muslim community once Muḥammad had died, and then began the process whereby the Muslim community established its influence beyond the frontiers of Arabia in what is today known as the Middle East, in such areas as Palestine, Egypt, Syria and Iraq.[9]

The Muslim community was thus established in an area which had previously been polytheistic and riven by tribal disputes. The unity which it introduced was both religious, in the sense that it was based on a belief in the unity or oneness of God, and practical, in the sense that it produced, for the first time in Arabian history, a united Arabian state. These two features were integrally related, in that belief in the unity of God was seen as necessarily leading to a unified society, and thus the symbiosis of belief and society, of religion and politics, was an essential element in the formation of the Muslim community.

Some similarities

Clearly as a result of their backgrounds and the contexts in which they worked there are a number of significant differences between Jesus and Muḥammad, between Christian origins and the establishment of the Muslim community. Most important among these are perhaps the fact that Jesus taught in a situation where there was an already well-established tradition of monotheism, while the environment in which Muḥammad taught was essentially polytheistic, and the fact that Palestine in the time of Jesus was under Roman occupation while Arabia in the time of Muḥammad was deeply divided along tribal lines. These differences, however, should not blind us to the fact that there are nevertheless some important similarities between their two careers.

Firstly, both Jesus and Muḥammad seem to have lived in an age of apocalyptic expectation, arising out of the widespread conviction that things in the world had gone awry, that only supernatural deliverance could resolve the difficulties encountered, and that such divine intervention was imminent.[10] For all the differences in the contexts in which they worked, therefore, which have been outlined already, there was this similarity. But it has to be conceded that Jesus and Muḥammad responded in different ways to these Messianic expectations, the former seeking to channel the interpretation of deliverance away from a this-worldly military understanding to a more other-worldly view, and the latter perhaps being readier to see the establishment of his community as part of the fulfilment of apocalyptic expectation.

More significantly, there are similarities between the two traditions with respect to the question of the sources of information concerning their origins. Put crudely, both sets of sources are from "the committed". Questions therefore arise with respect to their reliability and authenticity, and in the modern period fierce debates have sprung up, giving rise, with respect to both traditions, to "radical" and "conservative" opinions. The issue has come to the fore more recently with regard to the Islamic tradition than the Christian, because it was in the nineteenth/thirteenth century that the rise of historical criticism and its application to the Bible provoked discussion of Christian origins and the so-called quest for the historical Jesus, whereas it is perhaps books such as Patricia Crone and Michael Cook's *Hagarism*, already referred to above, which has provoked controversy over the question of the origins of the Islamic community.[11]

Part of the issue here is, of course, the different nature of the sources for the two traditions. Information of a basically biographical nature with respect to Jesus is found in the Christian scriptures themselves, especially the four gospel accounts, which may all date from within four decades or so of Jesus' death (i.e. before 70CE), and if not were almost certainly all composed before 100CE, whereas the earliest biographical information concerning Muḥammad is not scriptural (since the Qur'ān contains his message but very little about his life), but is rather found in later literature, especially the *sīrat rasūl allāh* (biography of the prophet of God). The earliest extant version of this is the biography of Ibn Isḥāq, who died in 768CE/151AH, in the edition of Ibn Hishām, who died in 833CE/213AH or 838CE/218AH, so the biographical information which is available to us concerning Muḥammad is considerably further removed from his time than is the case for the equivalent information with respect to Jesus.[12]

This debate in turn has sparked off a further modern debate concerning the extent of the originality of the two messages. The work of G. Vermes, E.P. Sanders and others on the Judaism of Jesus' day has given rise to considerable discussion of whether or not Jesus' teaching was similar to or different from other Jewish teachers of his day. Was he original, therefore, or was he not?[13] And a similar debate has arisen over the message of Muḥammad: was it new, or reliant to a greater or lesser extent on earlier religious ideas, including Jewish and Christian ones, or a new synthesis of existing ideas? And given the reports that exist of other individuals in the Arabia of Muḥammad's day who made claims to be prophets, a question also arises concerning the extent to which Muḥammad's message was unique in his own day or was simply part of a wider trend in the evolution of Arabian religion in a monotheistic and prophetic direction.[14]

This discussion is made more complicated by the contrast between the contents of the Christian and Muslim scriptures. The former include the earlier Jewish scriptures, a fact which, while allowing for Jesus' originality, emphasises at least a measure of continuity with earlier Jewish teachers. The Qur'ān, on the other hand, includes only the message of Muḥammad, which could be seen as heightening awareness of the distinctiveness of Muḥammad's message, yet much later Muslim opinion has emphasised that Muḥammad's message was not new, since it was simply a re-assertion of the message of earlier prophets.[15] In both traditions, therefore, the debates continue.

Conclusion

With their beginnings in different geographical areas and different circumstances, as well as separated in time by almost six centuries, it is not surprising if there are obvious differences between the origins of the Christian faith and the Muslim community, but some similarities can be discerned, even if the message of the kingdom of God within you, borne by small scattered Christian churches, and the message of submission to the one true God and obedience to his prophet within the context of a powerful Islamic state are clearly different in many respects.

NOTES

1 A thoroughly readable account of Jesus' life and ministry in the context of his time may be found in G. Theissen *In the footsteps of the Galilean*, SCM, 1987, which is notable as a study of Christian origins not least because Jesus is never actually referred to in the book at all. The author simply investigates his "shadow", that is his impact upon his contemporaries.

2 Later Christian attempts to make the birth of Jesus the starting-point of a new Christian calendar thus included an element of miscalculation, which more recent research has highlighted.

3 I recognise, of course, that this account is not one with which most Muslim commentators agree, but given that the philosophy of this book is that the sources used should, where possible, be those of the relevant religious community, Christian sources have been taken as being primary for this account.

4 A book whose title is a catchy summary of much Christian discussion on this theme is H. Montefiore *The womb and the tomb: the mystery of the birth and resurrection of Jesus*, Collins (Fount), 1992, in which the author, a bishop of the Anglican church, discusses the nature of Christian statements about the Virgin Birth of Jesus and his resurrection from the dead. The former he takes to be a mythical statement, and the latter a historical one.

5 The name Christian is not one which the followers of Jesus chose for themselves; rather it was given to them in the city of Antioch in Syria because they kept talking about "the Christ", a term which is simply the equivalent in Greek of the Hebrew term Messiah, meaning Anointed One. (See Acts 11:26). Given that the name was given shortly after Paul's conversion, it becomes appropriate, when talking of Paul, to refer to "the Christian movement" rather than the earlier "Jesus movement".

6 R.C. Zaehner *At sundry times*, Faber, 1958, p 27. Compare "Islam . . . is the prophetic religion par excellence" (p 161).

7 Many Muslims are under the impression that the Hijra took place on the first day of the first month of the first year of the Hijri calendar. In fact the Muslim calendar simply begins with the year in which the Hijra took place, the Hijra probably taking place on the twelfth day of the month of Rabīʻ al-awwal, the third month of the Arabic (and later Islamic) calendar in that year, which corresponds to 24th September 622CE.

8 For more detail on the career of Muḥammad see W.M. Watt *Muhammad: prophet and statesman*, Oxford U.P., 1961, M. Rodinson *Mohammad*, Penguin, 1971, M. Lings *Muhammad: his life based on the earliest sources*, Unwin, 1983, and M. Cook *Muhammad*, Oxford U.P., 1983. Of these four works, that by Lings relies most on traditional Muslim sources, while that by Cook is the most questioning of those sources. Fuller detail may be found in W.M. Watt *Muhammad in Mecca*, Oxford U.P., 1953, and *Muhammad in Medina*, Oxford U.P., 1956.

9 For further details concerning Muḥammad's first successors see F. Gabrieli *Muhammad and the conquests of Islam*, Weidenfeld and Nicolson, 1968, esp. pp 85–98. For a suggestive comparison between the roles of Paul for the Christian faith and ʻUmar ibn al-Khaṭṭāb for the Muslim community,

especially with reference to their significance for the process of the universalising their respective messages, that is taking them beyond the boundaries of those to whom they were originally delivered, see H. Lazarus-Yafeh "'Umar b. al-Khaṭṭāb – Paul of Islam?" in *Some religious aspects of Islam*, Brill, Leiden, 1981, pp 1–16.

10 More research has been done on apocalyptic thought as background to the time of Jesus than with respect to Muḥammad, but for the latter see B. Lewis "On that day: a Jewish apocalyptic poem on the Arab conquests" in P. Salmon (ed.) *Mélanges d'islamologie*, Brill, Leiden, 1974, pp 197–200.

11 For consideration of this theme with reference to Christian origins see E.P. Sanders *The historical figure of Jesus*, Allen Lane, 1993. There is a helpful discussion of the issue of sources for the early Muslim community in R.S. Humphreys *Islamic History – a framework for enquiry*, esp Chap 3, "Early historical tradition and the first Islamic polity", in which the work of Crone and Cook is discussed on pp 84–85. For an attempt to link the issues raised by the quest for the historical Jesus to the study of Islam see F.E. Peters "The quest of the historical Muḥammad" in *International Journal of Middle East Studies*, 23 (1991), pp 291–315.

12 The earliest Muslim biography of Muḥammad is available in English translation under the title *The life of Muḥammad*, translated by A. Guillaume (with material from other early Muslim historical works included), Oxford U.P., 1955. Further discussion of the issue of the different forms of the Christian and Muslim scriptures will be found in Chapter Two below.

13 See especially G. Vermes *Jesus the Jew*, 2nd ed., SCM, 1983, and E.P. Sanders *Jesus and Judaism*, SCM, 1985.

14 On Muḥammad, see J. Fueck "The originality of the Arabian prophet" in M.L. Swartz (ed.) *Studies on Islam*, Oxford U.P., 1981, Chapter Three.

15 It is for this reason that there is considerable reluctance among Muslims to have Muḥammad described as "the founder of Islam", since it is held that other prophets had also proclaimed the message of Islam well before his time.

2

SCRIPTURES

Introduction

Both Christianity and Islam have scriptures, which have been read, recited, memorised, studied, interpreted and reflected on in their respective communities since their earliest days. One of the most alarming features of any Christian-Muslim encounter, however, is the phenomenal ignorance of each other's scripture, so it is especially important for Christians and Muslims to realise that although both Christians and Muslims therefore use the term "scripture" the way in which that term is understood is widely different within the two communities. This is therefore one of the areas where it is most important to discern where there are similarities and where there are differences in understanding within the two traditions.[1]

Contents and form

Here the contrast is essentially the difference between the relative simplicity of form of the Muslim scripture, the Qur'ān, and the relative complexity of the Christian scriptures, which is testified to immediately by the use of the plural form, scriptures, when referring to the Christian tradition.[2]

The Qur'ān is thus the record of the prophetic revelations received by Muḥammad during the twenty-two year period of his career between his call in 610CE and his death in 632CE/11AH.[3] Moreover these revelations were in all probability collected together and edited into more or less the form in which they are found today within a period of some twenty-five years of Muḥammad's death.[4] The contents of the Qur'ān thus became known through the agency of one human being, Muḥammad, in a relatively short time.

The situation with respect to the Christian scriptures, by contrast, is far more complex. For a start the Christian scriptures include not only specifically Christian books, books that is which were written by Christian authors on recognisably Christian concerns. They also include a number of books whose origins lie in pre-Christian times and whose authors were Jews. There are thus two substantially different sections, or testaments, within the Christian scriptures. The contents of the first part, the Old Testament, are, in most cases, shared with Judaism, and are therefore sometimes referred to as the Hebrew scriptures, and they make up roughly three-quarters of the Christian scriptures. Only the contents of the remaining quarter, the New Testament, are therefore unique to Christians.

Each section, or testament, is in turn made up of a number of books, thirty-nine in the Old Testament and twenty-seven in the New Testament. In the Christian scriptures, therefore, there are a number of books, written by different authors, over the course of many centuries, perhaps as much as a millennium, and then later edited and collected together into the form in which they exist today.

In form, therefore, the Qur'ān is much more straightforward than the Christian scriptures. Overall it is approximately the same length as the New Testament, and it consists of 114 chapters, of widely-differing length it is true, but all in the same language, Arabic, and all bearing fundamentally the same prophetic message. There is some development in the detail of that message, so that some of the earlier sections of the Qur'ān, from the Meccan period of his career, contain short sharp warnings and calls to repent, along with stories, for example of earlier prophets, to reinforce the prophetic message of repentance in the light of imminent judgement, while some later sections, perhaps ten per cent, have been described as being legal in nature, and thus come from the latter part of Muḥammad's career, when he was responsible for the organisation and administration of a whole community in Yathrib.

The only significant complicating factor in understanding the Qur'ān is the fact that the arrangement of the chapters is based simply upon their length, so that after the first, or opening chapter (called the Fātiḥa) they proceed simply in order of length, with chapter two consisting of almost three hundred quite long verses, and some of the shorter chapters at the end of the Qur'ān consisting only of three or four short verses. This decision concerning how the chapters should be arranged seems to have been simply the decision of the early Muslim editors. Scholarly opinion differs over the extent of their further role in the process of compiling the Qur'ān, as in, for example, the compilation of individual chapters, but it is generally agreed that the process of compilation was completed by the first generation of Muslims after the death of Muḥammad.

Things are definitely not so simple with reference to the Christian scriptures. With reference to the Old Testament, first of all, here the books can be grouped into four main sections: firstly, the Law, or Torah, or Pentateuch, the last of which titles, based on a Greek word, indicates that five books are included under this heading; secondly, the Histories, or the Former Prophets, a further twelve books; thirdly, the Writings, a varied collection of five books; and finally the Later, or Latter Prophets, consisting of seventeen books. This is the usual Christian arrangement of these books, but it must be noted that it differs from the usual Jewish ordering of the thirty-nine books, which arranges them simply as the Torah, the Law, the first five books, followed by the eight prophetic books, including both Former and Latter prophets, and grouping the last twelve prophetic books of the Old Testament together as one book (called "The twelve"), followed by eleven books which make up the Writings.[5] And among Christians too there is further diversity, as although thirty-nine is the number of books which are universally accepted by Christians, there are a further seven books which are considered by some Christians to be scriptural, though of lesser (Deutero-canonical) status.[6]

The New Testament then also contains different types of book: at the beginning are four Gospel-accounts, which can most easily be categorised as biographies of Jesus, by four different authors; they are followed by a historical book, the book of Acts, which essentially chronicles the early history of the Christian church after the death of Jesus; then comes the largest group, of twenty-one Letters or Epistles, written by different leaders of the early church either to groups of Christians in particular cities, or to individual Christians. The authorship of thirteen of these letters has traditionally been attributed to Paul (nine to groups of Christians and four to individuals), seven are attributed to other early Christian leaders, and the source of the remaining one, the Letter to the Hebrews, is rather unclear. At the end of the New Testament there then comes the Book of Revelation, an apocalyptic vision which looks ahead in lurid terms to the end times and to the judgement.

Clearly, then, the Christian scriptures, compared with the Qur'ān, are anything but simple. They include the works of many different writers, produced over a considerable length of time, and, indeed, written in different languages, so that most of the Old Testament was originally written in Hebrew, and most of the New Testament in Greek, but Aramaic was also used for some of the Apocryphal books.

And whereas the Qur'ān, as we have seen, may be described as an essentially prophetic book, a great many different literary genres may be found within the pages of the Christian scriptures. In the Old Testament there is Law, especially in the first five books, and then there is history, telling the story of the experiences of the Jewish people as they journeyed around what is today described as the Middle East. There is also a considerable volume of prophecy, in two main forms. In the first the sayings and deeds of the early Jewish prophets such as Elijah and Elisha are outlined in narrative form by others, for example in the books of Samuel and Kings, and in the second the messages of later prophets such as Amos, Hosea, Isaiah and Jeremiah are recorded in books which bear their names (though this does not necessarily mean that they themselves actually wrote down their messages). In the Writings of the Old Testament there is then a huge variety of style, from the worship songs of the Psalms to the witty wise sayings of Proverbs to almost philosophical musings on life in general (Ecclesiastes) or on particular disastrous events (Lamentations). The New Testament too then contains a wide variety of types of literature – Gospel/biography, history, letters and apocalyptic vision.

For all the complexity of the Christian scriptures one saving grace is that the order of the books within them is roughly chronological with reference to the themes being described, though not necessarily to the order of their composition. Thus in the Old Testament the book of Genesis at the start of the Old Testament outlines the story of creation, the other books of the Torah refer to Moses, and the careers of the earlier prophets are outlined before the messages of the later ones, and in the New Testament the ministry of Jesus is described before the growth of the Christian community after his death and the ministry of Paul. In this respect, therefore, the Bible is perhaps more easily accessible to a first-time reader, at least a historically-minded one, than the Qur'ān, but overall this is probably outweighed by its otherwise greater diversity.

Compilation and editing

Because of the longer time-scale involved in the composition of the different books of the Christian scriptures, the process of editing and compiling them into the Christian scriptures as we have them today was also more complex and took longer than its equivalent for the Qur'ān.

With respect to the Qur'ān it is probably the case that some parts of it were written down before the death of Muḥammad in 632CE/11AH, with others existing in the memories of individual early Muslims, and that after a very brief period of oral transmission the whole scripture was written down and edited more or less into the form in which it exists today within some twenty-five years of Muḥammad's death. Muḥammad's first successors as leaders of the Muslim community seem to have taken the lead in initiating the process of collecting the messages proclaimed by him into book form, and while early editions of the Qur'ān were, according to the Muslim tradition, made by the first two caliphs, Abū Bakr and 'Umar ibn al-Khaṭṭāb, the authoritative collection was made by the third caliph, 'Uthmān, and this is why the text of the Qur'ān is sometimes referred to as the 'Uthmānic text.[7]

Even then, however, some variations in the text of the Qur'ān still remained. In the time of 'Uthmān, Arabic was written only in consonantal form, in other words without any vowels. The vowels, which take the form of small markings either above or below the consonants were thus only added later, in the time of the caliph 'Abd al-Malik (685–705CE/65–86AH). Because of this, given the extent to which the Islamic state spread geographically in its early centuries, different local traditions concerning how exactly the Qur'ān should be read, especially with reference to the vowels which should be used, grew up. Around 900CE/288AH, through the work of Ibn Mujāhid, seven readings were recognised as valid, the so-called canonical readings, and each of these had two permitted variants, so fourteen options were available, each considered equally authoritative. Variations were usually small, since they involved the use of different vowels for particular words, but the mere recognition of the possibility of some variation points to the acceptance of the fact that there had been some human role in the compilation and editing of the scriptural text. It had not simply been given to Muḥammad and inherited by the Muslim community with all the i's dotted and t's crossed, as it were; on some points of detail decisions had had to be taken by human editors and compilers, and they had not always agreed absolutely.

Further features of the text of the Qur'ān as we have it today were also added later. The formal division of the chapters into verses, for example, though in many cases based on the natural rhythms contained in the often poetic content of the message, was carried out later, and early commentators on the Qur'ān devoted a great deal of their time to working out the exact circumstances in which individual chapters, or indeed sections within individual chapters, had been revealed to Muḥammad. This work focused especially on the question of whether chapters should be thought of as belonging to either the Meccan or Medinan period of Muḥammad's career, and many editions of the Qur'ān now include this information as part of the title of each chapter.[8]

Perhaps the most significant development concerning the text of the Qur'ān, however, came with the development of printing and the publication, in 1924CE/1342AH, of the so-called royal Egyptian edition of the Qur'ān. It was called royal since it was prepared under the auspices of King Fu'ād of Egypt, and the influence of this edition may be seen simply in the fact that it is now the generally-accepted edition of the Qur'ān throughout the Muslim world. Significantly, however, a decision had to be made by those who prepared this edition as to which of the earlier canonical readings should be used, and their choice fell on the version of Ḥafṣ derived from that of 'Āṣim, and it is this one that has now become the standard or authorised version, in effect supplanting all the other canonical readings.[9] Its success can thus be seen in the fact that among most Muslims today there is no knowledge of the existence of the seven canonical readings, and the assumption is simply made that the version used by the Egyptian royal edition is the original text in every detail.[10]

With reference to the compilation and editing of the Christian scriptures, by contrast, again we find a greater degree of complexity. In the case of the Old Testament the period of oral transmission for some of the earlier books may have been as much as several centuries, but it seems that both legal and prophetic material was available in written form before the fall of Jerusalem in 587 BCE, and that the Law/Pentateuch was more or less complete by the time of Ezra and Nehemiah around 450 BCE. Individual prophetic books may well have been written down within twenty or thirty years of the prophet's death, and then the prophetic books were probably collected together over the course of the third century BCE. The idea of a third category of books, which later came to be known as the Writings, was established in the second century BCE, when the author of the prologue of the Book of Ecclesiasticus/Ben Sirach, probably around 130 BCE, referred to "the law, the prophets and the other books"; disagreement about exactly which books should be included in that grouping continued for some time, however.

Given that the Jewish community was scattered in different parts of the world by the time of Jesus, different Jewish communities had different collections of scriptures, but the Council of Jamnia in 90CE produced a standard canon, or collection, of scriptures, which essentially corresponds to the thirty-nine books of the Protestant Old Testament, though grouped together in a different order. The Council of Jamnia also produced a standard consonantal text, Hebrew, like Arabic, only coming to use vowels at a later stage of its development, and as a result different traditions of reading the text developed in different Jewish communities.

The vocalised text, including the vowels, was produced by the Masoretes in the middle centuries of the first millennium CE, and differences still persisted between the editions produced in Palestine and Babylonia, but the text which has become most widely accepted in the modern era is the Palestinian text of Ben Asher.

With respect to the New Testament, the four Gospel-accounts were probably written between 60 and 100CE, either by disciples of Jesus or by associates of the disciples of Jesus, and the Epistles were probably written between 50 and 100CE. The period of oral transmission before the accounts were consigned to writing is thus rather longer than was the case either with reference to some of the prophetic books of the Old Testament or with reference to the Qur'ān.

The collection of the different scriptures into the form of the New Testament also took some time. The four gospel-accounts had become generally accepted by the time of Irenaeus around 180CE; the Pauline epistles were assembled into a collection round about the same time; the main outline of the contents of the New Testament had been agreed by 200CE, as reflected in the Muratorian Fragment, and the final canon/collection of twenty-seven books is first referred to in the Festal letter of Athanasius in 367CE.

The process whereby the text of the Bible was divided up into chapters and verses, for ease of reference and of public reading took even longer, with the establishment of chapter divisions usually being attributed to Stephen Langton (died 1228CE/625AH), a lecturer in the University of Paris who later become archbishop of Canterbury. The further subdivision of the chapters into verses was accomplished first for the Old Testament, by Rabbi Isaac Nathan in around 1440CE/844AH, a system which (fortunately!) Christians adopted within a century or so; and then a system was established for the New Testament in Geneva around 1550CE/957AH, by Robert Stephanus. In a number of instances the divisions between verses are unsatisfactory as where, for example, a new verse begins in the middle of a sentence, but Stephanus' system does have the virtue of having become universally accepted, greatly aided by the development of printing shortly before his own time.

The whole process, then, was more complex and certainly took longer in the Christian community than it did within the Muslim community. But it is important to remember in seeking to make comparisons that analogies cannot be drawn between the collection of the Qur'ān and the collection of the Bible as a whole, since the latter is a collection of books, whereas the former is a single book. The only analogy which can accurately be drawn, therefore, is between the compilation of the Qur'ān and the compilation of an individual book within the Christian scriptures, and if one of the prophetic books of the Old Testament is used for the comparison, since they are closest in style and content to the message of the Qur'ān, then the process of compilation is actually extremely similar.[11]

It is also worth noting that with respect to neither the Bible nor the Qur'ān do we have original manuscripts available. Here too, as we might expect given its later composition, the tradition is stronger for the Qur'ān than for the Bible, as the earliest complete manuscripts of the Qur'ān date from the late 8th century CE/2nd century AH though there are fragments which date from the 7th century CE/1st century AH. For the Old Testament, by contrast, the earliest complete texts date from the 10th century CE/4th century AH, though the recent discovery of the Dead Sea Scrolls has made available texts of parts of all the Old Testament books except that of Esther from the first century BCE. The earliest complete text of the New Testament, the Codex Sinaiticus, dates from the fourth century CE, though fragments have been dated from as early as 120CE.[12] In the case of both scriptures, then, as well as a period of oral transmission of tradition before the scriptures were written in the first place, there is also a period of time during which written texts which are not available today were in circulation.[13]

Overall, however, we have to conclude that in form and content, and also with respect to the process of compilation and editing, there are obvious dissimilarities between the Muslim and the Christian scriptures. In most cases the contrast is between the relative simplicity of the Qur'ān – one message, received by one person, in one language, over a twenty-two year period and collected together within a further twenty-five years – and the relative complexity of the Bible – several dozen messages, received by many different people, in several languages, over many centuries, grouped together in two main sections or testaments, the first of which was collected together over several centuries and the second of which took several centuries to be finalised, even if its broad outlines were clear within a century and a half or so of the time of Jesus. Even if, therefore, both Christians and Muslims use the term "scripture", the importance of recognising that they each mean something rather different by it cannot be stressed enough.

Later developments in the understanding of "scripture"

In their origins and formation, then, there are some important differences between the Christian and Muslim scriptures. In later centuries, however, there are some intriguing parallels between the ways in which the two communities have developed their understanding of their scriptures.

This is true firstly with respect to the whole development of the concept and status of scripture. Over the centuries there developed within the Christian tradition an understanding of scripture as dictated by God.[14] This had as its consequence the idea that there was no involvement of the personality of the human vehicle through which the message was received, and even later there emerged the idea of the infallibility of scripture. The writings of James Barr are especially helpful on this, since he writes of how the "prophetic paradigm" of inspiration came to dominate Christian thinking in this area, despite the fact that it may not be at all appropriate for the Bible as a whole.[15]

In the Islamic tradition too a very exalted view of the status of Scripture developed, in particular the view that the Qur'ān was uncreated, existing with God even before its delivery to Muḥammad. This has had important consequences with respect to how the Qur'ān is understood and interpreted for it has given rise to the view that the message is eternally and universally valid, which in turn has produced some rather superficial exegesis which takes little or no account of the context within which the revelation was received, and has little explanation of the diversity of understanding which has evolved over the centuries.[16]

A second, more contemporary, parallel between the two traditions with respect to the understanding of "scripture" can be discerned in what can be called "the quest for external validation". What is involved here is the shared quest by more conservative Christians and Muslims for an external "independent" source of verification and authentication for the "truth" of scripture. The irony here is that each has located the source of authenticity/validation in a sense in the territory of the other, for conservative Christian opinion, especially in the West, has tended to find its "proof" of the truth of the Bible in the fulfilment of Old Testament prophecies in political developments in the Middle East, especially the creation of the state of Israel in 1948/1367, its spectacular victory in the war of 1967/1387, and so on.[17] This argument completely ignores the fact that the not inconsiderable lobbying power of supporters of this view in Western capitals may itself be one of the factors that have enabled these develop- ments to come about.

In balance to this conservative Muslims looking for external validation of the truth of the Qur'ān have developed a strong line of argument based on the view that the most telling evidence of the superiority of the Qur'ān to the Bible is its scientific statements, especially with respect to the creation of humankind, for, it is argued, the Qur'ān speaks of creation from a blood-clot (i.e. embryo) while the Bible speaks of creation from dust. One of the best selling Muslim books of recent years has thus been *The Bible, the Qur'ān and Science* by Dr. Maurice Bucaille, an eminent French surgeon who converted to Islam because of his having been convinced by precisely this argument, and in this work Bucaille argues that it is science which establishes the truth of the Qur'ān.[18]

This rather mechanical approach to the scriptures, which results in their being treated as some kind of heavenly truth-bank or data-base, can also be seen in the enthusiasm with which some Christians and Muslims have greeted the opportunities presented by the computerisation of the texts. Machine-readable versions of both Bible and Qur'ān have been prepared in a number of different places, with Hodder and Stoughton in Britain making the Biblical text available on disc and several different Muslim groups doing the same for the Qur'ān, in many cases combined with the Ḥadīth (Tradition).[19]

Similarities such as these, however, should not blind us to the perhaps more fundamental dissimilarities which exist between the two traditions, and this may be illustrated finally by their different approaches towards the possibility of their scriptures being translated. On this question the Christian tradition has generally displayed a far greater measure of flexibility.

Thus we have already seen the importance of the Septuagint, the translation of the Hebrew scriptures into Greek undertaken by seventy Jewish scholars in Alexandria in the third century BCE.[20] Even before the time of Jesus, therefore, the tradition of translating scriptures already existed in the Jewish community, even if later the Council of Jamnia in 90CE decided to include only books written in Hebrew in the canon of the Jewish Bible. With respect to the more specifically Christian scriptures, the New Testament, it is important to remember that any of the words attributed to Jesus in the four gospel-accounts are actually themselves already translations, since Jesus originally spoke Aramaic, and all the books of the New Testament were written in Greek. This shows clearly the transformation which took place in the early Christian community, under the guidance of Paul and others, whereby the message of Jesus came to be understood as being of significance not simply for Jews but for other peoples too.

Not only that but the New Testament itself also specifically encourages the idea of translation. In the last book of the New Testament, the book of Revelation, it is stated, in chapter 14 and verse 6, that the gospel is to be announced "to all the peoples of the earth, to every race, tribe, tongue, and nation", and this has been taken as a scriptural justification for the translation of the scriptures. Thus in the fourth century CE Jerome translated both the Old and New Testaments into Latin, and there was also a translation into Syriac in the early Christian centuries. In the Middle Ages, however, for a time the view became established that further translation was not permissible, and it was only during the Reformation in the sixteenth century CE/tenth century AH that the principle was once again established that translation into vernacular languages was not only permissible, but also desirable.[21]

In the Islamic tradition, by contrast, translation of the Qur'ān has not generally been encouraged. This is due in part to a number of statements in the Qur'ān which specifically refer to an Arabic Qur'ān (e.g. chapter 12, verse 2). Versions of the Qur'ān which have been prepared in other languages have not therefore traditionally been accepted as deserving to be called the Qur'ān; rather they should be described simply as interpretations of the Qur'ān.[22] Translations have been made in different periods, however, into Persian and Turkish in the medieval period, and into Persian and Urdu in more modern times in the Indian Sub-continent by Shāh Walīullāh (d 1762CE/1176AH) and his sons respectively.

The different attitudes of the two traditions to the question of translation is also reflected in their more general attitudes towards the study of their scriptures, especially in modern times. Many Christians have therefore been happy to apply a more inductive approach to the study of the Bible (what scripture means to me), leading to such activities as group Bible-study, whereas in the Muslim community a more deductive approach, relying for understanding on the interpretations of the great masters of the past, is more prevalent. But it should be stressed that this is also true of significant parts of the Christian world, it being particularly in Protestant churches that the inductive approach is most established. Additionally attitudes differ among Christians and Muslims towards the whole question of criticism of their scriptures. In general terms the idea of Biblical criticism is well-established in most western churches, though to a lesser extent in eastern churches, but any idea of an equivalent Qur'ānic criticism is viewed with considerable suspicion by most Muslims.[23]

Conclusion

With respect to Scripture, then, as with origins, we find some parallels and some significant differences between the two traditions. Looking at the two areas together, however, and especially the link between them, one really important distinction between Christianity and Islam does need to be highlighted, and that is the balance between person and book. In the Christian tradition, the apogee of revelation is a person, Jesus Christ, to whom the Christian scriptures bear witness. In Islam, by contrast, the apogee of revelation is a book, the Qur'ān, and the function of the person Muḥammad was simply to make known the message which came to be contained in the book.[24]

In looking for points of comparison between the two traditions, therefore, it is more accurate to compare not the persons of Jesus and Muḥammad but rather Jesus within the Christian tradition and the Qur'ān within the Islamic tradition as it is they which are the primary locations of revelation for each tradition. The role of Muḥammad as the vehicle through whom the revelation was made available in Islam is thus best parallelled by Mary, through whom Jesus came into being, in Christian conviction. Equally it is not strictly accurate to compare Bible and Qur'ān, since although they are the scriptures of both traditions their role within their respective tradition differs: in Islam the Qur'ān is the central revelation of God, whereas for Christians the Bible is rather the record or testimony of that central revelation which is the person of Jesus. A better analogy in Islam for the Bible is therefore the Ḥadīth, which will be discussed further below; this is the Tradition of Islam, which records, among other things, the details of Muḥammad's life and the practice of the early Muslim community.

The basic and fundamental statement concerning the different central focus of the two faiths, on person (for Christians) and book (for Muslims), however, should not close our eyes to the existence of a spectrum of opinion in both traditions on these questions, for some Christian groups do come close to a kind of Bibliolatry, to putting the Book first, and equally some Muslims, particularly those from the Indian Sub-continent, who because they are not Arabic-speaking have limited access to the Scripture, have elevated the person of Muḥammad to a kind of primacy, as Salman Rushdie discovered to his cost. In some circles this even involves going so far as to speak of a pre-existent Muḥammad, a kind of Logos figure.[25] In both traditions, therefore, there is a spectrum of opinion on this question, and even if the central focus of the spectrum of each is different that does not mean that the two spectrums do not appear to cross at certain points.

Notes

1 This is an area in which historically there has been much ignorance and misunderstanding among both Christians and Muslims. Some light has recently begun to be shed on the situation, however, not least by mutual study of both scriptures by Christians and Muslims together. See for example *The challenge of the scriptures*, Orbis, Maryknoll, 1989, a work which is the outcome of the researches and discussions over a number of years of the Muslim-Christian Research Group, a group consisting of French-speaking Christians (mostly Roman Catholic) and Muslims (mostly North African Arabs).

2 Although many Christians today talk of the Bible, in the singular, it is important to note that originally the term used was the Greek Biblia, which is a plural, meaning books, and only when this term was translated into Latin did the singular usage emerge as, coincidentally, in Latin Biblia is a singular, meaning book. This is the term which has later become established in other western European languages. See W.C. Smith *What is scripture?* SCM, 1993, p 13.

3 Some readers may find the use of the term "revelation" with reference to either the Qur'ān or the Christian scriptures problematic, perhaps because they are used to the term only being used to refer to their own scriptures or perhaps, if they are well-versed in modern western Christian Biblical scholarship, because the use of the term at all is sometimes rejected because of an overwhelming insistence on the human authorship of the works involved. Given the broadly phenomenological approach being adopted in this work, however, the term has been retained and used with reference to both scriptures partly because this is the way in which at least some parts of both scriptures seem to have wished to have been understood, and partly because of the prominence of this view of the scriptures during both Christian and Muslim history.

4 See the next section of this chapter for further detail on this process.

5 Additionally some books are categorised differently by Jews and Christians, so that, for example, Ruth, counted among the Histories/Former Prophets by Christians, is included in the Writings by Jews, and Daniel, a Later/Latter Prophet to Christians, is also among the Writings for Jews. See G.W. Anderson *The living world of the Old Testament*, 2nd ed., Longman, 1967, pp 4–5 and 554–559.

6 These have traditionally been included in Roman Catholic and Orthodox Bibles, but either omitted from Protestant ones or included as the Apocrypha, which literally means "hidden". These books are not included in the Jewish Bible of today, since they were not originally written in Hebrew, but they were included in the very important translation of the Jewish Bible into Greek, the Septuagint (so called because it was the work of seventy scholars), produced in Egypt in the third century BCE. The early Christians generally used the Septuagint, and it is this fact which explains why Roman Catholic and Orthodox Christians include these books in the Bible, while Protestants followed later Jewish opinion, and did not include them.

7 This is the traditional Muslim view on this question. Modern Western scholarship has disputed this, even on occasion producing the apparently

surprising opinion that the compilation of the Qur'ān as we have it today should actually be pushed back to the time of Muḥammad himself. See J. Burton *The collection of the Qur'ān*, Cambridge U.P., 1977.

8 One of the biggest technical difficulties for Westerners wishing to refer to particular verses of the Qur'ān is the fact that one of the earliest Western editions of the text, that prepared by Flügel in 1834, used a system of verse-numbering which corresponds to none of the Muslim systems. A number of English versions of the Qur'ān, however, particularly that by Arberry, still use Flügel's numbering, and so quotations from the text often need to be given two references, one to the generally-used Muslim edition and one to Flügel's edition.

9 On the question of the readings of the Qur'ān see W.M. Watt *Introduction to the Qur'ān*, Edinburgh U.P., 1970, pp 48–50.

10 An analogy may be noted here with reference to the situation in the English-speaking world whereby the Authorised Version of the Bible, the English translation of the Christian scriptures prepared in 1611CE/1020AH under the auspices of King James I of England, also acquired such a high status in the eyes of some of its users that it came to be thought of as itself being the original scripture. The situation is different from that of the Qur'ān, of course, in that the Authorised Version was a translation, rather than an edition of the original text, but stories exist of some devout and rather conservative Christians, confronted in the past century or so with the publication of other more modern English translations of the Christian scriptures, saying "if the Authorised Version was good enough for St. Paul (or even sometimes for Jesus), it is good enough for me"!

11 It is worth noting that some Old Testament scholars have specifically referred to the compilation of the Qur'ān in looking for an analogy of how the various prophetic books of the Old Testament were assembled.

12 The British Library in London is the location both of the earliest complete text of the New Testament, the Codex Sinaiticus, and of one of the two earliest complete extant manuscripts of the Qur'ān, Brit.Mus Or 2165.

13 In the light of this, there is an interesting historical parallel between the efforts of the third successor to Muḥammad as leader of the Muslim community, 'Uthmān (644–656CE/23–35AH), to establish a standard text of the Muslim scripture, and those of the Roman Emperor Constantine in the early fourth century CE to establish a standard text of the Christian scriptures.

14 Pope Gregory I (590–604), for example, held the view that "God had communicated to men through the elaborate allegories of the scriptural record whose human authors were no more than a pen in the hand of their real divine author". See M. Wiles *The remaking of Christian doctrine*, SCM, 1974, p 106.

15 See his *Fundamentalism*, 2nd ed., SCM, 1981, and *Escaping from fundamentalism*, SCM, 1984. See also J. Barton *People of the book? – the authority of the Bible in Christianity*, 2nd ed, SPCK, 1993, and the essay "The authority of scripture according to scripture" by J.D.G. Dunn in his *The living word*, SCM, 1987, pp 89–140.

16 See G. Widengren "Holy book and holy tradition in Islam" in F.F. Bruce and E.G. Rupp (eds.) *Holy book and holy tradition*, Manchester U.P., 1968, pp 210–236.

17 The most dramatic example of literature of this kind is *The Late Great*

Planet Earth by Hal Lindsey, Zondervan, 1970, which, after the Bible, is far and away best-selling Christian book of recent years. It is described by Malise Ruthven, who has also written on Islam, as "a mixture of biblical epic, science fiction and disaster movie" in his *The divine supermarket: travels in search of the soul of America*, Chatto and Windus, 1989, p 196.

18 First published in French by Editions Seghers in 1976, Bucaille's book has been translated into many other languages, including Arabic (dār al-ma'ārif, Cairo, 1978), and English (many different editions, of which I have used the 4th, published by Seghers in 1987). The main thrust of its message is also available in pamphlet form under the title *The Qur'ān and modern science*, also available in many different editions. A more recent publication is *What is the origin of man?*, Seghers, no date, but in this work the author's argument is altered to some extent so that the different scriptures are used together (rather than in opposition to each other) to suggest that science and religion are not inherently incompatible.

19 It is also worth noting that the last decade has seen cartoon versions of both scriptures being produced in different parts of the world. This development, however, has been considerably more controversial than the computerisation of the texts, especially with reference to the strip-cartoon version of the Qur'ān prepared by Yūsuf Ṣiddīq, a Tunisian writer, and published in France at the end of 1989.

20 See above, note 6.

21 At certain stages of the Middle Ages the interesting view known as the Four Languages Heresy became established, according to which the Bible could only exist in Hebrew, Aramaic, Greek or Latin, in other words in its original languages or in the language into which it had already been translated by Jerome. This view was eventually rejected, however, though it was only rather later, after several people such as William Tyndale (d 1536CE/943AH) had paid for it with their lives, that translation of the Bible into other languages became widely supported.

22 It is for this reason that many of the English renderings of the Qur'ān have been careful to use such titles as "The meaning of the glorious Qur'ān" (M.M. Pickthall) or "The Koran interpreted" (A.J. Arberry), but in the most recent printings of these versions publishers seem to be becoming less fastidious in their observance of this convention, with Oxford University Press now simply calling the Arberry version "The Koran".

23 On this see further my article "Each other's scripture", with a response by Hasan Askari, in *Newsletter of the Centre for the study of Islam and Christian-Muslim relations*, Selly Oak, Birmingham, No 5 (May 1981), pp 16–28.

24 Muḥammad is thus sometimes described in Muslim literature as the "voice-box of God" or the "larynx of God". His role, in other words, was simply to provide the physical instruments through which the message of the Qur'ān could be made audible and pronounced.

25 See the Appendix to V. Danner's *The Islamic Tradition*, Amity House, New York, 1988, for a list of the names of Muḥammad which point to what Danner calls his "transhistorical, spiritual reality". See also A. Schimmel *And Muḥammad is his messenger: the veneration of the prophet in Islamic piety*, University of North Carolina Press, 1987, especially the Appendix listing the noble names of the prophet.

3

THE DEVELOPMENT OF RELIGIOUS THOUGHT

Introduction

One further area in which the two traditions display certain parallels is that they develop after their origins and on the basis of their scriptures. Each develops partly as a result of internal discussion on certain contentious issues, and partly as a result of interaction with external influences and ideas. It is important to note, however, that developments springing from internal debate take different forms in the two traditions for a number of reasons, and while there is perhaps more similarity with regards to their development through interplay with external ideas, the sequential placement of such developments differs chronologically.

Early Christian thought

Internal

The internal debates which took place within the early Christian community focused mainly on what may loosely be called 'doctrine'. This resulted partly from issues concerning the relationship between the followers of Jesus on the one hand and the Jewish community on the other, issues which focused on the exact nature of Jesus and what was the nature of his relationship with God and partly from the fact that as a minority group within the powerful Roman state, sometimes tolerated by that state but sometimes persecuted by it, Christians were driven to develop doctrine as a means of shaping their identity and of defining the boundaries of their community. The Christian creeds are therefore perhaps the most significant product of this early period of Christian thought.

As we have already seen, Jesus and all of his first disciples were

3

THE DEVELOPMENT OF RELIGIOUS THOUGHT

Introduction

One further area in which the two traditions display certain parallels is that they develop after their origins and on the basis of their scriptures. Each develops partly as a result of internal discussion on certain contentious issues, and partly as a result of interaction with external influences and ideas. It is important to note, however, that development springing from internal debate takes different forms in the two traditions, for a number of reasons, and while there is perhaps more similarity with regards to their development through interplay with external ideas, this process took place out of synchronisation chronologically.

Early Christian thought

a) Internal

The internal debates which took place within the early Christian community focused mainly on what may loosely be called doctrine. This resulted partly from issues concerning the relationship between the followers of Jesus on the one hand and the Jewish community on the other, issues which focused on who exactly Jesus was and what was the nature of his relationship with God and partly from the fact that as a minority group within the powerful Roman state, sometimes tolerated by that state but sometimes persecuted harshly by it, Christians were driven to develop doctrine as a means of stating their identity and of defining the boundaries of their community. The Christian creeds are therefore perhaps the most significant product of this early period of Christian thought.

As we have already seen, both Jesus and all of his first disciples were

Jews. They were thus firmly monotheists, coming from a community which had been monotheist for centuries. As a result of the crucifixion of Jesus, however, in which the leaders of some of the Jewish schools of thought of the day were implicated, relations between the Jewish community and the Jesus movement did not take long to become strained. At first, even after the death of Jesus, his followers continued to worship in Jewish synagogues and in the Temple in Jerusalem, but once they had become known as Christians and the decision to make Jesus known among non-Jews too had been taken then the two communities began to go their separate ways.[1]

The Christians thus proclaimed their conviction that Jesus had been the Messiah, God's anointed servant and the Saviour of those who responded to his message, while the Jewish community continued to reject these claims. It was not long, therefore, before the Christians began to articulate more systematically their view of who Jesus was.

An important contributory factor to this process was the intellectual milieu in which the Christian church grew up. The Eastern Mediterranean area in the time of Jesus had been deeply influenced by Hellenistic culture in the wake of the conquests of Alexander the Great in the fourth century BCE. In the wake of those conquests Greek culture and the Greek language had become widespread throughout the region, and it was for this reason that some members of the Jewish community had seen fit to translate the Hebrew scriptures into Greek, the result of their efforts being the Septuagint.[2]

One of the major issues confronting the Jewish community in the centuries preceding the time of Jesus, therefore, was the question of how it should respond to Hellenistic influences and ideas: were they to be welcomed and viewed positively, or were they to be seen rather as negative and threatening? Not surprisingly, opinion was divided. But when the Christian movement began to establish itself, having taken the decision to make Jesus known beyond the boundaries of the Jewish community and to produce its scriptures in the Greek language, it was almost inevitable that to a greater or lesser extent the way in which the early Christians expressed their faith would be influenced by Hellenistic ideas.

One of the areas affected by this development was Christian explanation of who Jesus was, the area technically known as Christology. In seeking to explain their views on this question, what the early Christians did was to draw upon certain trends of thought which had developed in some Jewish circles in the three centuries or so before the time of Jesus, with particular reference to certain Messianic and other intermediary figures between God and human beings. This involved such figures as Enoch, who was referred to in the book of Genesis, chapter 5, verse 24, as someone who walked with God and was then taken to be with God. On the strength of this statement the view developed that because of his miraculous ascension Enoch had become a kind of intermediary figure between God and humankind who had undertaken a heavenly journey with the angels and gained wisdom so that he became the initiator of wisdom on earth.

In addition to such individual figures as Enoch (and Enoch, incidentally, is one of the Old Testament figures who is referred to also in the Qur'ān, where he is named Idrīs), personifications of certain key virtues also became prominent and came to be thought of as having some intermediary role between God and human beings. Thus Wisdom (Sophia) began to be identified with this role, and Wisdom was thus a prominent feature not only of some of the Writings in the Old Testament but even more so in some of the Jewish writings which were not in the end accepted into the Hebrew Bible but were included in the Septuagint, such as The Wisdom of Solomon and the Book of Ecclesiasticus (or the Wisdom of Ben Sirach). The idea of the uncreated Torah was another concept which, in some Jewish writings, came to occupy an intermediary role. And so too did the idea of the Logos, the Word, which in the work of Philo, a Jew living in Alexandria at around the same time as Jesus, came to fulfil a mediating role too.

All of these ideas were part of the background against which the early Christians attempted to elaborate and formulate their view of who Jesus was. When combined with the idea of covenant which was prominent in the Old Testament with reference to the relationship between God and his people Israel, so that, for example, some of the prophets referred to God as the "father" of his people, these ideas led to the emergence of Christian use of what might be called the language of relationship in order to clarify the status of Jesus. In particular, it was stated, he enjoyed a special relationship with God, to the extent that he could be called the son of God, as well as, for example in the Gospel according to John, the Logos, the Word of God.

In the New Testament writings, therefore, we see a number of attempts to point to the special status of Jesus. The claim, for example, that he had been raised from the dead[3] was one way of pointing to Jesus' special relationship with God. So too were other ideas, such as his miraculous conception and birth, or his ascension to be with God after his resurrection.

Once this kind of language had become established, further reflection was necessary in order to clarify the exact nature of the relationship between Jesus and God. Was Jesus in some sense divine, or was he simply a chosen human being? If he was in some way divine but also human, how did the two parts of his nature relate to each other? These questions quickly became the source of considerable controversy within the early Christian community, and the mechanism which was adopted to resolve the tensions was the holding of a number of Church Councils.

The first Council, held at Nicaea in 325, dealt with questions raised by the Egyptian priest Arius, who had suggested that Christ was created and subordinate to God; the Council concluded that Christ was uncreated and divine, eternally begotten of the Father and the same in being as the Father. The second Council, held at Constantinople in 381, then dealt with Apollinarius of Laodicea (in Syria) who, on the basis of decisions of the Council of Nicaea, had argued that Christ was not fully human, since he was motivated by the Logos rather than by a human mind; the Council affirmed Christ's full humanity. The third Council, held in Ephesus in 431, addressed the views of the Syrian monk Nestorius, who had affirmed both the full divinity and the full humanity of Christ but was accused of suggesting that his two natures somehow operated separately so that when, for example, healing it was Christ's divine nature operating whereas when suffering it was in his human nature that he was afflicted; the Council affirmed the unity of Christ in response. And the fourth Council, held at Chalcedon, near Constantinople, in 451, pronounced on the opinions of Eutyches, a monk in Constantinople, who while accepting that Christ had two natures nevertheless argued that the human nature was absorbed into the divine so that the divine predominated; the Council affirmed that two natures remain in one person in Christ.[4]

The deliberations of each of these Councils were passionate and often acrimonious, given that it was clearly an essential item of Christian belief which was under discussion and the unity of the Christian church which was at stake. The Councils' decisions, not surprisingly, were not universally accepted, and so the risk of division within the Christian community was great. After the first Council it looked for some decades as if the views of Arius were actually going to become more widely accepted than those of the Council. After the second Apollinarius' views remained widely influential, especially in what came to be known as the Alexandrian school of thought concerning Christology.[5] But it was after the third and fourth Councils that long-lasting institutional division took place and separate churches were established in different parts of the Christian world.[6]

A consensus of the majority of Christians eventually emerged around a view which stated that Jesus was both fully human and fully divine, the two natures being combined in one person.[7] But this raised certain further difficulties, not least connected with the question of whether this meant that Christians had somehow qualified monotheism, and when this was combined with discussion of a third person of significance, the Holy Spirit, further discussion concerning the nature of God was inevitable.[8]

The concept of the Spirit of God was not one which was invented by Christians since the Old Testament refers to the Spirit of the Lord coming upon people on a number of different occasions. Jewish writings in the centuries before the time of Jesus also refer to such a spirit. It is in the New Testament, however, that there were fuller references to the Spirit, usually described there as the Holy Spirit, with the Gospel according to John in particular suggesting that Jesus himself spoke of a Spirit who would come after him and give guidance and comfort to the followers of Jesus, and in the Book of Acts it was the Holy Spirit who was responsible for arousing the disciples from their inertia after the disappearance of Jesus and giving them fresh enthusiasm for the task of making the message of Jesus widely known. (Acts 2:1–13)

Once the Holy Spirit had become an important part of Christian teaching and discussion similar questions to those about the relationship between Jesus and God began to be asked about the exact nature of the Spirit's relationship to God, and to Jesus. It was in the context of this discussion, therefore, that Trinitarian language began to be used of God, the suggestion being that there was only one God, but that there were three Persons within that one God.[9]

Early internal discussions within the Christian community thus focused on these doctrinal issues, and the Christian Creeds, which were intended to serve as authoritative statements to resolve these questions, were the main outcome of these discussions. This is not to say that there were not other areas of controversy too, but it is to say that issues of doctrine were the most significant internal focus of early Christian thought.[10]

A number of other issues also preoccupied Christian thinkers in the early centuries. On the one hand there was the question of the organisation and leadership of the Christian community, on which issue the early centuries saw the emergence of three types of church leader, bishops, presbyters and deacons, but the exact detail of the division of responsibility between them is not clear. At the highest level the deliberations of the various Councils of the Early Church eventually resulted in the recognition of five senior figures of authority in the church, who eventually became known as Patriarchs, based in Jerusalem, Antioch, Alexandria, Rome and Constantinople, and this reflected the tendency towards the establishment of a hierarchical organisation within the church.

On the other hand there was also the vital question of the appropriate attitude to be adopted by Christians towards political authorities, especially the Roman Emperor. At times the early Christians emphasised the importance of submission to and respect for the Roman authorities, but at other times the emphasis was much more on obeying God rather than man and a much more negative attitude towards the authorities was taken up. In large part, not surprisingly, Christian thinking on this subject was affected by the attitude of the authorities towards the young Christian community: if the authorities were tolerant the Christians were submissive, but in any era of persecution or harassment a far darker view of the state came to predominate among the Christians.[11]

Finally, the Early Church also had to wrestle with the ideas and practices of a number of groups which are usually described as extremist since they took an aspect of Christian teaching and developed it in such a way that it was given a prominence out of all proportion to its place in the New Testament and the opinion of the majority of the Christian community. Thus the Gnostics laid claim to special knowledge of God which led to salvation and the Montanists claimed that the Holy Spirit gave special guidance to their leaders, who were therefore called upon to alert people to the imminent end of the world, but each of these groups was condemned as being in error, or heretical.[12]

b) External

Alongside these discussions within the Christian community there were also parallel discussions concerning the attitude which Christians should adopt towards other intellectual traditions, especially the Hellenistic/Greek one of Socrates, Plato and Aristotle. We have seen already how Hellenistic culture challenged and influenced Jewish thought in the period before the time of Jesus, and how Hellenistic ideas had some influence on the internal development of Christian thinking. Like the Jewish community, therefore, the Christian church had to work out how it was going to evaluate and assess the worth or otherwise of this tradition.

In the early Christian centuries what actually evolved with reference to this question is that a wide spectrum of Christian opinion developed.

Some Christian thinkers were basically negative in their attitude towards the Greek heritage. Tertullian, for example, in North Africa in the third century, simply asked "What has Athens to do with Jerusalem?", implying, in other words, that the tradition of Greek philosophical thinking, with its birthplace in Athens, was of absolutely no relevance to Christian revelation, with its locus in Jerusalem. Other Christian thinkers, however, were by no means so negative, with Justin Martyr (c100–165), someone who had investigated a number of schools of Greek philosophy before being converted to Christianity, arguing that Christianity was the true philosophy, so that he continued to wear his philosopher's robe as a Christian teacher. And Clement of Alexandria at the start of the third century also took a broadly positive attitude towards the legacy of Greek philosophy.[13]

It was not always so, however. After Christianity became the official religion of the Roman Empire in the time of Constantine early in the third century CE, the development of a close association between the church and the political authorities seems to have led over a number of decades to a gradual waning in Christian intellectual curiosity and willingness to interact with other traditions of thought, so that, for example, in 529, the Byzantine Emperor Justinian closed the philosophy school in Athens (though rather than being completely extinguished it simply moved to another part of the world, Jundishapur in the Persian Empire, where the Syriac-speaking Christians of the Nestorian church ensured its survival and continued vitality). In the West, that is the Western half of the Roman Empire, traditions of learning and scholarship all but disappeared when the Empire was overrun and collapsed in 476CE, with Boethius (d c 524) being generally seen as the last creative philosophical thinker in the West for several centuries.

In the West, then, the intellectual hatches were, as it were, battened down, partly as a result of external threats and partly as a result of the breakdown of the political, economic and social order established by the Romans, and it was only later, with the renaissance of learning beginning in the twelfth century CE/sixth century AH, partly as a result of influence from the Islamic world, that the tradition was revived.

In the early Christian centuries, then, and also, in the West at least, since the renaissance of learning beginning in the twelfth/sixth century, Christian thought has broadly taken a positive view of the importance of interacting with wider intellectual and philosophical trends. A relatively open attitude towards other cultural traditions has thus been a feature of much of Christian history, but it is true that alongside that attitude a different, more negative, attitude has generally been evident, and at some periods of Christian history that more negative attitude has been dominant. As we turn to the Islamic community, we will see a similar rhythm evident over the course of the centuries.

Early Muslim thought

a) Internal

In the early Islamic community, partly as a result of the different circumstances in which it developed because of its link with the state, the issues which concerned and stimulated Muslim thinking were rather different from those which pre-occupied the first generations of Christian thinkers.

The first two questions which emerged were rather practical in nature, involving as they did questions which went so far as to cause armed conflict within the Muslim community. The first involved the question of the leadership of the community – who should lead the community, and what was the nature of their leadership; and the second focused on the issue of the boundaries of the Muslim community – who was a Muslim.[14]

When Muḥammad died in 632CE/11AH the question of who should succeed him as leader of the Muslims[15] was settled by the inner group of Muslims, Muḥammad's closest associates, who selected from among their own number Abū Bakr. When he died two years later a similar process took place, which resulted in the selection of another of the group 'Umar ibn al-Khaṭṭāb. On his death after ten years the selection fell on 'Uthmān, a member of the Umayyad clan within the tribe of Quraish. 'Uthmān's twelve year rule was seen by later Muslims as consisting of six positive years followed by six negative years since towards the end of his rule he began to be suspected of nepotism, having given a number of high (and lucrative) offices to his own relatives. In 656/35 'Uthmān was therefore murdered by a group of mutinous soldiers from Egypt, and a dispute arose concerning the succession.

On the one hand in this dispute were the protagonists of 'Alī, Muḥammad's cousin and son-in-law, who was widely recognised as being a model of piety and devotion but who, it seems, had not up until this point been considered for a position of leadership. Because of concern among some in the community about 'Uthmān's worldliness, however, 'Alī was put forward now and he seems to have been widely accepted at first, but he made no effort to bring the murderers of 'Uthmān to book, and so 'Uthmān's relatives, the powerful clan of Umayya, became restive.

Conflict broke out between the supporters of 'Alī[16] and the clan of Umayya in 657/37, and the situation was soon complicated by the emergence of a split among 'Alī's supporters, as a result of which a third party, the Khawārij emerged.[17] They claimed that as a result of a tactical error by 'Alī in his conflict with the clan of Umayya he had forfeited his claim to leadership, and that a future leader should therefore be chosen from among their number. After a series of military engagements involving all three groups, 'Alī was himself murdered, in 661/40, by one of the Khawārij, and the leading representative of the clan of Umayya, Mu'āwiya, became the generally-accepted leader of the Muslim community. When he died in 680/60 he was succeeded by his son Yazīd, and leadership remained with his Umayyad dynasty for almost a century, but this did not mean the end of the dispute about the leadership for 'Alī too had his descendants who continued to lay claim to the position.

The three views which emerged during this conflict and were then codified more systematically in the wake of it were thus firstly that of the Khawārij, who argued that leadership should rest with one of their number; secondly that of the Shī'a (party of 'Alī), whose view was that it should rest with 'Alī and his descendants; and thirdly that of the clan of Umayya, whose view was that it should rest with them. The main criterion for leadership which each group put forward was respectively spiritual merit (the Khawārij), blood relationship to Muḥammad (the Shī'a, since 'Alī was Muḥammad's closest surviving male relative), and, after some time, since their initial claim rested simply on military victory, membership of the same tribe as Muḥammad (the Umayyad clan).

The second question which occupied the attention of the early Muslim community was the related one of "who is a Muslim?" This arose because the Khawārij, in rather a similar way to their elitist approach to the question of leadership, reckoned that they alone were to be regarded as true and authentic Muslims. Others, in their view, might claim to be Muslim but they had in fact compromised the purity of their faith in some way and so they should be regarded as *kāfirs*, unbelievers, who should be fought against. It was for this reason that 'Alī was murdered by one of the Khawārij.

The Shī'a do not seem to have entertained a similarly narrow view of who was a Muslim; in other words they did not appear to suggest that their opponents were not Muslim, and equally the Umayyads did not adopt a narrow sectarian and exclusive view, and so in the early Muslim community as a whole the view which eventually came to predominate was the broader one that anyone who claimed to be a Muslim should be recognised as such. This view came to be identified with a school of thought known as the Murji'a, whose title literally means "those who defer judgement", on the basis that such a decision should be left to God.[18]

Following on from these two early issues, three further areas of discussion emerged in the first Muslim centuries, and on one level they may appear to be what might be called more theological, or more intellectual and theoretical issues, but as we shall see, in the context of the Muslim community they also had important consequences in other areas.[19]

The first of these more theoretical questions to be discussed involved the relationship between human free-will and divine predestination. This was a question which had earlier been discussed by Christians, St. Paul on the question of why the Jews had rejected Jesus, and Augustine on the question of why Rome had fallen when it had earlier been claimed that it was an instrument of the divine will.[20] Given the stress in the Qur'ān on the greatness and omnipotence of God, however, it was perhaps an especially difficult issue for the Muslim community.

Around 700/80 discussion of the issue began more systematically, and two schools of thought emerged: firstly the Qadariyya, who emphasised the real ability of human beings to choose, in other words their possession of free-will, and secondly the Jabriyya, the proponents of predestination.[21] Each group was able to point to certain passages in the Qur'ān in support of their view, so that the Qadariyya emphasised those scriptural passages which pointed to the need for humans to repent in the light of the fact that they would be judged by God while the Jabriyya stressed those passages which referred to human beings guided or being led astray by God. A number of attempts were made to resolve this paradox, including those of Ḥasan al-Baṣrī (d 728/110), who suggested that God did not so much predestine as command, so that God might have foreknowledge of but did not necessarily determine human actions, and the great theologian al-Ash'arī (d 935/324) who put forward the idea of *kasb*, namely that God did indeed predestine human actions, but human beings nevertheless acquired responsibility for them.[22]

What made discussion of this issue more than simply a matter of theological significance was the fact that the Umayyad dynasty gave its support to the proponents of predestination, for the simple reason that if God did indeed predestine, then clearly Umayyad rule had been predestined, and if that were the case then any attempt at overthrowing that rule, for example by different Shī'ī groups, was illegitimate. Theology and politics were thus closely intertwined.

A second issue involved the question of the attributes (*ṣifāt*) of God.

Again questions of how certain statements of the Qur'ān were to be understood were significant here, for example references to God sitting on his throne (2:255), and God being the seer and the hearer (40:21). Were these statements to be understood literally, or metaphorically?

One important contributor to the debate on these questions was the group known as the Mu'tazila, whose name literally means "those who secede", but whose preferred name for themselves was *ahl al-'adl wa'l-tawḥīd*, the people of justice and unity. The reference to justice indicates that on the question of free-will and predestination, their concern to preserve the idea of the justice of God led them to incline towards free-will, since if God punished wrong-doing, when it had been predestined, this was clearly unjust. And the reference to the unity points to their concern to preserve the monotheism of Islam absolutely rigidly.

The problem with the Qur'ān's references to the attributes of God, for the Mu'tazila, was firstly that if they were understood literally they ran the risk of anthropomorphism, suggesting that God was in some way like human beings, with similar characteristics and attributes, and the Mu'tazila were keen to preserve the difference (*mukhālafa*) of God from human beings, as well as to emphasise his unity. This latter was important since some Christian thinkers in the world of Islam argued that the Christian idea of the Trinity could be explained by using the language of attributes as an analogy in order to explain how it was that one God could exist in different persons, and this the Mu'tazila were keen to reject.

Their view was eventually rejected by the main body of the Muslim community, however, to a large extent as a result of the opposition to them of Aḥmad ibn Ḥanbal, (d 855/241) who preferred a more literal interpretation of the Qur'ān and a more tradition-based, as opposed to the reason-based views of the Mu'tazila, general understanding of Islam. Aḥmad ibn Ḥanbal thus insisted that the Qur'ān should be taken as it stands *bi-la kayf* (without asking how).[23]

The third issue then concerned the exact status of the Qur'ān itself, in particular the question of whether it was created or uncreated. Again statements from the scripture itself could be provided in order to support either view: "we have made an Arabic Qur'ān" (43:3) might seem to point to the logic of viewing the Qur'ān as created, but "the essence of the book is with us" (43:4) could be taken as meaning that the Qur'ān had always existed in essence with God, even if it was delivered to Muḥammad at a particular time and place.

This issue too became not simply an intellectual theological one but also a political one because one of the caliphs of the 'Abbāsid dynasty, which had taken over from the Umayyad dynasty in 750/132, al-Ma'mūn, in 833/218 chose to make the view that the Qur'ān was uncreated the official view of the state and to institute a kind of inquisition (*miḥna*) in order to ensure its universal acceptance. His reason for doing this seems to have been that with reference to the discussion concerning authority within the Muslim community, the view that the Qur'ān was created was more conducive to greater power resting with the political authorities whereas the view that the Qur'ān was uncreated would give more power to its interpreters, namely the religious scholars, the *'ulamā'*.

As is often the case with any attempt at coercion of opinion in matters of religion, al-Ma'mūn's policy completely backfired, and, to a large extent as a result of the opposition of Aḥmad ibn Ḥanbal, not only the *miḥna* but the whole idea of the created Qur'ān was completely discredited in the eyes of the majority of the Muslim community, and the predominant view came to be the one which insisted that the Qur'ān was uncreated. The Mu'tazila continued to insist that this view ran the risk of compromising *tawḥīd*, the unity of God, because if the scripture was uncreated, then there was the risk that it might come to be seen as a second divinity besides God; this was precisely the error which the Muslim community had accused Christians of being guilty of because of their beliefs about Jesus and the Trinity, but their protests were either ignored or set aside.[24]

These then were the major issues which dominated religious thought in the early Islamic period, and we have seen how in many cases issues of theology and intellect also involve issues of practical importance with respect to the organisation of the Muslim community. Many of the issues which preoccupied the early Muslim community are thus rather different from the internal issues which were of primary significance in the early period of Christian thinking. When we turn to Islamic thinking on the relationship between Islam and other intellectual traditions, particularly those of Greek reasoning and philosophy, however, we find here perhaps rather more similarity between the courses which discussion took within the two communities.

b) External

In the early Islamic centuries the Muslim community, like the Christian community before it, encountered and had to react to the Greek tradition. In the Muslim community, again as in the Christian community, a wide spectrum of opinion developed on this question, with some Muslim thinkers proving quite positive and open towards Greek philosophy and science and others demonstrating rather more mistrust towards it. Thus a Muslim thinker who valued the Qur'ān and the Muslim tradition as the supreme sources of knowledge and guidance, such as Aḥmad ibn Ḥanbal, had quite a negative attitudes towards the study of Greek philosophy, but a number of other Islamic thinkers, together known as the *falāsifa* (plural of *faylasūf*, philosopher) were far more positive and tried to produce a synthesis of Islamic revelation and Greek reason.[25]

After almost five centuries, however, the relative openness towards Greek philosophy which had existed in the earliest Muslim centuries, at least in the minds of some Muslim thinkers, began to be superseded by a more negative attitude, and so in a development which seems a remarkable parallel to that which took place in the Christian world in the fifth and sixth centuries, the hatches began to be battened down on the Greek tradition, and external influences became more suspect. To a considerable extent in the world of Islam this was due to the influence of one of the most important Islamic thinkers of any century, al-Ghazālī (d. 1111/505), who, having studied philosophy, ultimately rejected its usefulness in favour of knowledge derived from revelation and prophecy. This view was outlined most comprehensively in his work *tahāfut al-falāsifa* (the incoherence of the philosophers).

The interesting feature here, therefore, is the extent to which the periods of relative openness to the achievements of Greek philosophy in the Christian and Muslim worlds did not coincide. Christians, having been relatively open in their early centuries, became less so, with some exceptions, in the two centuries or so before the establishment of the Muslim community. In its early centuries, then, Islam too was relatively open to the Greek tradition, to the extent that today the earliest texts available of a number of important Greek philosophical and scientific works are Arabic translations of these works made in the ninth/third and, to a lesser extent, tenth/fourth centuries in the medieval Islamic world.[26]

A thousand years ago, therefore, the extent of the difference in knowledge of the Greek tradition in the Western Christian and Islamic worlds has been estimated by R.W. Southern. He reckoned that in the tenth/fourth century, a Western European scholar such as Gerbert, who later became Pope Sylvester II (d 1003/393), would have been able to acquire as much knowledge of Greek philosophy and science as could have been acquired by a reasonably educated Muslim scholar such as his near contemporary Ibn Sīnā (Avicenna) (d 1037/428) by the age of sixteen.[27]

As, however, the Islamic world then began to batten down the hatches on this tradition, at the very same period the Western Christian world then began once again to open up to these influences, and the irony here is that one of the major factors contributing to this change of attitude was the influence of some important Islamic thinkers, especially in Spain. Probably the most important of these was Ibn Rushd (Averroes) (d 1198/595), who despite his attempts to answer al-Ghazālī's critique of philosophy, notably in his *tahāfut al-tahāfut* (the incoherence of the incoherence), referring to al-Ghazālī's work "the incoherence of the philosophers", actually became far more influential in Western Europe, through the translation of many of his works into Latin, than he was in the world of Islam.[28]

In broad terms this is then how the situation has remained up until today, with at least the Western Christian world continuing to take seriously the importance of interacting with the Greek tradition and its modern descendants, and the Islamic world remaining more suspicious of that tradition.[29]

Conclusion

In looking at the development of religious thought in the Christian and Muslim communities, then, we have seen how with respect to the issues which they confronted as a result of internal disagreements the two traditions developed rather differently. Christian discussion tended to focus on matters of doctrine, particularly concerning the person of Jesus and his relationship with God, and also the relationship between the Holy Spirit and both God and Jesus; given the minority position of the Christian community within the Roman Empire for its first three centuries, it was belief which served as its main boundary marker, and hence the creeds had a particular importance. In the Islamic community, which from the time of Muḥammad himself enjoyed considerable political power and influence, different issues emerged, some more practical and some more theoretical, but even the latter had important practical implications. The two traditions, then, had different internal stimuli to intellectual development.

One issue, however, which they both encountered and to which similar responses evolved, concerned the question of how to react to external intellectual influences, especially those coming from the Greek philosophical tradition. On this question a spectrum of opinion developed in both traditions, with the relative openness of some thinkers in the early period of each tradition in each case giving way after five centuries or so to a less sympathetic view. On this question, therefore, the two traditions developed in similar ways, but out of synchronisation chronologically.[30]

Both traditions did, then, develop, and so one of the most persistent Muslim criticisms of the Christian faith, namely that over the course of the centuries it became corrupted by deviating from the original teachings of Jesus may therefore also be made of the Muslim tradition, since there too there was development over the course of time. 'Abd al-Jabbār (d 1025/415), a Muslim judge and theologian whose summary of early Christian history was that "if you look carefully you will find that the Christians became Romans . . . but you will not find that the Romans have become Christians", could perhaps be answered with the suggestion that in the course of early Islamic history something rather similar occurred, but with the Persians, who are generally described as having converted to Islam, exercising a huge influence on the early intellectual development of the Islamic tradition, and thus Persifying it. But was this a corruption or a development? And, of course, whichever answer is given must be applied equally to both traditions, so that there are no double standards.[31]

Notes

1 See E.P. Sanders et al (eds.) *Jewish and Christian self-definition*, SCM, 3 Vols, 1980–1982, and J.D.G. Dunn *The partings of the ways: between Judaism and Christianity and their significance for the church and Christianity*, SCM, 1991.
2 See Chapter Two above on this.
3 See Chapter One above on this.
4 For a more detailed outline of both the personalities and the issues involved in these discussions see F. Young *From Nicaea to Chalcedon*, SCM, 1983, and for an even more comprehensive discussion see J.N.D. Kelly *Early Christian doctrines*, 5th ed., A and C Black, 1977.
5 This school has traditionally been presented as being in opposition to the Antiochene school, whose views were closer to those of, for example, Nestorius in emphasising the full integrity of the human nature of Jesus.
6 More detail is given on these divisions in Chapter Six below.
7 The so-called Chalcedonian definition of the person of Jesus, which won majority, but not universal, acceptance in the fifth century CE, included the following words about Jesus: "perfect in Godhead and perfect in humanity, truly God and truly human . . . . of one substance with the Father as regards his Godhead, of one substance with us as regards his humanity . . . . begotten of the Father before all ages as regards his Godhead, ... born from the Virgin Mary (God-bearer) as regards his humanity, one and the same Christ, Son, Lord, unique, to be acknowledged in two natures, without confusion, change, division or separation . . . ."
8 In looking at Christian thinking about both of these issues – the nature of Jesus as God and human, and the understanding of God as Trinity – it is important to remember that there is a very strong traditional Muslim antipathy

to these ideas. This may be explained, however, by the fact that Muḥammad proclaimed the message of Islam in a polytheistic society and given the overwhelming insistence of that message on belief in only one God, this may be something of an obstacle in developing an appreciation of what the Christian ideas actually mean.

9 Part of the difficulty in rendering this language comprehensible in modern times is caused by a change, over the centuries, in the idea of Person. Today the idea of Person is closely related to the idea of Individual, so that Person becomes a kind of separate and distinct identity. In the past there was less emphasis on these concepts and so the idea of three Persons in one God was less paradoxical than perhaps it appears today, when it may appear that language about the Trinity defies logic: the correct terminology is as expressed in Christian worship, "we believe in Father, Son and Holy Spirit . . . let us worship Him (singular!)". An additional difficulty is that when Christians say their Creeds (their affirmations of belief) in the context of worship, the statements about the different persons of the Trinity are usually set out in three different paragraphs: thus the paragraphs of the Nicene Creed begin respectively: "We believe in one God, the Father . . . .", "We believe in one Lord, Jesus Christ . . . .", and "We believe in the Holy Spirit . . . .", which might appear to suggest a rather qualified view of belief in one God. The true monotheistic conviction of Christians might therefore be made more clear if the Creed was set out as follows:

"We believe in one God: the Father . . . .
one Lord, Jesus Christ . . . .
the Holy Spirit . . . ."

10 On the development of the Creeds see F. Young *The making of the creeds*, SCM, 1991, and for more detail J.N.D. Kelly *Early Christian creeds*, 3rd ed., Longmans, 1972.

11 On this aspect of Christian thought, and also for some comparisons between Christian and Muslim political thinking, see my article "Some reflections on Christian and Islamic political thought" in *Islam and Christian-Muslim relations*, 1 (1990), pp 25–43.

12 On these, and other, issues in early Christian thought see S.G. Hall *Doctrine and practice in the early church*, SPCK, 1991 and M. Brox *A history of the early church*, SPCK, 1994.

13 See further H. Chadwick *Early Christian thought and the classical tradition*, Oxford U.P., 1966.

14 For more detail on the historical background to these questions see B. Lewis *The Arabs in history*, 6th ed., Oxford U.P., 1993, Chapter 3, esp pp 61–64.

15 The technical term used for this position was *khalīfa*, usually anglicised as caliph, which literally means deputy or representative.

16 The term used for 'Alī's supporters was the Shī'a, literally meaning party; for the later development of this group see below Chapter Six.

17 This term literally means "those who went out" from 'Alī's party, and a widely-used one word term for them is "seceders".

18 A parallel may perhaps be drawn here with some of the discussions which took place in the Western part of the Christian church at the time of the Reformation in the sixteenth/nținteenth century. Given the differing

definitions circulating at the time about who was or was not an authentic Christian the view emerged in some Christian circles that a certain agnosticism on the question was perhaps appropriate, and so anyone who outwardly claimed to be Christian should be recognised as being such.

19 On these questions see W.M. Watt *Islamic philosophy and theology*, 2nd ed., Edinburgh U.P., 1985, and, for more detail, W.M. Watt *The formative period of Islamic thought*, Edinburgh U.P., 1973.

20 On this see especially Paul's letter to the Romans, Chapter 9–11, and St Augustine's *City of God*.

21 The terminology is slightly confusing here since the Arabic words which gave rise to the names of both of these schools, *qadar* (determination) and *jabr* (compulsion), both mean predestination. What seems to have happened is that the proponents of free-will were given the title Qadariyya not because they believed in determination but because they talked so much about it, so it is really a kind of nick-name.

22 Islamic and Christian history provide similar anecdotes of opponents of predestination performing actions intended to illustrate the ludicrous nature of the views of their opponents in slightly provocative ways: thus in medieval Baghdad al-Ash'arī was slapped by 'Alī al-Nāshi' during the course of a disputation between them, and when al-Ash'arī asked him why he had done this al-Nāshi' replied that it was God's doing so why was he angry if the action had been predestined by God? al-Ash'arī exclaimed that it was not God's but his doing, and it was beyond the bounds of decency in a disputation, but the audience laughed. In the same way a celebrated nineteenth/thirteenth century English preacher, in the heyday of debate between the Arminians (who argued for free-will) and Calvinists (who argued for predestination), is supposed to have poured water or milk down an opponent's neck during a breakfast-time discussion in order to make a similar point. On the former see G. Makdisi *The rise of the colleges*, Edinburgh U.P., 1981, p 135, but I have been unable to find a reference for the latter.

23 This statement can perhaps be seen as an Islamic parallel to the question of Tertullian referred to above: "what has Athens to do with Jerusalem?"

24 There is thus an intriguing parallel here between Christian discussion of the nature of Christ and Muslim discussion of the nature of the Qur'ān. The pre-existence of the former and the uncreatedness of the latter could both be seen as compromising monotheism, but this did not prevent these beliefs coming to be accepted by the majority of their respective communities, each of which continued to insist that they were true monotheists.

25 See especially M. Fakhry *A history of Islamic philosophy*, 2nd ed., Longmans, 1983.

26 F. Rosenthal, in his work *The classical heritage in Islam*, Routledge and Kegan Paul, 1975, lists the Greek writers some of whose works have been lost in the original language but have been preserved in Arabic on pages 11–12.

27 See R.W. Southern *Western views of Islam in the Middle Ages*, Harvard U.P., 1962, pp 9–12. A further example of the far greater intellectual sophistication of the Islamic world in that time is the growth and development of the institution of the university. On this see G. Makdisi *The*

growth of the colleges, Edinburgh U.P., 1981. It is not widely known that many customs still practised in modern western universities have their origin in the medieval Islamic world: examples are the idea of a university degree, or licence; the institution of chairs for professors in certain subjects; the idea of their delivering inaugural lectures; the organisation of universities into faculties; and the fact that, in English at least, we still talk of academic circles.

28 On Ibn Rushd see D. Urvoy *Ibn Rushd*, Routledge, 1991.

29 This is not to ignore such movements within the Islamic community as modernism, nor the rather different attitudes to the Greek tradition which are evident, for example, in Eastern Christianity, but rather to draw a contrast between the situation in the two communities in general. See Chapter Eight below for further discussion of more modern developments.

30 Perhaps one of the easiest ways to highlight this is simply to point to the dates which the two communities have reached in their respective calendars. The year 2000 of the Christian calendar will begin in the year 1420 of the Muslim calendar, and the year 1400 of the Muslim calendar fell in the year 1979 of the Christian calendar, and a comparison of the attitude of most Christians towards Greek philosophy in 1400/802 and of the majority of the Muslim community today reveals more similarity than would a comparison either between the two communities' attitudes in that year or their attitudes today.

31 'Abd al-Jabbār's sentence may be found in a translation by S.M. Stern in "'Abd al-Jabbār's account of how Christ's religion was falsified by the adoption of Roman customs" in *Journal of Theological Studies*, 19 (1968). p 140. A further piece of evidence in support of the rather provocative thesis presented in this paragraph is provided by the dress worn by at least some religious teachers in the two traditions, since the ecclesiastical robes used by many Western churches (e.g. purple for bishops) are based on ancient Roman imperial models, and the robes worn by traditional Islamic legal scholars derive from ancient Persia.

4

LAW AND ETHICS

Introduction

In this area too we can discern some parallels and some distinctions between the two traditions. Both refer in some way to morality, so that both discourage murder, theft and adultery and encourage concern for the vulnerable, respect for property, and support of the family, but the mechanism used by the two traditions to achieve these ends differs, with the Islamic community laying the primary emphasis on law, with ethics as subsidiary, whereas within the Christian tradition the order of priority is reversed, and the Islamic community perhaps laying more stress on the communal aspect of morality and the Christian community stressing the individual dimension to a greater extent.

Islamic Law

As we have seen already, in the time of Muḥammad Arabia was a tribal society, where each tribe was ruled, in a sense, by its own custom or *sunna*, rather than by any generally-accepted code of law. As a result of the career of Muḥammad, however, a supra-tribal religious community was established, which quickly came to dominate most of Arabia and which not long after the death of Muḥammad expanded so that it controlled much of the area known as the Fertile Crescent, that is Syria[1] and Iraq, and also Egypt and Iran.[2]

As a result of this new situation a tendency which had begun in the latter half of Muḥammad's career came to be accentuated. In the years after the Hijra when, in Yathrib/Medina, Muḥammad was in a position of some influence and power, his message, as recorded in the Qur'ān, had begun to include what might be called legislative, or legal, material. Roughly-speaking some ten per cent of the Qur'ān may be described as fitting in to this category, and it included guidance or regulations concerning such issues as the ordering of life within the Muslim community, for example sexual morality, the punishment of a number of crimes such as theft, and the inheritance of property, and also the ordering of relationships between the different communities living in Yathrib, for example the non-Muslim Arab tribes, the Jewish tribes of the city, and the Muslim community.[3]

Given that the Qur'ān was considered to be divine guidance, and not simply the message of Muḥammad, this legal material clearly had a special status and authority, and after the death of Muḥammad, which removed the living voice of prophecy from the community, the Qur'ān's legal guidance continued to be important. This was especially the case since the prophet's successors as leaders of the Muslim community, the caliphs, found themselves having to provide guidance and regulations not only for a newly-united Arabia but also for a state whose boundaries stretched over a considerable area beyond Arabia too.[4]

The business of making law therefore came to be a matter of considerable significance and importance for the early Muslim community. Caliphs, their legal representatives in different towns, the *qāḍīs*, and religious teachers and scholars all came to devote much attention to this question. At first, perhaps even for as long as the first century of Muslim history, law developed on a rather ad hoc and flexible basis, but after the replacement of the Umayyad dynasty by the 'Abbāsid dynasty in 750/132, the process of elaborating the law more systematically accelerated.

In part this was simply a result of the contrasting policies and approaches of the two dynasties. The Umayyads, descendants of one of the leading clans of Mecca, ruled what has been described as primarily an Arab empire from their headquarters in Damascus. The 'Abbāsids, who traced their ancestry back to an uncle of Muḥammad, Ibn 'Abbās, by contrast, laid far more emphasis on the religious basis for their rule, that is their relationship with the prophet, and the shift of the capital to Iraq, and eventually to the new city of Baghdad, founded in 762/145, symbolised an intention to organise the affairs of the empire on a new basis. In addition, its existence for over a century gave a certain sense of security to the Muslim state, and the resulting ending of fears for its survival allowed its rulers to begin to develop new ideas and institutions. The beginnings of conversion to Islam among the conquered population, which under the Umayyads had in general retained, and indeed been encouraged to maintain, its previous religious allegiance, also caused a shift in emphasis from the Arab nature of the empire to a more specifically Islamic identity.

Law, then, came to play a central role in this process of the elaboration of Islam. In part this was because of the foundations for legal development which existed in the Qur'ān and in the latter half of Muḥammad's career, in Yathrib/Medina. In part it was also due to the lack of a generally-accepted legal system in Arabia, yet alone in the larger Islamic empire.[5] Other factors were the practical, rather than the speculative, nature of Muḥammad's message, and the fact that the early caliphs encountered legal questions as a matter of some urgency, whereas the more theoretical questions which came to the fore as a result of the Muslim encounter with Greek philosophy and wisdom did not really arise until the 'Abbāsid period. It has also been suggested that Jewish influence, or the influence of Jewish converts to Islam, in the early Muslim period contributed to the process whereby law became a matter of primary significance.[6]

The way in which Islamic Law developed went something like this. In the Qur'ān there were references to divine guidance, and also to "the straight path", as in, for example, Chapter One, verse Six. There was also, in the Qur'ān, a reference to the Arabic word *sharī'a*, literally meaning path (45:18) As the early Muslim community developed, this was the word which came to be used to describe the system of guidance, of divine law, which occupied such an important place within Islam.[7]

The first foundation of the Sharī'a was the Qur'ān. Upon this foundation Islamic Law developed three further principles which, together with the Qur'ān, came to be known as the four principles, or foundations, of the Sharī'a. These were the Ḥadīth (Tradition), *ijmā'* (consensus), and *qiyās* (analogy).

The Ḥadīth, firstly, is the record of the custom (*sunna*) of Muḥammad himself and the first generation of the Muslim community, whose practice came to be recognised as paradigmatic for later Muslims. The form which this record takes is a number of collections of sayings (ḥadīths), which are regarded as being sayings originating either from the prophet or from his early companions. Six collections of ḥadīths are generally regarded as authoritative by Sunnī Muslims, the two most significant being those of al-Bukhārī (d 870/256) and Muslim (d 875/261).

At the start of each ḥadīth is an *isnād*, usually translated as chain of transmission, though perhaps genealogy might be a simpler explanation: it consists of a list of who heard this saying from whom, going back over several generations to either Muḥammad or one of his companions. It was this *isnād* which then enabled the collectors of the Ḥadīth, al-Bukhārī, Muslim and the others, to assess the reliability or otherwise of individual ḥadīths and thus work out whether or not they were worth including in their authoritative collections.[8]

The justification for taking the Ḥadīth as an authoritative source of guidance lay in the oft-repeated Qur'ānic phrase "Obey God and the prophet" (e.g. 33:33, 4:58), and the Qur'ānic statement that Muḥammad was a good example to follow (33:21). The justification for the third source of the Law, *ijmā'*, in turn lay in a ḥadīth attributed to Muḥammad "My community will not agree on an error". This was taken to justify the view that if at a later stage the community came to a consensus on a point of law, then that consensus became part of the structure of the Sharī'a.

Consensus, of course, did not emerge at once. What seems to have happened in the early decades of Islamic history was that the caliphs and the *qāḍīs* (judges appointed by the caliphs in the different provinces of the Islamic empire) used their individual reasoning to formulate legal pronouncements. This was known as *ra'y* (individual opinion), and was justified in part by the early story of a provincial governor declaring that in reaching decisions on matters of law he would follow first the Qur'ān, then, if that was not clear, the example of Muḥammad, and then, if that too was not clear, his own reason. The problem with *ra'y*, however, was that it naturally tended to diversity and, ultimately, if taken to extremes, to anarchy. It was thus the achievement of the great systematiser of Islamic Law, al-Shāfi'ī (d 820/205), to counteract these possible consequences of *ra'y* by introducing the idea of *ijmā'*. This resulted in a much greater degree of harmonisation, standardisation and coherence, and gave the Islamic community an invaluable theoretical tool for allowing and yet controlling change and development.[9]

The fourth principle of the Sharī'a, *qiyās*, analogy, was also introduced by al-Shāfi'ī as a way of moderating and controlling *ra'y*. New legal problems and issues would obviously continue to arise, and by advocating the use of *qiyās*, al-Shāfi'ī's intention was to limit the use of individual reason by suggesting that new guidance could only be evolved on the basis of analogy from existing points of law. The scope for radical innovation was thus severely curtailed.[10]

In theory, therefore, the Sharī'a, on the basis of these four foundations, provides a comprehensive system of guidance for Muslims for all areas of life, including not just individual behaviour or the areas which might be described in the West as involving private morality, that is relationships within the family, but also public life, the organisation of society and relationships between communities and nations. In reality, despite the claim that the Sharī'a is a divinely-originated law (as opposed to a law which is the product of human evolution), it has not always been taken seriously by the holders of political power in the Islamic world, and so it has often been an ideal of what ought to happen in a perfect world rather than a serious model for the conduct of the affairs of this world.[11]

In the Islamic tradition there is also, it should be stressed, an important tradition of ethics (*akhlāq*), represented, for example, by the writings of Miskawayh (d 1030/421).[12] The development of this tradition is closely associated with the growth of the philosophical tradition within Islam, stimulated by the growth in knowledge of and interest in the Greek tradition of philosophy and science. In general terms, however, in the Islamic community the study of and interest in ethics has taken second place to the study of law, and the situation is thus the reverse of that which has by and large been the case in the Christian community, where, as we shall see, it is generally ethics which has been primary.

Christian ethics

In investigating this subject, some consideration must first be given to the relationship between Christianity and Judaism. On the one hand, as we have seen already in looking at the subject of scripture, the Christian community has included within its holy book certain writings whose origin lies within the Jewish community, namely the books of the Old Testament. Some of the key moral pronouncements of the Old Testament, therefore, particularly the Ten Commandments, recorded in Exodus 20:1–17 with alternative listings in Deuteronomy 5:1–21, are also considered to be authoritative by Christians.[13] These teachings come mostly in the section of the Old Testament which is known as the Law/Torah, namely the first five books of the Old Testament.

On the other hand, in the Inter-Testamental period, that is the two or three centuries before the life of Jesus and the composition of the New Testament, considerable further development in thinking about morality and law took place within the Jewish community, on the foundation of the Torah, and this is reflected in the Mishnah, a codification of the oral tradition which had been elaborated on the foundation of the Torah. And the school of thought within Judaism which laid most stress on the importance of punctilious observance of the Law, in the sense of Torah and later elaboration of Torah, was the Pharisees.

As we have seen in looking at Christian origins, the Pharisees were one of the groups with whom, on some issues, Jesus came into conflict, and who, as a result, were involved in the controversies which led eventually to the trial and execution of Jesus. Jesus, it could thus be said, was representative of the other major tradition within the Old Testament and within Judaism, the prophetic tradition, which sought to complement a stress on the importance of observing the Law with a balancing stress on the need for internal purity.[14] It should not surprise us, therefore, if there seem to be some significant differences in emphasis between Jesus and at least some aspects of the Judaism of his day concerning morality.

These differences were reinforced through the influence of Paul, who had originally been a Pharisee but who as a result of his dramatic conversion to the Jesus movement came to hold significantly different opinions. Thus in a number of his letters in the New Testament Paul discusses in detail the relationship between what he calls the Law and the Spirit, and since for him this was a crucial issue for the question of salvation, that is how human beings could be considered acceptable by God, it was evidently a primary concern for him.[15]

Among the effects of this discussion in early Christianity were firstly an acceleration of the process by which the Jewish and Christian communities came to develop separately.[16] And secondly the growth of a tendency in the Christian community as a whole to view Law rather negatively, perhaps most particularly as a feature of a relatively less developed stage of religious evolution.[17]

These theological foundations for Christian thinking were then further reinforced by the context in which the Christian church grew up, namely the Roman Empire, which was already the possessor of a highly-developed and sophisticated system of law, whose influence continues in many Western legal systems up until today.[18] It was this combination of religious ideas and context which was thus responsible for the relative lack of interest in Law in the early Christian community.

This did not mean, however, that there was no Christian concern for issues of morality. It is true that it was not long before some of the teaching of Paul about freedom led to an apparent casting aside of any concern with morality in some of the early Christian communities, for example that in Corinth, and so Paul found it necessary to explain how freedom from the Law did not mean freedom to behave however one wished.[19] Later Christian thinkers too have sometimes had to tread a delicate line between emphasising Christian freedom and lapsing into antinomianism.[20] But a clear tradition of Christian thinking about morality did exist.

Positively, then, the form which Christian thinking on moral questions did take was the study of ethics or, as it is sometimes called, moral theology. On the one hand this was based on certain scriptural foundations, such as the Ten Commandments, but in the New Testament these were refined and developed along the lines of becoming positive statements of principle, as opposed to negative prohibitions. Thus Jesus himself, according to the New Testament, summarised the Commandments in terms of two principles: to love God with all one's heart, mind and soul, and to love one's neighbour as oneself.[21] Moreover in the so-called Sermon on the Mount (Matthew 5–7) he outlined nine positive ideals whose practitioners, he said, would be blessed by God – the Beatitudes. The same Sermon also laid great stress on the importance of the inner intention, rather than stressing simply the outward action.[22]

On the other hand, Christian thinking also drew considerably on the Greek tradition of ethics, which was one element of the wider Greek tradition of philosophical reflection, and the relative openness of at least some Christian thinkers in the early centuries towards this tradition is part of the explanation of why Christian thought developed in this way. Thus the influence of Aristotle's discussion of virtues may be seen in the medieval Christian traditions concerning the seven virtues and the seven deadly sins, or vices.

The virtues were generally listed as follows: firstly faith, hope and love, which have scriptural foundation in 1 Corinthians 13:13, as the fundamental virtues, and secondly prudence, justice, temperance and fortitude as the cardinal virtues. More modern Christian thinking has sometimes focused on another scriptural list, the fruit or harvest of the Spirit referred to by St. Paul in his letter to the Galatians: love, joy, peace, patience, kindness, goodness, fidelity, gentleness and self-control are here listed as the marks of authentic Christian character (Galatians 5:22–23). The seven deadly sins, by contrast, were anger, pride, lust, sloth, gluttony, avarice and envy. This list was also influenced again in part by scriptural precedents, such as the saying of Jesus in Matthew 15:19–20: "for out of the heart come evil thoughts, murder, adultery, fornication, theft, false witness, slander; these are what defile a man".

These lists illustrate the tendency of Christian thinking to concentrate on principles, rather than the detailed prescriptions concerning the desirability or otherwise of particular actions which may be seen in the textbooks of Islamic (or Jewish) Law. This is also seen in the medieval tradition of expressing the moral life as consisting simply in terms of the imitation of Christ, but Christian writers such as Ambrose (d 397) and Gregory (d 604) in the West did attempt to produce more systematic outlines of the detail of Christian moral obligations and duties, while in the East John of Damascus (d 750/132) summarised early Christian thinking on the moral life by using many of Aristotle's concepts.

In some cases it may also appear that Christian ethics has concentrated unduly on individual behaviour.[23] But there is also a strong tradition of Christian thinking on social and political issues, and this is often highly critical of "the powers-that-be", so that Christian thinkers have often explicitly opposed and condemned the actions of governments and political leaders. One of the most dramatic examples of this in the early Christian centuries involved Ambrose, the bishop of Milan, who in 390 ordered Theodosius, the Roman Emperor of his day, to perform public penance for having ordered the suppression of a rebellion in Thessalonica in an unnecessarily harsh way, as a result of which three thousand people were killed.[24]

The one aspect of Christian morality which is occasionally referred to as being in some way analogous to Islamic Law, in that it is sometimes referred to as "sacred" or "divine law" as opposed to "civil law" (which is the law administered by the state) is canon law. This is an area where parallels hardly exist in reality, however, since canon law is simply law which is internal to the Christian community, in other words which regulates the internal affairs of the church. It might involve, therefore, matters of church government and administration, appointments to positions of leadership and responsibility within the church, and matters concerning church property and land. It is not, therefore, "sacred" or "divine" in the sense that Islamic Law is considered to be ultimately of divine origin.[25]

Generally, then, despite their common concern with issues of morality, the mechanisms by which the Christian and Muslim traditions work out and formulate moral guidance for their members are different: in the Islamic tradition it is Law/Sharīʿa which has generally served as the primary source of guidance for Muslims, whereas in the Christian community, by contrast, ethics has been the main focus of attention.

A case-study: Christian and Muslim thinking on the position of women in society

Despite the differences in emphasis between the two traditions in terms of where they look for guidance on moral questions, there are, of course, certain issues which confront both communities equally, and of these perhaps the most burning contemporary issue concerns the role of women in society, including the question of their role in public life, both political and religious. It may be instructive, therefore, to look at how the two traditions address these questions.

Both traditions, first of all, find certain statements in their scriptures which are relevant to this question. In the Christian scriptures, for example, Paul offers specific guidance in his letter to the Galatians: "In Christ there is neither Jew nor Gentile, slave nor free, male nor female" (Galatians 3:28). This might appear to be a clear statement concerning the full equality of all within the Christian church, regardless of ethnic origin, social status and gender. On the other hand, addressing a different group of Christians, in Corinth, in another of his letters, Paul seems to offer a rather different piece of advice: "While every man has Christ for his head, a woman's head is man" (1 Corinthians 11:3). Later in the same letter he also suggests that women should wear a veil on their heads (11:10), and that they should be silent in church and subordinate (14:34). These teachings are echoed in Paul's letter to the Ephesians (5:21–24), where wives are exhorted to be subject to their husbands since the husband is the head of the wife, and in his first letter to Timothy (2:9–12), where Paul states that women should adorn themselves modestly, should keep silent, and should be given no authority over men.

The obvious question, therefore, is simply which of these statements is primary and which is secondary. Is the first statement, seemingly more positive concerning the role of women, a general principle which outlines the long-term aspiration of the Christian community and the second group of statements, seemingly pointing towards a more subordinate position for women, a temporary concession towards the culture of Paul's day? Or is the first statement concerned simply with the very general principle of the spiritual equality of men and women before God while the second statement outlines the eternally valid pattern for Christian worship and the organisation of the Christian community in this world, where men lead and women are silent participants?

In a very similar way, the Qur'ān contains a number of statements about women's role. Chapter Thirty-three, verse thirty-five, for example, seems to lay explicit emphasis on the equal role of men and women in a way which is virtually impossible to translate adequately into English since the Qur'ān is able to make powerful use of the fact that Arabic has separate masculine and feminine plural nouns: "men and women who submit to God, men and women who believe, men and women who obey, men and women who are truthful, men and women who persevere, men and women who are humble, men and women who give alms, men and women who fast, men and women who guard their modesty, and men and women who remember God often, God has prepared for them forgiveness and a vast reward". On the other hand the Qur'ān states that men are a degree above women (2:228), that men are in charge of women (4:34), that under certain conditions men may take up to four wives (4:3), that daughters inherit only half the amount of sons (4:11), that the testimony of a woman to a financial transaction has only half the value of that of a man (2:282), and that, while it is important for both sexes to be modest, there is a special responsibility upon women to dress modestly (24:30–31 and 33:59). The question again is therefore raised: which of these sets of statements takes priority over the other? Does the general principle of equality have precedence, offering fundamental guidance for the later Muslim community, or are the various statements implying some measure of female subordination the ones which are the more important for subsequent generations?

On these foundations each community has then developed further traditions and patterns. In the Muslim community, in the Ḥadīth, some sayings seem to limit the role of women to certain spheres. Despite the prominent role which some women seem to have had in the time of Muḥammad himself, notably his first wife Khadīja and his third wife ‘Ā’isha, a gradual process seems to have begun whereby, for example, it was stated that women are not required to pray in the mosque and that women are not permitted to be political leaders.[26] The possibility of women occupying positions of religious leadership hardly seems to have been considered, though there were exceptions to this, such as Khadīja bint al-Baqqāl (d 1045/437) and Khadīja al-Shahjaniya (d 1068/460), both of whom were avid students of the art of the sermon in medieval Baghdad, and Rābi‘a al-‘Adawiya, one of the early Sufis.[27] But in general terms the opportunities for women to be involved in the public life of the Islamic community, either as political figures or as religious teachers seemed to become fewer rather than greater as the centuries passed.

Something broadly similar took place in the Christian community too. Jesus' inner group of disciples included a number of women, but none attained a position of leadership in the Christian community as it developed after his death. None of the books of the New Testament was written by a woman. None of the great thinkers of the early Christian church, the Church Fathers (!) was a woman. Traditions grew up to the effect that political leadership should not be entrusted to a woman, so that Queen Elizabeth I of England, for example, had to work hard to establish her credibility and her right to rule, and the idea of a woman occupying a position of religious leadership never seems to have been entertained at all. Some of the great mystics of the Christian tradition, it is true, were women, but in the more formal public life of the church women did not usually play a significant part.[28]

In modern times, then, both communities have seen traditional patterns challenged, both in theory and in practice. Christian feminist writers have argued that since there is a clear and specific statement in the New Testament concerning the equality of men and women in the Christian community there is no reason why women should be excluded from any position, including those of leadership, within the church.[29] During the course of the last century or so, a number of Christian churches have therefore permitted women to serve as ministers and priests.[30] Women have also become far more prominent in positions of leadership within different parts of the Christian community.[31] Equally, in some Western societies in which Christianity has traditionally been the dominant faith, women have been elected as political leaders.

In the Muslim community too, feminist writers have argued forcibly that some traditional Muslim pronouncements about the position of women in society need urgent rethinking and revision. It has been suggested, for example, that the tradition about anarchy being caused by having a women as political leader is not authentic, and that the Muslim community should return to the situation in the days of Muḥammad himself, where women were given more prominent roles than they have been given subsequently.[32] One of the most interesting features of the Muslim community in the former Yugoslavia, whose existence has been forcefully brought to a far wider public appreciation than was the case a few years ago by the recent events in Bosnia, is the very positive attitude taken to the role of women: thus in 1981 the first woman, Nermina Jasarevic, graduated from the Islamic Theology Faculty in Sarajevo (Bosnia), and by 1986 the first woman Imams had been trained and the first sermon preached in a mosque in Skopje and Kumanavo (Macedonia), both of which were radical changes from the pattern of most of the Islamic community throughout most of its history.[33] Finally, in those parts of the world where Islam has traditionally been the dominant faith, women have also come to positions of political leadership, the most famous example being Benazir Bhutto, who became Prime Minister of Pakistan for the first time in 1988.[34]

In both the Christian and Muslim communities, therefore, the question of the position of women in society is one which is currently receiving much attention and causing much discussion. Traditional patterns are being challenged by some thinkers and re-asserted as authoritative vigorously by others, and the discussions involve issues as fundamental as the interpretation of scriptural statements, the authority of traditions from the past, and the extent to which past centuries have seen cultural patterns exerting their influence on, rather than being set aside by, religious teachings. The issue is therefore one which poses a great challenge to Christian and Muslim opinions in the fields of law and ethics.

Conclusion

So there are, as ever, some parallels and some distinctive features between the two traditions in this area of law and ethics, with the former being more significant for the Islamic tradition and the latter playing a greater role within the Christian community.[35]

A further general comparison then needs to be made between the Christian and Muslim traditions with respect to their central disciplines, in the sense of academic study and general focus: it is important to note in particular that in the Christian tradition the central focus is much more on the areas which were investigated in Chapter Three, namely the development of religious thought, whereas in the Islamic tradition it is the subject matter of this chapter, namely Law, which is thought to be much more significant. Thus it could be said that in the Christian tradition the central discipline is theology, whereas in the Islamic tradition the central discipline is law.

This in turn is significant with respect to the means by which the two communities establish their boundaries: the Christian tradition has tended to do this by means of creeds, that is by belief, and so to expect orthodoxy (right belief) of its members; the Muslim community by contrast, has tended to stress right behaviour, or orthopraxy (right practice). This does not mean that Muslims are not concerned with creeds, or that Christians are unconcerned with practice, but as a general statement of the relative significance which is attached to the two areas, it must stand.

Notes

1 Syria here means the historical entity of Syria, sometimes described as Greater Syria, which stretches from the Euphrates to the borders of Egypt.

2 For further details of this process, see Chapter Seven below.

3 What is generally recognised as being one of the earliest documents of Islamic History apart from the Qur'ān, the Constitution of Medina, also addresses these questions of relationships between the different elements of the population of the city. See R. B. Serjeant "The Constitution of Medina" in *Islamic Quarterly*, 8 (1964), pp 1–16, and F.M. Denny "Ummah in the Constitution of Medina" in *Journal of Near Eastern Studies*, 36 (1977), pp 29–47.

4 The question of the exact nature of the authority wielded by the early caliphs is a matter of on-going scholarly discussion, as although the main

(Sunnī) Muslim view is that the caliphs were simply administrative and political leaders, with no spiritual authority of their own, some Shī'i thinking, and some modern Western scholarship, has recently suggested that in the case of the first four caliphs at least, administrative/political and spiritual authority were combined to a greater extent than the mainstream of later Muslim thought has recognised. See P. Crone and M. Hinds *God's caliph: religious authority in the first centuries of Islam*, Cambridge U.P., 1986.

5 The contrast here with the growth of the Christian church within the Roman Empire, with its highly-developed system of law, is clear.

6 See S.D. Goitein *Jews and Arabs: their contacts through the ages*, Schocken, New York, 1955, Chapter Four, esp. pp 59–61.

7 The word *sharī'a* may only occur once in the Qur'ān but it is worth noting that the word "theology" does not occur at all in the Christian Bible!

8 The Ḥadīth is thus sometimes compared with the New Testament in that similar questions arise as to the authenticity of some of their contents – did Muḥammad really say this/ did Jesus really say this (especially some of the statements attributed to him in the Gospel according to John)? They are also similar in that the time-scale of their composition is much more similar than the time-scale involved in the composition of the Qur'ān, on which see the conclusion to Chapter Two above. On modern discussion of the authenticity of the Ḥadīth see A. Rippin *Muslims: their religious beliefs and practices*, Vol 2, Routledge, 1994, Chapter Four, which makes it clear that, contrary to some opinion, it is not only Western writers who have questioned the authenticity and value of the Ḥadīth.

9 *Ijmā'* is also a concept which seems to have no obvious parallel within the Christian community, where, as Chapter Six below will show, traditions of authority tend to involve either scripture or particular institutions of religious teaching, but one possible parallel may perhaps lie in the Anglican Christian idea of the "reception" of doctrines and practices: this basically means that doctrines and practices, however they are formulated, are not technically authoritative until they have been "received", that is agreed, by the Christian community, and this does, in theory, give an influence to the community of believers similar to that which, ideally, *ijmā'* also does.

10 One of the most famous examples of this process centres on coffee, which was discovered and introduced to the central part of the Islamic world in the sixteenth/ninth century, after its discovery in the Yemen. Given its novelty it was necessary for Islamic legal scholars to decide on its permissibility or otherwise, and after some considerable discussion their conclusion was that by analogy with alcohol, which was specifically prohibited in the Qur'ān (5:90), coffee too should be prohibited. Two problems resulted from this judgement: firstly, modern scientific opinion now knows that physiologically alcohol and coffee are not strictly analogous in their effects, indeed they may have exactly opposite effects; and secondly, by the time that the Islamic legal scholars had reached their decision so much time had passed that the practice of drinking coffee had already become immovably established in the Muslim community. See J. Kritzeck (ed.) *Anthology of Islamic literature*, Penguin, 1964, pp 377–378 (an extract from Katib Celebi's *The balance of truth*).

11 This is one of the reasons for the persistent call of many Islamic revivalist groups for the implementation of the Sharīʻa, an act which is seen by their members as being the solution to many of the current problems in Islamic societies. See further Chapter Eight below.

12 On the tradition of ethical thinking in Islam see especially M. Fakhry *Ethical theories in Islam*, Brill, Leiden, 1991, and G.F. Hourani *Reason and tradition in Islamic ethics*, Cambridge U.P., 1985.

13 The importance of these texts can be seen in the attempts by some Muslims to point to a kind of equivalent in the Qur'ān, Chapter 17:22–39, with parallel passages such as Chapter 6:151–153, where the text can be interpreted as pointing to a similar listing of ten commandments. There are differences of detail, however.

14 Compare 1 Samuel 16:7 where, in looking for a king for his nation Samuel is told that "man looks on the outward appearance but the Lord looks on the heart" and the call of the prophet Joel to "rend your hearts and not your garments" (2:13).

15 See especially E.P. Sanders *Paul and Palestinian Judaism*, SCM, 1977, and *Paul, the law and the Jewish people*, Fortress Press, Philadelphia, 1983.

16 See Chapter Three above for further discussion of this issue.

17 The work of the modern German theologian Hans Küng on Judaism may perhaps serve as a modern example of this: despite his undoubted concern to move beyond Christian caricature of Judaism and to present a more sympathetic and understanding Christian view, a number of Jewish reviewers have commented that the one area of Judaism which Küng conspicuously fails to demonstrate much sympathy for is Rabbinic Judaism, because of its concern with the minutiae of Law. On this issue, then, the parting of the ways between the two communities seems to have run so deep that there is an almost insuperable barrier to mutual understanding. Küng's book *Judaism*, the first volume of a trilogy, the remaining volumes of which will treat Christianity and Islam, was published by SCM in 1992; for a Jewish comment see Tony Bayfield's review in *The Church Times*, on 27th March 1992. Another example, at a different level, of the difficulty faced by those from a Christian background in trying to identify sympathetically with the idea of law in religion is the persistent tendency of British undergraduates, when writing about Islamic Law, to use the word "legalistic" when what should really be used is simply "legal".

18 The experience of the trial of Jesus, in which the actions of the Roman governor Pontius Pilate could be seen as representing a miscarriage of justice rather than the ideal of justice which Rome liked to think of itself as representing, might have been expected to alienate the Jesus movement from Roman law, but once the decision had been made by the early Christians to make the message of Jesus known among non-Jews (on which see Chapter One above) they did not hesitate to appeal to Rome for justice. See especially Acts 25:1–12. where Luke tells of how Paul adopts precisely this course.

19 See especially Paul's advice to the Christians in Corinth, especially that contained in Chapters Five to Seven of his first letter to them.

20 An example of this might be the suggestion of Augustine of Hippo that Christians should "love God and do what you will". His assumption that

love for God would ensure that Christians would not behave in a way displeasing to God was not always grasped fully by later generations of Christians.

21 This was one of Jesus' sayings which is not unique as this summary was also given by a number of his contemporaries. See Chapter One above.

22 There is a clear parallel to this emphasis in Islamic teaching, where the stress on *niyya* (intention) is also intended to balance any over-emphasis on the outward.

23 This is certainly an accusation which Muslim writers have often made against Christianity, especially when they are discussing the relationship between Islam and the West. For some examples of such a critique, see my article "The Muslim critique of the West" in *Anvil*, 4 (1987), pp 113–126.

24 A more modern attempt by a Christian thinker to apply Christian principles to the affairs of the state and of the world is Hans Küng's *Global responsibility*, SCM, 1991, in which he seeks to develop a universal ethic of which one important element is peace and dialogue between the different religious communities of the world.

25 Only certain churches, Orthodox, Roman Catholic and Anglican actually possess a tradition of canon law. Protestant churches, because of their different attitudes towards and relationships with the state generally do not possess canon law. In modern times the subject of canon law has been enjoying something of a revival in some quarters, as seen in the fact that in Britain it is now possible to read for a degree in the subject, at the University of Cardiff.

26 On traditions about women praying separately see R. Levy *The social structure of Islam*, Cambridge U.P., 1969, pp 99, 126 and 131, and on women in positions of political leadership see F. Mernissi *Women and Islam: an historical and theological enquiry*, Blackwell, 1991, especially Chapters Two and Three.

27 On the first two of these, see G. Makdisi *The rise of humanism in classical Islam and the Christian West, with special reference to Scholasticism*, Edinburgh U.P., 1990, pp 178 and 187. On the Sufis, see Chapter Five below.

28 See Chapter Five below for some comments on Christian mysticism. The fact that in both the Christian and Muslim communities it was among the mystics that women sometimes found greater opportunity for involvement may say something important about not only the ideas but also the social organisation of mystical groups, which sometimes seem to have served as alternative spiritual societies.

29 A convenient introduction to this discussion is Ann Loades "Feminist Theology" in D. Ford (ed.) *The modern theologians*, Vol II, Blackwell, 1989, pp 235–252. For more detail see D. Hampson *Theology and feminism*, Blackwell, 1990, and A. Loades (ed.) *Feminist theology: a reader*, SPCK, 1990.

30 For a convenient summary of the debate on this subject see O. Chadwick *The Christian church in the Cold War*, Penguin, 1992, pp 153–158.

31 Britain's first woman Professors of Theology and Religious Studies, Morna Hooker, Frances Young and Ursula King, were appointed to the Universities of Cambridge, Birmingham and Bristol respectively during the 1980's/1400's.

32 On this theme see especially F. Mernissi op. cit. See also the works of Rifaat Hassan, especially "Made from Adam's rib: the woman's creation question" in *al-Mushir*, Rawalpindi, Pakistan, 27 (1985), pp 124–155. For a general discussion of feminism in Islam see A. Rippin *Muslims: their religious beliefs and practices*, Vol II, Routledge, 1993, pp 115–126.

33 See S.P. Ramet "Islam in Yugoslavia today" in *Religion in Communist lands*, 18 (1990), pp 233–234.

34 Newspaper headlines on the occasion of her election serve as interesting evidence of the double standards which are sometimes applied to different societies. A headline in "The Times" (18th November 1988) thus referred to Miss Bhutto's election as a "historic step for Muslim women", and the following article referred to "a remarkable historic double in the modern Muslim world: the first woman leader of Pakistan and the first female leader of a Muslim country", perhaps implying that centuries of oppression and discrimination were being set aside but seeming to forget that it was less than a decade since Britain had elected its first woman Prime Minister (Margaret Thatcher in 1979); in the context of the centuries-long histories of Christianity and Islam a nine year difference between the two is surely not terribly significant. But other examples of such double standards could easily be found: when J.F. Kennedy was elected President of the United States of America, some British newspapers ran headlines such as "Americans elect Roman Catholic as President", seeming to suggest that this was a major leap forward for such a religiously-bigoted Protestant nation, but completely forgetting that Britain has never had a Roman Catholic Prime Minister. And when Bob Hawke, the Prime Minister of Australia, was ousted from his position by a coup within his own Labour party, some British newspapers ran headlines which referred to such things as stabbing in the back, as if this was to be expected in such an uncivilised place as Australia, completely forgetting that a very similar series of events had taken place in Britain just a few months previously in order to oust Mrs Thatcher from power.

35 An absolute contrast should not be drawn between the two traditions, however, as can be seen from the recent occasion when an Anglican priest in Telford called for criminals to have their hands chopped off as a deterrent for others, after his church centre was vandalised. He claimed to have conceived the idea while watching the Saudi Arabian team play football during the World Cup. See *British Muslims monthly survey*, Birmingham, Vol II, No 6, p 14. This is also, of course, an interesting example of the tension between the ideals of the Christian faith, as expounded in the Sermon on the Mount (Matthew 5 – 7), and the realities of life in the Christian community.

5

WORSHIP AND SPIRITUALITY

Introduction

These are subjects which are obviously crucial to both traditions. The Qur'ān affirms that God created humankind and the *jinn* (spirits) in order to worship him (51:56), and there are many exhortations throughout the Bible to worship the Lord God. As might be expected in the light of their different origins there are significant differences in form between Christian and Muslim worship, but there are perhaps some similarities in what might be described as their philosophy of worship, and when we come to look at spirituality we shall find that this is one of the areas in which there has been fruitful interaction between Christians and Muslims over the centuries.

Christian worship

As is the case in so many other areas too, Christian worship cannot really be understood without looking at its Jewish antecedents. Jesus, after all, was a Jew, and both he and his first disciples worshipped in both the Jewish synagogue and the Jewish Temple until the parting of the ways between the Jewish and Christian communities towards the end of the first century.[1]

Jewish worship itself was not a static phenomenon, as it had gone through several phases of development before the time of Jesus. At its heart, though, were two central institutions. On the one hand was the Temple in Jerusalem, built in the 10th century BCE by King Solomon as the place where the Jewish rituals of sacrifice were enacted, both as thank-offerings and for the purpose of atonement, and also the place where hymns of praise, the Psalms, were sung to God. The Temple was destroyed in 587BCE, when Jerusalem was besieged and occupied by

Nebuchadnezzar the king of Babylon, and shortly afterwards the Jews were carried off into exile in Babylon.

There, without any Temple as a focus or worship, a new religious institution developed as a place of worship, the synagogue, a word which literally means place of assembly. The origins of the institution are obscure, but it seems to have developed as a place of community meeting and also as a place in which the reading of scriptures and communal prayer came to play a prominent role.[2]

Some time after 539BCE groups of Jews returned to Palestine, and a Jewish community was thus re-established there. A Second Temple was constructed by the returnees, but it was destroyed in 167BCE, and a Third was then begun by Herod the Great in 19BCE. Both Temple and synagogue are therefore part of the background to the life of Jesus, as seen, for example, in such parts of the New Testament as Luke 4:16–21, where Jesus is asked to read the scriptures in the synagogue in Nazareth, and Matthew 21:12–13/Luke 19:45–46 where Jesus, in the best prophetic tradition, is highly critical of some of the activities which were going on around the Temple. And in its early days the members of the Jesus movement also participated in the worship of both synagogue and Temple.[3]

A third significant element of Jewish worship, whose origins precede those of both Temple and synagogue, was the role of certain rituals which took place in the home. Probably the most important of these was the weekly meal which took place at the start of the weekly Sabbath, or holy day, in other words on Friday evenings. The foundation of this ritual was that it was a commemoration firstly in general terms of creation and secondly, more specifically, of an event which was seen as formative of the whole Jewish community and tradition, namely the Passover, when, as described in the Book of Exodus, the ancestors of the Jews were miraculously delivered from Egypt.

The meal involved both the drinking of wine and the breaking of bread. In addition to this weekly ceremony the Passover was also commemorated annually on 14th Nisan, when the story of the events of the Exodus was re-told, and the Passover meal involved the consumption of both wine and unleavened bread.

Jewish worship, then, was based on these three elements, which developed at different stages of Jewish history. All three were significant at the time of Jesus, though it was not long after that that one of the three, the Temple, was destroyed, in 70CE, and since that time Jewish worship has therefore been centred on a combination of the synagogue and the home.

It was against this background of Jewish worship, and the developing separation between the Jewish and Christian communities, that the patterns of Christian worship unfolded. At first, since Christians were a minority community within the Roman Empire, and a community sometimes persecuted at that, Christian worship tended to take place within homes, and it seems to have developed along the following lines: the two focal points were firstly readings from the scriptures, involving both Gospel accounts and Epistles, and also readings from the Old Testament, and secondly a kind of fellowship meal, involving the breaking of bread and the drinking of wine.[4]

The Jewish antecedents of each of these elements is obvious, but the form of Christian worship obviously differed from the Jewish pattern in that different, distinctively Christian scriptures, were read, and new, distinctively Christian, interpretations came to be given to the fellowship meal. In particular the breaking of bread and the drinking of wine came to be seen as symbolic representations of the death of Jesus and of incorporation and membership of the Christian community, which came to speak of itself as being, in some way, the body of Christ. New levels of meaning were thus added to a ritual which was not, in fact, Christian in origin at all.

Christian worship, like Jewish worship, therefore evolved over the centuries, with development taking place particularly rapidly in association with such events as Christianity becoming the official religion of the Roman Empire in the fourth century CE, as a result of which for the first time buildings were set aside publicly for Christian worship, as churches. But throughout Christian history the two main elements of Christian worship have always remained paradigmatic, to a greater or lesser extent, and so most Christians still retain a pattern of worship which involves firstly what is sometimes called "The Ministry of the Word", that is readings from scripture, sometimes with an associated sermon, and secondly "The Ministry of the Faithful", which involves participation in a sacred meal which in some way either re-enacts or commemorates the death of Jesus. Different Christian groups sometimes lay more stress on one or the other of these elements, with traditional Roman Catholic and Eastern Orthodox Christians tending to lay more stress on the sacred meal, and Protestant Christians tending to emphasise the Ministry of the Word, but in most Christian groups both elements are still regarded as significant, even if the balance between them differs.[5]

In one specific respect Christian worship did differ from Jewish worship and that concerned the day of the week on which the main act of Christian worship took place: instead of the Jewish Sabbath Christians worshipped on the following day, Sunday, the justification for this being that it was on that day, the first day of the week, that the resurrection of Jesus from the dead was thought to have taken place. It was on this day, therefore, that the celebration of the Lord's Supper, as it was called in the New Testament (1 Corinthians 10:16) took place.

Later Christian history has also seen further elaboration of the understanding of worship so that, for example, traditions concerning pilgrimage to certain places which have particular associations with aspects of Christian history have grown up. The most important of these are focused on Jerusalem and Palestine, the places where Jesus himself lived and taught and the places where many other events described in the Bible, both prior to and subsequent to Jesus' time, took place. For this reason Palestine (as it then was) is still described by many Christians as "The Holy Land", and pilgrimages to it are organised from all parts of the Christian world. Other centres which at a later stage acquired special significance for Christians also function as places of pilgrimage, the most important example being Rome.

Traditions concerning festivals at different times of the year have also grown up in the Christian community, with the two major festivals, Christmas and Easter, commemorating the birth, and the death and resurrection of Jesus respectively. The Christian community worldwide is not unanimous about the dates on which these should be celebrated, with Christmas being celebrated on December 25th in the West but January 6th in most of the East, and with Easter moving around in springtime in both West and East, occasionally coinciding but sometimes being separated by as much as six weeks. Other festivals commemorate either important events or important individuals in the history of the Christian church, with the most important probably being Pentecost, originally a Jewish festival held fifty days after the Passover, but significant for Christians because it is on that day that they commemorate the special descent of the Holy Spirit on the early Christians, described in the second chapter of the book of Acts.

In addition to specific rituals and acts of worship the Christian tradition has also insisted that in one sense the whole of life is to be considered as worship, so that, for example, the giving of money should also be considered as an aspect of worship. In this, as in so many other areas, Christians were simply continuing a tradition which had grown up in Judaism in the form of the tithe (giving ten per cent of wealth) and then, in the centuries immediately prior to the time of Jesus, through almsgiving (the general principle of generosity to the poor).[6]

As regards the setting in which public acts of Christian worship take place, namely church buildings, the consequences of all this are as follows. For all the inevitable variety of style which has grown up in different centuries and in different parts of the world, Christian churches usually have two central features which serve as focal points. On the one hand there will usually be a pulpit and/or lectern, reading desks from which the scriptures are read and the sermon preached. In addition to these, usually behind them, there will usually be a table, often called an altar, at which the sacred meal consisting of bread and wine, will be prepared as the central focus of the Ministry of the Faithful.

Christians sometimes stand, sometimes sit, and sometimes kneel for worship, so the furniture will vary in different churches, with Eastern churches tending to have seating only around the outer walls and Western churches tending to have seats, or pews, for worshippers. In addition Protestant churches tend to be plainer in their style of decoration and to focus more on pulpit and/or lectern, largely because of the stress that is placed on the importance of the word, whereas Orthodox and Catholic churches may be more highly decorated and the focus of attention will rest more on the altar. This reflects differences of theology as well as of tradition.

Muslim worship

There are some important differences between the patterns of Christian and Muslim worship which it is worth noting immediately. Christian worship, as we have seen, has developed over the centuries, and also exhibits some measure of diversity, not least as a result of the acceptability of the use of different languages. Muslim worship, by contrast, in all of its fundamental elements, has remained more or less the same over the whole course of Muslim history and over the whole geographical extent of the Muslim world, and one cause of this is the community's insistence on the use of the Arabic language in the different rituals of worship.[7]

It is generally stated that there are five particular acts of worship associated with the Muslim community, and these are sometimes described as the "five pillars of Islam".[8] One, the first, involves a kind of intellectual assent, and the remaining four are actions which Muslims should perform. This balance perhaps makes clear a point made earlier about the balance between belief and practice in the two communities, with the Christian community tending to lay more stress on right belief and acceptance of creeds, so that it is preoccupied with orthodoxy, and the Muslim community tending to emphasise right action and behaviour, and being primarily concerned with what has been called orthopraxy.

The first act of worship involves *īmān*, faith, which is encapsulated in the *shahāda*, or declaration of faith, which Muslims make on various occasions. This simple creed consists simply of two phrases, the first being "I declare that there is no god but (or except) God", in other words that there is only one God, and the second being "I declare that Muḥammad is the prophet of God", each of these phrases being from the Qur'ān (37:35 and 48:29 respectively).[9] For anyone wishing to convert to Islam, the recital of the *shahāda* three times with sincerity in the presence of two witnesses is enough for that person to be considered a Muslim.

The second act of worship centres on prayer, *ṣalāt*, but whereas prayer in the Christian tradition tends to mean a primarily verbal activity, involving speaking to, and occasionally listening to, God, prayer in the Muslim tradition primarily means a physical act of prostration before God.[10] In more detail this takes the form of a series of ritual prostrations five times a day, with accompanying phrases which should be recited.[11]

The third act of worship involves giving, known as *zakāt*, which literally means purification. What this involves is the giving, sometimes on a monthly basis and sometimes on an annual basis, of a proportion of a Muslim's wealth, to charitable causes. This may include the care of the poor and the needy, such as widows and orphans, and provision for the spread of Islam. Traditionally one fortieth (2.5%) of a Muslim's wealth (not income) is the proportion which it is suggested that Muslims consider giving, but there is some variety in the detailed regulations which have evolved in different places at different times.

The fourth act of worship is fasting, *ṣawm*, which takes place during one month of the Muslim calendar, the month of Ramaḍān, between the hours of dawn and sunset. During this time nothing should enter the body of a Muslim, so that Muslims should abstain not only from food and drink but also from such things as having injections.

Finally, the fifth action is pilgrimage, *ḥajj*, which if at all possible Muslims should participate in once during their lifetime. In more detail what this involves is taking part in a series of rituals in Mecca, the birthplace of Muḥammad, during the twelfth month of the Muslim calendar, some of the rituals focusing on incidents in the life of Muḥammad himself, some commemorating events longer ago in the life of Abraham (Ibrāhīm), and some having a more general spiritual significance.[12]

With respect to the antecedents of these acts of Muslim worship, it is not always possible to be specific, but a number of possible influences may be discerned, including on the one hand Jewish and Christian influences, and on the other pre-Islamic Arabian influence. Thus the ideas of giving and fasting may owe something to Jewish and Christian practice, as may some aspects of prayer, given that in its earliest days, until 624/2 the Muslim community prayed in the direction of Jerusalem, like Jews and Christians. But the fact that in that year the direction of prayer changed to that of Mecca, together with the prominence of prostration in prayer, and also the basic pattern of the pilgrimage to Mecca point to Arabian influences on the pattern of Muslim worship as well.[13]

The pattern of Muslim worship, once fixed in the early days of the community, has not substantially changed. As we have seen there were some changes in the time of Muḥammad himself, and much of the detail of Muslim worship is not found in the Qur'ān but is rather based on the example of Muḥammad as recorded in the Ḥadīth, but once the pattern had been established in the Muslim community it has by and large remain fixed.

For the Muslim community the main holy day of the week, the day on which if at all possible Muslims should take part in congregational prayer in the mosque for the noon prayer, is Friday. The reason for this seems to have been partly a desire to distinguish the Muslim community from the already-existing Jewish and Christian ones but more importantly because it was on Friday that Adam was created. Friday is not necessarily, in the Islamic understanding, a day of rest.[14]

As in the Christian tradition so also in the Muslim tradition the passing of time in each year is marked by certain festivals, and the two most important Muslim ones are the *'īd al-fiṭr*, the feast of the breaking of the fast which falls at the end of the month of Ramaḍān, the tenth month of the Muslim calendar, and the *īd al-aḍhā*, the feast of the sacrifice, which occurs at the climax of the *ḥajj* (pilgrimage) in the twelfth month of the Muslim calendar. Because the Muslim calendar is based on the lunar cycle, these festivals do not always fall at the same time in the Western (solar) calendar, but in 1995 they fell respectively at the end of February and in the middle of May, and in each succeeding year they will advance by some ten days relative to the Western calendar. There are also other lesser festivals such as the *mawlid al-nabī*, the birthday of the prophet Muḥammad (which Sunnī and Shī'ī Muslims celebrate on the 12th and 17th the month of Rabī' al-awwal, the third month of the Muslim calendar, respectively), and the *laylat al-isrā' wa'l-mi'rāj*, the night of the journey/ascent of Muḥammad to Jerusalem and the seventh heaven, celebrated on 27th Rajab, the seventh month of the Muslim calendar.[15]

The layout of the mosque, the place of communal worship in the Muslim community, is fairly simple. The main focus of attention is the *miḥrāb*, the niche or alcove which indicates the direction of Mecca, towards which prayer is directed, and the only other major feature is the *minbar* or pulpit, from which a sermon is usually preached during the noon prayer on Friday. In some mosques both *miḥrāb* and *minbar* are highly ornate and decorated, but the general pattern of mosques, despite considerable regional variety as a result of different climates and building styles, is a fairly simple one. Given that Muslim prayer involves physical prostration the main body of the mosque consists simply of an open space in which prayer can be performed, and the only decoration in the mosque usually takes the form of either calligraphy, the stylised representation of verses from the Qur'ān, or the use of coloured tiles.

Christian and Muslim spirituality

On the foundation of formal, public worship other, perhaps more informal or more individual patterns of devotion and spiritual life have developed in both communities, and it is important to take some account of these. On one level certain obvious devotional practices such as the reading and study of scriptures are found among both Christians and Muslims. In Islam, for example, there is the well-established tradition of the Qur'ān being divided into seven sections, which can be read on the basis of one section per day so that the whole Qur'ān is read during the course of a week, and also the division of the scripture into thirty sections, so that it can be read, or publicly recited, on the basis of one section for each day of the month of Ramaḍān. And in the Christian community there is a whole range of ways in which the Christian Bible may be divided up and read on the basis of daily portions or extracts over the course of a year or, more often because of the length of the Bible, over a number of years. More detailed attention, however, will be given to a number of other areas of spirituality.

a) Mysticism

This area is one in which, over the course of the centuries, there has been very interesting interaction and mutual influence between Christian and Muslim mystical writers, with the influence sometimes going one way and sometimes the other. Thus in the early centuries of Islam, when the different traditions of Islamic thought were still evolving, some of the early Sufis, Muslim mystics, were influenced by the ideas and practices of Christian monks. Just as Christian monasticism had evolved as a kind of alternative Christianity, a protest against some of the trends towards worldliness which emerged once Christianity had become the official religion of the Roman Empire in the fourth century CE, so Sufism emerged in part as a protest against the worldliness which the Sufis saw as beginning to affect the Muslim community once it had become powerful and successful in its early conquests.[16]

It was not surprising, therefore, if Sufis learnt from and adopted some of the ideas and practices of the Christian monks. One story involves a Sufi visiting a monk and marvelling at his spectacular feats of asceticism.[17] Sufism was not a monolithic or uniform movement, however, and other influences on it came from Persian Zoroastrian and Indian Hindu and Buddhist sources.[18]

At a later stage, then, the ideas of some of the Sufi mystics seem to have been influential upon some of the most significant Western Christian mystics. The locus of this exchange was at the western end of the Islamic world, in the twelfth to fourteenth/sixth to eighth centuries, when especially in Spain there was a relatively open attitude towards interaction and interchange of ideas between the two communities.[19] Among the first Christian mystical writers to be influenced to some extent by Sufi ideas was Ramon Lull (d 1316/716), a former knight who after a dramatic conversion to the Christian faith dedicated his life to making the Christian faith known among Muslims, and partly as a result of his influence Sufi ideas have also been discerned in the works of the later Spanish Carmelite St John of the Cross (d 1591/999).[20]

Thus there are some uncanny parallels between the sayings of some of the Sufi Muslims and some of the Christian mystics. On the one hand we have the saying of the Sufi al-Ḥallāj (d 922/309), "I am the truth", as a result of which he was crucified, as elaborated by Jalāl al-dīn Rūmī (d 1273/672): "This is what is signified by the words . . . 'I am the truth'. People imagine that it is a presumptuous claim, whereas it is really a presumptuous claim to say . . . 'I am the slave of God', and 'I am God' is an expression of great humility. The man who says . . . 'I am the slave of God' affirms two existences, his own and God's but he that says . . . 'I am God' has made himself non-existent and has given himself up and says 'I am God', i.e. 'I am naught, He is all: there is no being but God's". This is the extreme of humility and self-abasement."[21] And on the other hand we have the sayings of Christian mystics such as Julian of Norwich (d 1420/823), "I saw no difference between God and our substance", and St. Catherine of Genoa (d 1510/916), "My God is me, nor do I recognise any other me except my God himself".[22]

It is also interesting to note that to the already-mentioned Qur'ānic verse which states that God created humankind and the spirits to worship him the Sufis sometimes add the phrase "and to know him", which is remarkably close to the well-known Protestant Christian statement of faith that "man's chief end is to glorify him and to enjoy him for ever".[23]

In this field of mysticism we thus see, at different periods of history, interaction between Christians and Muslims, with ideas and practices passing both ways at different times, and also some very striking parallels in some instances between Christian and Muslim concepts and experiences.[24]

b) Sacrifice

Moving ahead to the modern period, again a number of examples of intriguing parallels between Christian and Muslim spirituality may be discerned. One such example might be seen in a comparison between two pamphlets, one Christian and one Muslim, on the subject of sacrifice. Both pamphlets have as their main title simply "Sacrifice", but they have different sub-titles, the Christian one being "a challenge to Christian youth", and the Muslim one being "the making of a Muslim".

The Christian pamphlet was first published in 1936, in London, by the Inter-Varsity Fellowship, an interdenominational Christian group working particularly among university students. Its author, Rev. Howard Guinness, was one of the mentors of the IVF, and the pamphlet proved extremely popular, with a second edition being produced six months after the first, a third edition in 1945, a fourth in 1950, and a fifth in 1961, each edition having been reprinted a number of times before a new edition became necessary. The most recent reprint was in February of 1966.

The Muslim pamphlet was published in 1985 by the Islamic Foundation, and its author Khurram Murad was then the Director of the Foundation. The pamphlet was developed from an address given by the author at Friday prayers at the West Coast Conference of the Muslim Students' Association of the USA, held in Los Angeles in July 1979,

What we have here, therefore, are some intriguing parallels: we have two pamphlets, admittedly written at different times and in different contexts, but bearing the same main title, addressed to similar student audiences, written by authors who come from what could be described as similar "conservative" backgrounds within their respective traditions, and published by organisations which, coincidentally, are now both based in Leicester.[25] Given that on many university campuses in Britain today the largest religious societies are often the Muslim Students'

Society, the British equivalent of the American organisation to which Khurram Murad's address was originally given, and the Christian Union, the local branch of the successor to the Inter-Varsity Fellowship, the Universities and Colleges Christian Fellowship, a study of the two pamphlets may reveal some interesting truths about campus religion today, as well as about the Christian and Muslim understandings of sacrifice.

Guinness' pamphlet investigates the theme of sacrifice in five chapters, with an epilogue to bring things to a conclusion. The chapter titles are poverty, love, discipline, experience and power, with the first three chapters elaborating on the main elements of sacrifice, the fourth being more autobiographical with the author outlining the various stages of his own growth as a Christian and a number of crises which contributed to that process, and the fifth outlining the goal of the whole process of making sacrifices, namely the receipt of the power of the Holy Spirit. The Epilogue then simply urges young Christians to respond to the challenge of the pamphlet, to live dangerously in the service of Christ and even be ready to fling away their lives for the love of Christ. Readers are invited right at the end to sign and date their assent to a prayer: "Out of gratitude to Thee, my Lord and Saviour, who though Thou wast rich yet for my sake didst become poor, I now surrender myself to Thee to be filled with Thy Holy Spirit that I may, from today, live a life of sacrifice."[26]

It is in the first three chapters, then, that the author's understanding of sacrifice is most fully elaborated. Discussion of poverty points to the need for willingness to give up career and financial security for the sake of Christian work. This might include taking out citizenship of another, less developed, country, in order to work there and show solidarity with local Christians. As well as financial generosity, and such disciplines as keeping careful accounts, sacrifice might also involve self-denial in such things as vacations. Discussion of love dwells at some length on the need for care in relationships between the sexes to ensure that such relationships do not distract from Christian vocation and that they are properly founded on mutual respect and true affection. Seven questions are given which are intended to help readers discern whether or not a relationship should be pursued, and it is stressed on a number of occasions that such things as broken engagements are to be avoided if at all possible. Discussion of discipline then focuses on the need for discipline in every aspect of life – mind, heart, will, body, and spirit. Examples of such discipline are regular private prayer, the absence of any spirit of criticism of others, careful use of time, regularity in answering letters, tidiness, being methodical in determining reading material, a sensible pattern of sleep, moderate eating and keeping fit.

The pamphlet by Khurram Murad is not arranged formally into chapters, but there are three main sections, with an introduction and a conclusion. The central sections address three main questions – why sacrifice?, what is sacrifice?, and how to sacrifice? Crucial to the first question, in the author's view, is the fact that Islam is a path of struggle, both on a personal and on a collective level. The whole man, his inner personality, his environment, his society and the entire world is to be brought to the path of God, and this process may be compared to building a wall. The second section suggests that there are two types of sacrifice, which the author calls tangible and intangible sacrifices; the former are such things as time, worldly possessions and money, and even life itself, and the latter include familial love, friendships, and attachment to one's own views and opinions, feelings and emotions, taste and temperament, and ego. Such sacrifices are continual and may not produce obvious results. The section on how to sacrifice stresses such characteristics as love for God, remembering God, living in God's presence and being ready to meet God; sacrifices should be made with gratitude and humility, and with a careful watch on their motivation. Two specific aids are *ṣalāṭ* (prayer) and *ṣabr* (patience and the will to sacrifice), and two models who may be followed are Abraham and Muḥammad. On two occasions (pp 13 and 29) three principles of sacrifice are stated: something is a sacrifice only if it is loved or valued; it is more difficult to sacrifice abstract things than concrete ones; and it is only possible to sacrifice things if it is done out of love for something of greater value.

There are thus some similarities and also some differences between the two pamphlets. Overall it is perhaps the central section of Murad's pamphlet and the first three chapters of Guinness' pamphlet which are most easily comparable as they each elaborate certain specific examples of sacrifice – time, money and even life, for example.[27] In other respects, however, there are interesting differences between the two.

Firstly, Guinness is far more ready to refer to personal experience in order to explain his argument: thus the whole of his fourth chapter is autobiographical and his experience serves as his own personal testimony concerning his theme.[28] Murad, by contrast, is much more diffident, and all that the reader learns of his biography is what is given of it on the back cover of the pamphlet.[29]

Secondly, Guinness' emphasis is throughout rather more exclusively on the individual dimensions of sacrifice, whereas Murad does also stress a communal dimension; in part this may reflect a Western individualism rather more than a necessary characteristic of the Christian faith, but it is certainly there in the pamphlets, and it may be seen perhaps most clearly in the two writers' discussions of the family. Here Guinness writes in such a way as to suggest that part of a Christian's sacrifice may be not to have a family, in other words not to marry and remain single. Murad, by contrast, even where he is explaining the need for sacrifice in the context of familial relationships, may argue for the need to withdraw from contact with unsympathetic relations but he never goes on to argue that there should be a withdrawal from the family as such; a balance may need to be maintained between the demands of following the path of God and the needs of wives and children, but it is never stated that one of the former might be to renounce the family altogether.

Thirdly, there is an important distinction between the two authors' outlining of the purpose of sacrifice. For Guinness sacrifices are made for Christ, whereas for Murad their purpose is for the advancement and revival of Islam,[30] and this perhaps points to an important difference between the two faiths in general, namely the Christian focus on the person of Christ in contrast to a greater Muslim concentration on the system of Islam.[31]

Fourthly, Murad's pamphlet contains more specific guidance on methods which may be employed in order to enable readers to undertake sacrifices. This is found especially in his third section which is entitled "How to sacrifice", and the inclusion of this section could be seen as evidence of a tendency in some Christian spiritual writing to rely rather heavily on exhortation to certain actions, in contrast to the tradition in Islam of putting forward a disciplined programme of action towards the desired end.

It would thus not be true to say anything more than that there are some parallels between the two authors' views. But even the existence of some parallels is a suggestive pointer towards the existence of at least some common ground between the two communities in the field of spirituality.

c) Letters from prison

The same is also true of our last focus of comparison between the two traditions. This takes the form of an investigation of two slightly fuller publications of the past half century which take the form of letters and reflections from prison. The works concerned are firstly Dietrich Bonhoeffer's "Letters and papers from prison", first translated into

English by Reginald Fuller in 1953 and subsequently republished in a number of different editions, and secondly Muḥammad Fadhel Jamali's "Letters on Islam", first published in 1965 and translated into English by the author in 1967.[32]

Bonhoeffer, a Lutheran pastor, was imprisoned during the Second World War on suspicion of involvement in anti-Nazi activities in Germany, and after two years in prison he was executed for these activities on 9th April 1945. Jamali, an active politician in Iraq, eight times the Foreign Minister and twice Prime Minister in the years between 1945 and 1958, was imprisoned and sentenced to death in 1958 when the regime which he had represented was overthrown by a military coup involving the secular Ba'ath party. The sentence was not carried out, however, and he was released and permitted to go into exile in Tunisia in 1961.

Bonhoeffer's letters were to his parents and to his friend Eberhard Bethge (sometimes with his wife Renate), and along with the letters he sometimes included such things as a Wedding Sermon for the Bethges (pp 5–10), some prayers for his fellow-prisoners (pp 28–32), a report on the first year of his life in prison (pp 79–83), thoughts for the baptism of the Bethges' son Dietrich (pp 96–102), and a number of poems (pp 110–112, 117–119, 126–127, 133–134, 144–145, and 146). Jamali's letters were to his son Abbas, and generally they are more systematic in form as the author set out on his writing with the specific intention of outlining to his son the salient points of Islam, in his understanding.[33] The section of Bonhoeffer's book which is closest in style to Jamali's letters is probably that on pages 96–102, where he writes some thoughts for his godson, Dietrich Bethge, on the occasion of his baptism.

Despite the superficial similarities between the two works, there are inevitably significant differences between them. For example, the background against which Jamali wrote, for all the uncertainty concerning his own fate, was one in which there was less general unpredictability about the unfolding of events in the wider world, to which there are hardly any references in his letters, whereas Bonhoeffer, writing in a situation in which a world war was raging around him, includes more references to aspects of that wider conflict, such as the effect of a number of air-raids on his fellow-prisoners (pp 16–17, 33–34, 34–35, 36, 38, 39, 58–59, 60–61, 62, 72–73, 76, 82–83, and 117), his thoughts on hearing of the D-day landings (p 113), and his concerns for Eberhard Bethge who had been called up for military service in Italy (pp 73–74 and 102–105).

In addition the two writers seem to have rather different understandings of their own suffering. Referring to the commutation of his death sentence, Jamali simply says: "It was the will of Allah the Sublime that I should remain alive and not be hanged, for my sentence of death was commuted after a year and a half, and my freedom was restored after I had been three years in prison" (p vii), and he elaborates on this with the words: "No man or group of men can change what Allah has destined. If my time had come to die, then death would have been inevitable. While under sentence of death I felt that the blessing of faith and the spiritual peace which goes with it is the most precious treasure in this life. Poor is the individual who is devoid of faith, for he is no more than a bankrupt man devoid of the greatest blessing which ennobles humanity; for faith gives man the assurance of spiritual survival so that he will not fear death or worry about trivial matters in life" (pp vii–viii). There is here, then, a strong insistence on the need simply to submit, with faith, to whatever might happen.

Bonhoeffer, by contrast, seems to struggle more with the problems arising from his suffering, and wrestles his way towards locating some kind of meaning for them in the precedent or paradigm of Jesus' suffering. He even goes so far as to speak of God's suffering: "God lets himself be pushed out of the world on to the cross . . . . . . only the suffering God can help" (p 130), so Christian discipleship is to be taken up into the sufferings of God in Christ. Suffering becomes a station on the road to freedom (p 134), and this theme is powerfully expressed in some of Bonhoeffer's poems:

Men go to God when they are sore bestead,
Pray to him for succour, for his peace, for bread,
For mercy for them sick, sinning, or dead;
All men do, Christian and unbelieving.

Men go to God when he is sore bestead,
Find him poor and scorned, without shelter or bread,
Whelmed under the weight of the wicked, the weak, the dead;
Christians stand by God in his hour of grieving.

God goes to every man when he is sore bestead,
Feeds body and mind with his bread;
For Christians, pagans alike he hangs dead,
And both alike forgiving. (p 127)

It is this conviction which gives Bonhoeffer his confidence, as expressed in the final words of the abridged edition of the letters:

While all the powers of good aid and attend us,
boldly we'll face the future, come what may.
At even and at morn God will befriend us,
and oh, most surely on each newborn day! (p 146).[34]

All this points us to what is perhaps the most significant difference between the two writers, and that is that Jamali's focus is very much on God and on the system of Islam, whereas Bonhoeffer's is much more on the person and example of Christ. Jamali thus sings the praises of the system of Islam as a way of life and as total system of guidance, with his first nine letters elaborating on the need for faith, letters ten to twelve focusing on Islamic creeds, thirteen and fourteen explaining the value of Islamic rituals, fifteen to nineteen outlining the Islamic social system, twenty to twenty-two focusing on Islamic morality, and finally twenty-three and twenty-four discussing nationalism and the modern world respectively. Bonhoeffer, by contrast, stresses a more individual kind of transforming faith, and this more personal emphasis perhaps explains why, as with Guinness and Murad, there is a greater element of autobiography in Bonhoeffer's letters, including several references to his fiancée Maria (e.g. pp 22, 25, 26, 35, 40–41, 53–54, 109 and 143), with Jamali appearing far more diffident and modest concerning his own person and experience.[35]

As John Bowker remarks, however, both Bonhoeffer and Jamali point to the importance of faith, a clear conscience, and loyal friends, and in their shared experience of suffering, therefore, they did find at least some common anchoring points.[36]

Conclusion

With respect to both their formal, communal rituals and to their informal, more personal and private devotional practices, then, there are obvious differences but also some similarities between Christian and Muslim practices. On the one hand the outward forms of the two communities' worship are quite different, but on the other when attempts are made to locate the inner intention of this worship and its meaning some common ground may be discerned. Equally, with respect to more informal spirituality there are significant differences of emphasis between the two traditions, but to balance this there are some areas where similar language, with respect to sacrifice and suffering, is used and others, especially in the field of mysticism, where concepts and ideas have quite clearly been exchanged between Christians and Muslims. Once again, therefore, we find some divergence and some convergence.[37]

NOTES

1 See Chapters One and Three above for more detail on these developments.
2 See Chapter Two above for further detail of the process by which the Jewish scriptures were collected.
3 See, for example, Acts 3:1 (the Temple) and Acts 14:1 (the synagogue).
4 An early statement about the worship of the Early Church can be found in Acts 2:42: "they devoted themselves to the apostles' teaching and fellowship, to the breaking of bread and the prayers".
5 For more detail on these and other differences within the Christian community see Chapter Six below. For more detail on the development of the patterns of Christian worship see C. Jones, G. Wainwright and E. Yarnold (eds.) *The study of liturgy*, 2nd ed., SPCK, 1992.
6 See, for example, the commendation of alsmsgiving in some of the books of the Apocrypha of the Old Testament such as Tobit (1:3; 4:10–11,16; 12:8–9).
7 The question of the use or otherwise of different languages in the two traditions is closely related to the question of the permissibility or otherwise of translating scriptures into different languages. See Chapter Two above on this question.
8 There are some small differences in the form of worship between Sunnī and Shī'i Muslims, but in the context of the generally identical pattern of worship in the two groups they are pretty insignificant.
9 The first of these declarations can be parallelled in Jewish scriptures such as Isaiah 44:6 ("besides me there is no god"), but it is obviously the second phrase which makes explicit the different convictions of Muslims from those of Jews or Christians.
10 This idea is not completely foreign to the Christian tradition as in the great encounter between a human being and God described in the book of Revelation at the end of the New Testament, the author fell prostrate and bowed down before God.
11 A useful visual aid which illustrates the pattern of Muslim prayer has been produced by the Audio-Visual unit of the University of Leeds, under the title "Friday prayer at the mosque". Some of the rituals which are seen towards the end of the video, however, are characteristic of the particular Muslim group involved in the project, and are not performed by all Muslims.
12 Many of the rituals, of course, combine aspects of these different levels of meaning.
13 Just as Christian worship owed much to Jewish patterns of worship, Islamic worship therefore owes at least some debt to pre-existing patterns of worship, as, for example, in the fact that the Ka'ba, the cubical shrine in Mecca towards which Muslims now pray and around which part of the *ḥajj* rituals are performed, already existed and occupied a prominent place in pre-Islamic (polytheistic) Meccan worship.
14 See A. Rippin and J. Knappert (eds.) *Textual sources for the study of Islam*, Manchester U.P., 1986, p 63.

15 On Muslim festivals in general see H. Lazarus-Yafeh *Some religious aspects of Islam*, Brill, 1981, Chapter Three, and on the festival of Muḥammad's birthday in particular, which is the occasion of some controversy among Muslims as to its permissibility, see N.J.G. Kaptein *Muḥammad's birthday festival*, Brill, Leiden, 1993.

16 For further detail on this, see Chapter Seven below.

17 See A.J. Arberry *Sufism*, George Allen and Unwin, 1950, p 37, where the Sufi Ibrāhīm ibn Adham describes how he learnt the knowledge of God from a Syrian monk called Simeon.

18 There is something of a parallel here with the growth of philosophy (on which see Chapter Three above) and also the growth of medical and scientific knowledge in the medieval world of Islam, in all of which fields Muslims drew not just on Greek but also on Persian and Indian expertise.

19 Again there is an obvious parallel here with the process whereby Islamic philosophical, and also scientific and medical knowledge was transmitted to Western Europe through the translation movement in Spain and Sicily. See Chapter Three above for more detail on this.

20 See M.A. Palacios *St John of the Cross and Islam*, Vantage Press, New York, 1981, where it is suggested that St John may have been particularly influenced by the Sufis Ibn 'Aṭā' Allāh of Alexandria (d 1309/709) and Ibn 'Abbād of Ronda (d 1390/793), and *El Islam Cristianizado*, Editorio Plutarco, Madrid, 1931, where the influence of the Spanish Sufi Ibn 'Arabī (d 1240/638) is posited. For a more recent comment on the question of Muslim influence on the Christian mystics of Spain see F. de B. de Medina "Islam and Christian spirituality in Spain: contacts, influences, similarities" in *Islamochristiana*, 18 (1992), pp 87–108 (especially pp 97–105).

21 R. A. Nicholson *Rumi, poet and mystic*, George Allen and Unwin, 1950, p 184.

22 See respectively A. Louth *The wilderness of God*, Darton, Longman and Todd, 1991, p 73, and G. Hughes *God of surprises*, Darton, Longman and Todd, 1985, p 161.

23 Comparison may also be made between Oliver Cromwell's advice to "trust in God and keep your powder dry" and the Arabic proverb "trust in God and tie up your camel"!

24 Another parallel might perhaps be the tendency for mystical thinkers to be regarded with some suspicion by the institutions of religious leadership in both the Christian and Muslim communities, as seen in the experiences of a Sufi such as al-Ḥallāj and a Christian mystic such as St John of the Cross. The impatience of mystics with the outward details and form of religion is in large part responsible for this tension, which led to the rather unkind anonymous comment that "mysticism begins in mist and ends in schism"!

25 In the case of the Christian pamphlet it is actually the Universities and Colleges Christian Fellowship, the descendant of the original publisher, which is now based in Leicester.

26 In the context of any comparison with Islam, the use of the word "surrender" is very suggestive. Compare the observation of Wilfred Cantwell Smith that the Catholic Encyclopaedia (1913 edition) defines religion as "the voluntary subjection of oneself to God"; see *The meaning and end of religion*, SPCK, 1978, p 113.

27 For an interesting survey of the concept of giving up one's life for the faith

in Christianity and Islam see M.M. Ayoub "Martyrdom in Christianity and Islam" in *Newsletter of the Centre for the study of Islam and Christian-Muslim relations*, (Birmingham), No 14, November 1985, pp 4–14, reprinted (with minor changes) in R.T. Antoun and M.E. Hegland (eds) *Religious resurgence – contemporary cases in Islam, Christianity and Judaism*, Syracuse U.P., 1987, pp 67–77.

28 In the fourth edition of the pamphlet, published in 1950, a new section was added to the end of Chapter Four, in which Guinness very movingly described events in his life which had unfolded in the intervening twenty-four years, particularly the onset of lymphosarcoma, a disease of the glands, for which there was no cure.

29 In the first paragraph of Chapter Four Guinness is also hesitant about referring in such detail to his own experience, but he proceeds to do so on the grounds that it may be helpful to some others.

30 For further elaboration of the author's views on one aspect of this see his pamphlet *Da'wah among non-Muslims in the West*, Islamic Foundation, Leicester, 1986.

31 Another minor difference can be seen in some of the language which the two writers use: Murad's references to the ego, for example, are testimony to the growth in the use of Freudian language in the interval between the first publication of the two pamphlets, while some of the rather spartan practices commended by Guinness in the first edition of his pamphlet were toned down somewhat by means of additional foot-notes in later editions (e.g. note 1 on p 41 about cold baths and the acknowledgement in note 1 on p 23 that ignorance about sex among young Christians was becoming less common!)

32 The most recent, and fullest, English edition of Bonhoeffer's letters, the 4th edition, was published by SCM in 1971. I have made use of the Abridged Edition, published by SCM in 1981, partly because of its popularity and wide circulation, and partly because its form (without foot-notes and references, and arranged simply in chronological order rather than according to theme) best conveys the immediacy of its author's concerns and most closely resembles the format of Jamali's letters, which were published by Oxford University Press in 1965 and reprinted by the World of Islam Festival Trust in 1978.

33 The published version of the book also includes three appendices, two of which consist of letters to other people, the first to another son of the author, Usameh and the second to another, unnamed young man, and the third being the text of an address to the Young Men Muslims' Association in Baghdad.

34 This is a line of thought which has been further developed by more recent German Protestant theologians, especially Jorgen Moltmann in his *The crucified God*, SCM, 1974.

35 For biographies of the two figures under discussion see E. Bethge *Dietrich Bonhoeffer – theologian, Christian, contemporary*, Collins, 1970, and H.J. Almond *Iraqi statesman – a portrait of Mohammed Fadhel Jamali*, Grosvenor Books, Salem, 1993.

36 See J. Bowker *Problems of suffering in the religions of the world*, Cambridge U.P., 1970, p 135. I am indebted to this work for the idea of comparing the ideas of the two writers.

37 Another example of both congruity and distinctiveness in the area of spirituality in the two traditions is their whole discussion of spiritual warfare. Within the Christian tradition on this, for example, St Paul, in his letter to the Ephesians (6:10–20), does not hesitate to use military metaphors, and the words used in the rite of baptism (initiation into the Christian faith) often exhort new Christians to "fight valiantly under the banner of Christ", and this is parallelled by the Sufis in Islam, who speak of their attempts to make spiritual progress in life as the "greater *jihād*". On the other hand the (probably more widely-known) use of the word *jihād* is to refer to a military struggle for the defence of Islam (not, as is often thought by non-Muslims, a war of aggression for the furtherance and spread of Islam), and this is parallelled by the Christian tradition's discussion of the idea of the Just War. An interesting comparison can also be made between two notices seen on the campus of the University of Ibadan in Nigeria, the first outside the mosque and the second outside the Arts Faculty building:

"'I am a fanatic'
When you're oppressed
You should keep mute
Compromise your rights
Your personality and your freedom
You'll be praised and
name-tagged 'a civilized person'
But when you're oppressed
You start to fight
You compromise not your rights
nor your liberty, nor your freedom
They will call you a fanatic,
a fundamentalist or extremist . . . .
Yes
I am a fanatic
or whatever name you prefer
But
only
to
oppressors.

Y.M. Adamu (Geography Department)

"The saints called to be *militant* (my emphasis) are: peculiar, wonderful and prepared unto every good work"

SCM (Student Christian movement)

For further discussion of this whole area see J.T. Johnson and J. Kelsay (eds.) *Cross, crescent and sword: the justification and limitation of war in the Western and Islamic tradition*, Greenwood Press, Westport, 1990, and *Just war and jihad: historical and theoretical perspectives on war and peace in Western and Islamic tradition*, Greenwood Press, Westport, 1991.

6

UNITY AND DIVERSITY

Introduction

One feature of both Islam and Christianity which cannot be denied, and which is an obvious similarity between them, is that they both have an ideal of unity within the community of their adherents. In Islam the doctrine of *tawḥīd*, the unity of God, is meant to be reflected in the practical unity of the *umma*, the Muslim community, and likewise in Christianity there is the ideal of "one church, one faith, one God", to quote the words of a well-known Christian hymn. In reality, however, both traditions fail to live up to their self-proclaimed ideals.[1]

The Islamic community

Within the *umma*, the Muslim community, there is one major rift, that between Sunnī and Shī'ī Muslims. As we have seen already this rift has its roots in the early years after the death of Muḥammad, and arose over the question of the leadership of the community.[2] It involved both a question of the identity of the leader – who should occupy that position – and a question of the nature of the authority of the leader, especially whether or not the leader had authority in spiritual matters.

Once that rift had taken place, and the Shī'a,[3] or party of 'Alī, had been created, it should not surprise us if the two groups developed in different ways. Shī'ī Muslims have usually been in the minority within the Muslim community as a whole, but the main body of the community did not evolve a coherent system of thought until probably the third century of Islamic history (the ninth century CE), and it did not acquire its name of Sunnī Islam till even later, when the usage grew up whereby the main body of the Muslim community came to be known as the *ahl al-sunna wa'l-jamā'a*, the people of the custom/tradition (of the

Prophet) and the consensus (of the community).[4] These terms were meant to draw a distinction between the Sunnīs, an abbreviation of the title, and the Shī'īs, who had a different version of the tradition of the prophet and rejected the consensus of the community.[5]

Today between 10 and 15% of the world's Muslims are Shī'ī and the vast majority of the remaining 85–90% are Sunnī. There is only one region of the Islamic world in which Shī'ī Islam is the established, or state religion, and that is Iran, where Shī'ī Islam was selected for this purpose by the Safavid dynasty in 1501/907. Shī'ī Muslims also make up the majority of the population of Iraq, but they are not the politically dominant group there, and there are also significant numbers of Shī'īs in Lebanon, where they are the largest Muslim group and possibly 30% of the total population of the country, and in India and Pakistan, where they make up some 10–15% of the Muslim population.

The most important differences which have developed between Sunnī Muslims and the main body of Shī'ī Muslims since their original split over the question of the leadership of the Muslim community are as follows. Firstly they differ over the idea of the Mahdī: this was a concept which grew up among Shī'ī Muslims in the wake of an event which took place in 873/260, when the twelfth in the line of Imams, that is those whom the Shī'īs considered as the rightful leaders of the Muslim community, went into occultation or hiding.[6] Shī'īs later came to believe that this Imam was the Mahdī, which literally means the Guided One, and who would return at the end of time to introduce an era of justice, in other words that he would be a kind of Messiah figure.

In response to this idea Sunnī Muslims accepted the concept of a Mahdī figure, but gave a different identity to the Mahdī, namely Jesus/'Īsā, who, Sunnī tradition asserted, would return at the end of time and do a number of things such as marry, smash the sign of the cross, and become a Muslim, the obvious purpose of these traditions being to assert the validity of Islam over and against that of Christianity.

Shī'ī Muslims also developed a rather different structure of leadership within the community, especially in Iran after 1501/907, where a kind of religious hierarchy evolved with Mullahs (the Persian word for teacher) as the lowest level, and a council of six Ayatollahs (literally signs of God) as the highest level of authority. In Shī'ī Islam as it has developed in Iran, therefore, it is possible to speak of the existence of a religious hierarchy in a way which is not really applicable to Sunnī Islam, where the '*ulamā*' (the Arabic word for teachers/scholars) are not organised in quite such a strict hierarchy, although in practice each region or country tends to have a supreme figure to whom people look for guidance on matters of religion.[7]

With respect to ceremonies and rituals Shīʿī Muslims have one distinctive annual ceremony which is not shared by Sunnīs, and which for that reason is often the occasion of the greatest tension between the two communities in those parts of the Muslim world such as the Lebanon where the two groups live alongside each other. This ceremony is the *taʿziya*, or passion play, which takes place on the tenth day of the first month of the Muslim calendar, Muḥarram, and commemorates the death of the third Shīʿī Imam, al-Ḥusain, in the year 680/61. Al-Ḥusain had been involved in a movement of protest against the Umayyad caliph Yazīd, and when this developed into an armed revolt, the caliph gave orders for it to be crushed. An over-zealous lieutenant, ʿUmar ibn Saʿd, took his orders further than had been intended, and al-Ḥusain, along with all of the seventy armed men with him, was killed, and his severed head was then brought back to the caliph. Sunnī Muslims, while retaining respect for al-Ḥusain as a grandson of the prophet and sometimes expressing some regret for the manner of the actual killing of al-Ḥusain, nevertheless interpret his death as being just treatment of a revolt against legitimate authority, but in Shīʿī minds al-Ḥusain was an innocent victim of an unjust government and therefore a martyr.

Shīʿīs therefore commemorate his death each year, and the form which this takes is simply a rather stylised re-enactment of the events leading up to the confrontation between Yazīd's soldiers and al-Ḥusain, followed by the martyrdom of the latter.[8] As part of the ceremony, however, some Shīʿīs, usually young males, beat themselves with chains or swords, drawing blood and sometimes fainting, as a sign of their identification with al-Ḥusain in his sufferings, and so the ceremony becomes a time of high emotion and tension.[9]

On the basis of the event of al-Ḥusain's death and the ceremony which commemorates it, Shīʿī Muslims differ from Sunnīs in a number of related areas too. For example Shīʿī Muslims have a rather different understanding of suffering from that of Sunnīs in that Sunnī Islam tends to have what might be called, by analogy with some modern forms of Protestant Christianity, especially in North America, a "success mentality", whereby it is asserted that devout observance of the principles of the faith will lead to material success in this world, whereas Shīʿī Islam, by contrast, given its memory of the fate of the virtuous al-Ḥusain, knows that this is not necessarily the case: the righteous may suffer, and so suffering is not necessarily interpreted as being a sign of disapproval from God. Rather it may earn spiritual merit, just as al-Ḥusain, through his suffering, is seen by Shīʿīs as being able to intercede with God for his followers.[10]

As a result of their view of the death of al-Ḥusain, Shī'ī Muslims also have a distinctive understanding of martyrdom so that under certain circumstances they will actively seek martyrdom, seeing this as being a direct following in the footsteps of al-Ḥusain. Sunnī Muslims, by contrast, may share certain convictions concerning the reward available to martyrs, as seen, for example, in the tradition that anyone who dies fighting for Islam will proceed immediately to Paradise, but as a generalisation among Sunnīs there is not the same tradition of actively seeking to be martyred as exists in Shī'ī Islam.[11]

The two communities also differ in some details of other areas too: Shī'ī Muslims have their own collections of Ḥadīth, their own legal traditions and stipulations, their own traditions of interpretation of the Qur'ān, their own schools of thought in theology, their own shrines and places of pilgrimage, and their own customs in prayer, but these are all relatively minor differences within patterns which are fundamentally the same for both Sunnīs and Shī'īs, and so Shī'īs have sometimes been described as heterodox, that is a variety within the main stream of the Muslim tradition, rather than as unorthodox.[12]

Within each of the two main groups within the Muslim community there is also some diversity, and some further subdivision. Thus among Sunnī Muslims there are four well-established schools of law, the Ḥanafī, Mālikī, Shāfi'ī and Ḥanbalī, each with its own particular emphasis and tradition, but each recognising the others as authentically Muslim.[13] There are also many different Sufi groups, called *ṭarīqas* (literally paths), each group with its own rituals and leadership structures, but in the case of most of these they are recognised as simply variations of practice within the Muslim community. In addition there was also the well-established tradition in the medieval period that there were seventy-three schools of thought in theology, a view which was based upon a tradition attributed to Muḥammad in which he stated that after him that number of schools would emerge.

Then in more recent times other new schools of thought and movements have emerged. In the eighteenth/twelfth century in Arabia the reform movement known as the Wahhābī movement was established, taking its name from its first preacher Aḥmad ibn 'Abd al-Wahhāb (d 1792/1206), calling upon Muslims to set aside certain well-established traditions and return to the earliest sources of Islam, the Qur'ān and the Ḥadīth, for guidance. In the nineteenth/thirteenth century many new movements grew up in the Indian Sub-continent, arising out of the urgent need to respond to the new challenges brought about by British rule and Western ideas. Examples of these are the Ahl-i-Ḥadīth (People of the Tradition), with rather similar views to the Wahhābīs; the Deobandis, named after the important seminary at Deoband, who see themselves as the guardians of the classical tradition of Islam; and the Barelvis, named after Maulānā Aḥmad Rizā Khān Barelvi (d 1921/1339), heavily influenced by Sufism, laying great stress on devotion to the person of Muḥammad, and enjoying widespread support in the rural areas of the Sub-continent.[14]

The twentieth/fourteenth century too has seen new movements growing up among Sunnī Muslims, with many of them seeking to purify and reform the world of Islam, but advocating different programmes to that end. Thus in the Indian Sub-continent again a movement such as the Tablīghī jamā'at (literally Preaching Group), founded by Muḥammad Ilyās (d 1944/1363), advocates a programme of individual conversion and purification as the way to restoring the proper practice of Islam, while a group such as the Jamā'at-i islāmī, founded by Abu'l-A'lā Mawdūdī in 1941/1360, advocates a more systematic programme for the purification of the whole of society through education and political action. In the Middle East the Ihkwān al-muslimūn, established by Ḥasan al-Bannā' in Egypt in 1928/1347, adopts a broadly similar approach to that of the Jamā'at-i-islāmī. All three of these groups have become hugely influential outside their counties of origin in other parts of the Muslim world.

Within the Sunnī world, then, there is some diversity, and an increasing number of new movements is also making its presence felt. Among Shī'īs there is perhaps even more diversity, and the process of sub-division has proceeded further.[15] In most cases splits have occurred over the simple question of who is the rightful claimant to be the Imam and thus assume the position of the leadership of the community. The main split among Shī'īs occurred in 765/148 over precisely this question, when after the death of the sixth Imam some accepted the claim to the succession of his eldest son Ismā'īl while others accepted the claim of his younger son Mūsā.

The main body of Shī'īs took the latter view, accepting Mūsā and then five further Imams until the twelfth Imam, al-Mahdī, went into occultation in 873/260. They therefore became known as the Ithnā'asharī (literally Twelver) Shī'īs, or sometimes Imami Shī'īs, while the followers of Ismā'īl became known as the Ismā'īlī Shī'īs, or sometimes the Sab'iyya (literally Seveners) since they claimed that Ismā'īl should have been recognised as the seventh Imam. They did not, however, believe that he went into hiding, and so Ismā'īlī Shī'īs have generally (though not always) believed in an Imam who is active in the world at any particular time. Considerable further sub-division about his identity, however, has taken place among the Ismā'īlīs during subsequent centuries.[16]

There is also a third group of Shī'īs, the Zaidīs, who take their name from Zaid bin 'Alī (d 740/122), whom they consider to be the fifth Imam. Of all the Shī'īs this group was the one which was closest to Sunnī thinking on many issues, and over the centuries Zaidīs enjoyed considerable influence in the Yemen, which was ruled intermittently by a Zaidī Imam until 1962/1382.

In addition to Sunnī and Shī'ī Muslims there is a third group which needs to be remembered, and it has already been mentioned in connection with the events which took place in the immediate aftermath of the death of Muḥammad, namely the Khawārij (literally those who went out, or seceded).[17] Their attempt in that early period to argue that they alone were the true Muslims and that the leader of the Muslim community should be led by the best Muslim, who was to be found among their number, was not successful, and although they were defeated militarily in the central regions of the Islamic world they did continue to exist in some of the more remote parts of the Middle East, especially in Oman in south-eastern Arabia and on the island of Jerba off the coast of Tunisia.

Their original views were moderated in these areas in order to ensure survival, but those early views are also of note in modern times because on some points the opinions and methods of some of today's Islamic revivalist groups have been described as a resurgence of Khārijī views. This language is used particularly because of some groups' tendency to assert that they alone are true Muslims and that it is therefore an obligation upon them to use violence in order to overthrow the existing political and religious authorities and establish a truly Islamic state.[18]

Finally, from different groups which we have examined, at different stages of their history, further extreme groups have split off, and these will be mentioned although their relationship to the main body of Islamic opinion is sufficiently tenuous as to mean that they would not normally be described as Muslim. The two most significant groups of this type which came into existence in medieval times are the Druzes, found mainly in Lebanon, Syria and northern Israel, a secretive Ismā'īlī offshoot who believe that an eleventh/fifth century Fāṭimid ruler, al-Ḥākim, was a divine incarnation, and this was the message preached by al-Darāzī, who gave his name to the group; and the Alawīs or Nusairīs, found mainly in Syria, who have their origins in Imami Shī'ī Islam and are accused by their opponents at least, of going so far as to treat 'Alī, the first Shī'ī imam, as divine.[19] More recent times have seen the emergence of two other groups: firstly the Aḥmadiyya, a group established in 1889/1306 in India, whose roots lie in Sunnī Islam but which is considered suspect by most Sunnīs because of the accusation that the founder of the group, Mīrzā Ghulām Aḥmad of Qādiān (d 1908/1326) claimed to be a prophet, and secondly the Bahā'īs, whose roots lie in the Iranian Shī'ī tradition but which is suspect to most Muslims because of the claim of the founder Bahā'ullāh (d 1892/1309) to be the figure through whom all the religious traditions of the world will be brought together in a kind of synthesis.

In the Muslim community, then, despite the ideal of unity within one *umma* the reality has been the coming into a being of a number of significant divisions among Muslims, and also, within different groups, the existence of a fair amount of diversity. Relationships between the different groups have on different occasions been tense and even hostile but in general terms despite their differences most groups have been ready to acknowledge that the members of other groups should at least be recognised as being Muslim, and so in the midst of diversity and even disagreement the Muslim community has succeeded in preserving a remarkable degree of unity. Especially important in this has been the form of its worship which, as noted in Chapter Five above, has remained the same both across the centuries and across the whole geographical span of the Islamic world, so that for a Muslim from, say, Indonesia or the Philippines, there is no obstacle to participation in prayer in a mosque in Morocco or Senegal. It is largely due to this fact that the Muslim community has succeeded in retaining a far greater measure of unity than has been managed by the Christian community, to which we now turn, although in the world of today Muslims are perhaps beginning to face some of the factionalism and dissension to which the Christian church has been subject for some time.[20]

The Christian community

In the history of the Christian church too, there is one major rift within its membership, and this rift has in turn has been followed by the growth of further divisions in subsequent history. This main division is the split which grew up between Eastern and Western Christians, beginning in the fourth century and coming to its formal conclusion in the eleventh/fifth century.

The split between Eastern and Western Christians derives in part from the increasingly close association which grew up between the Christian church and the Roman Empire after the conversion of the Emperor

Constantine to Christianity in 312. Once that had taken place, Christianity became the official religion of the empire, and so when, in 395, for reasons of administrative convenience, the Empire was divided into an eastern and a western half, there was pressure for the church to follow suit.

It was not simply, however, a question of church following state, since there were several other factors already in existence which supported this trend. On the question of authority, for example, there were five early centres of the Christian church which were regarded by Christians as having special influence and status because of their role in the history of the community. Of these five centres four were in the eastern part of the Roman empire – Jerusalem, Antioch, Alexandria and Constantinople – while only one – Rome – was in the western half. One effect of this was that different understandings of authority developed. The East tended to have a more dispersed, or conciliar, understanding, so that no one centre could come to decisions on its own and if decisions were to have genuine authority they needed to be agreed by all centres, while the West tended to develop a more centralised understanding of authority since its one centre had no rival.

This difference between East and West on the question of authority was reinforced by differences of language and theology. In the East the most widely-used language was Greek, which had been the language of philosophical reflection, while in the West Latin, the language of law, was more common. The different languages had some influence on the Christian theologians who wrote in them, and one consequence of this was that Greek-speaking theologians tended to express their Christian faith in terms of divinisation or deification, so that the central affirmation of Christian doctrine for them involved Jesus' Incarnation, the process by which God became human so that humans might become divine, whereas Latin-speaking theologians saw the focal point of Christian teaching as being Redemption, involving a kind of legal transaction whereby through the death of Jesus God bought back a sinful humanity. Each thus expressed the Christian message in a framework of thought which was appropriate for the language which they used.

This in turn affected the understanding of worship which grew up in the two parts of the Christian community, with the East focusing on what came to be called the Eucharist, the thanksgiving for the mystery of the Incarnation, as a result of which it became possible for Christians to be transported, in some way, into the presence of God, while the West focused on what came to be called the Mass, the re-enactment of the sacrifice of Jesus on the cross, as a result of which Christians could be purged of their sin and have their relationship with God restored.

All of these differences, then, were developing in the early Christian centuries and the split of the Roman Empire into its two halves in 395 in a sense gave some more explicit form to the process of bifurcation. Further development took place in the following century when the western half of the Roman Empire collapsed in 476 and the church in Rome was left in a rather vulnerable position, still retaining spiritual authority but now separated from the political authority of the empire, and needing to develop new links with the political authorities which grew up in the West, mostly the leaders of a number of tribes which had invaded the Empire. In the East, however, the Roman Empire survived, becoming known as the Byzantine Empire after the old name for its capital, Constantinople, and there the old link between church and state continued for almost another millennium, until the fall of Constantinople to the Ottoman Turks in 1453/857.

The Eastern and Western churches did not formally split, however, until 1054/446, when mutual threats and condemnations were issued and the so-called Great Schism took place. In reality this only gave explicit form to a divergence which had developed over the course of the previous centuries, but the harsh language used in the proclamations gave a much clearer form to the division.

In addition to this major split in the Christian community, further subdivision then took place within each of its two halves. In the East the focus of disagreement was a particular point of doctrine, namely the nature of Christ, which has been investigated already in Chapter Three, and although the West was also involved the arguments took place mainly in the East. It was thus in the East that after the Councils of Ephesus (431) and Chalcedon (451) lasting institutional division within the Christian church took place with separate churches becoming established which claimed to represent the views of those whose opinions had been rejected at the Councils.

In particular a church which represented the views of Nestorius was established in parts of Syria and also further east in Iraq and Iran, beyond the Byzantine frontier. This Nestorian church was later responsible for spreading the Christian faith across Asia, even as far as China. After the Council of Chalcedon a number of churches which held to the opinions of Eutyches were established in parts of Syria and also in Egypt, and these Monophysite churches (so called because of the charge that they believed in only one nature (*physis*) in Christ) were influential also further to the south and east in Africa, especially in Ethiopia.

Modern research has suggested that with respect to these further subdivisions within Eastern Christianity it was not only doctrine which was responsible, for other factors such as language and regional feeling were also partly responsible. The Nestorian church, for example, used the Syriac language for its worship and in its theological writings, and among the Monophysites too a number of different local languages were used, such as Coptic (in Egypt), Syriac (in Syria), Armenian, and Amharic (in Ethiopia), and the use of these different languages points to the extent to which local resentment against the Greek-speaking Byzantine Empire was a factor in these doctrinal disputes.

The end result of these disputes was thus the emergence of a number of different churches within the Eastern Church. All tend to describe themselves as Orthodox churches, in the sense of being Eastern Christians and sharing a broadly similar philosophy and style of worship, but within this group there are clearly significant differences of doctrine, and the Nestorian and Monophysite churches together are sometimes described as either the Oriental Orthodox or the non-Chalcedonian churches to make it clear that they differ from what became the main body of the Eastern Christian church, the Byzantine and later Greek Orthodox Church and its descendants, in particular in that they did not accept the judgements of the Council of Chalcedon.[21]

Partly as a result of all these disputes there grew up in the Eastern church a tradition of there being one hundred heresies (errors of belief), and thus when John of Damascus (d 749/132), who is sometimes described as the last of the Fathers of the Eastern Church, came to write about Islam, he discussed it as the one hundred and first heresy in an appendix to his work outlining the opinions of the hundred.[22]

A similar division, but over a different question, took place within the Western church too, but some centuries later. This was a division which came to be expressed in the whole movement known as the Reformation in the sixteenth/tenth century. At the heart of the Reformation was the question of authority, and this was discussed, and sometimes fought over, on a whole range of different levels. On the one hand the Reformation was a movement of protest against the religious authority of the Papacy in Rome which, according to the Reformers and some of their precursors such as John Wycliffe in England and Jan Hus in Bohemia, had become corrupt and needed to be purged and reformed. Some within the Western Church, such as Erasmus and Ximenes, saw the need for reform of some kind themselves, and tried to work towards that, but for others the situation was already too dire for that to be possible, and the alternative locus of authority suggested by the Reformers was the Bible, which was put forward as the standard or criterion against which all subsequent Christian teaching was to be judged.[23]

On another level the Reformation was also a movement of protest against the political authority and influence of the Papacy. This was particularly the case in northern Europe where for several centuries tensions had existed between the centralising tendencies of the Papacy and the desire of both peoples and kings for more autonomy. The payment of ecclesiastical taxes to Rome was one focus of resentment here, as was the desire for more local say in the appointment of senior figures within the church. Nationalism was thus a further factor in the growth of the Reformation.[24]

The Western Church thus became deeply divided in the sixteenth/tenth century between Roman Catholic southern Europe and Protestant northern Europe, with the middle belt (running across Europe from west to east) scarred by some of the conflicts which resulted from the division. At different times Ireland, England, France, Germany, Austria and various parts of Eastern Europe too were riven by armed conflict as political and religious authorities tried to use force to extend the sway of their particular understanding of the Christian faith. According to some estimates a half of the population of some parts of Germany was killed in the Wars of Religion of the sixteenth/tenth and seventeenth/eleventh centuries.

Within Western Christianity there is also evidence of the development of diversity and of further sub-division. Within the Roman Catholic Church even before the Reformation diversity was evident in the establishment of different monastic orders, groups within the church which took upon themselves the cultivation of what came to be called "the religious life" in a rather more total and specialist way so that communities of monks and nuns were formed which were set apart from the world, in a geographical and spiritual sense, to devote themselves to the worship of God in a particularly thorough and systematic way, based on a highly-disciplined routine of prayer and work.[25]

The earliest monastic order in the West was the Benedictine order, based on the Rule of St Benedict (d 547), and many orders which emerged later began as attempts at reform within that order. In reality, as is often the case, the end result was simply the creation of new orders which attempted to return to the original rule and practice it more thoroughly than the main body of Benedictines. Perhaps the best example of this process is the establishment of the Cistercian order which grew out of attempts to purify the Benedictine order in the twelfth/sixth century.

In later centuries other orders also became established under the authority of the Papacy, some of the most famous being the Mendicant Orders, the Franciscans and the Dominicans, established in the thirteenth/seventh century by Sts. Francis of Assisi and Dominic for the dissemination of the Christian faith through example and learning respectively, and the Jesuits, established in the sixteenth/tenth century under the personal authority of the Papacy with the express purpose of opposing the Reformers by all means possible. The Jesuits thus became one of the main elements of what came to be known as the Counter-Reformation, the movement whose purpose was the re-establishment of Catholicism as widely as possible in Europe.

These Roman Catholic Orders are sometimes compared with the Sufi orders in Islam in that they have their own distinctive practices and roles yet they are not usually mutually exclusive or antagonistic towards each other, all co-existing within the broad confines of their wider religious community, Christian or Muslim. Some of the divisions which have grown up among Protestant Christians, however, are more akin to those among Shīʿī Muslims in that disagreement has resulted not merely in diversity but rather at times in formal separation and even mutual antagonism.

Some of these divisions within Protestantism are the result of differences in opinion between individual Reformers in the sixteenth century. Some Protestant churches thus look to Martin Luther (d 1546/952) as their authority while others look to John Calvin (d 1564/971), who refined and took further many of the ideas of Luther. This can be seen particularly in Calvin's insistence on the idea of *sola scriptura* (Scripture alone) as authoritative, and his view that political authorities should be subject to the guidance of religious authorities.

Regional and national factors are also important in the growth of different Protestant churches since the influence of one or other of these thinkers became more dominant in particular parts of Europe, often as a result quite simply of personal contacts with one or other of the geographical centres of the Reformation, and the result of this was that, for example, in Scandinavia, the main Protestant churches are Lutheran whereas in Scotland the national church is Calvinist.

Further disagreement also grew up among Protestants on a number of other questions such as the internal government and organisation of the church. This gave rise to such further divisions among Protestants as that between Presbyterians and Congregationalists who, while both being in the "Reformed" (as opposed to Lutheran) tradition which can be traced back to John Calvin, argued respectively that there should be some kind of central church authority and that the supreme authority should be the individual congregation of Christians.[26]

In what is sometimes called "The Radical Reformation" further issues which were raised were the significance of rituals such as baptism and the question of whether or not Christians should be pacifists. These issues were raised primarily by the question of how the teaching of the New Testament should be understood, and how it should be related to the growth of subsequent traditions since in both cases the practice of the first generation of Christians, as recorded in the New Testament, had been to baptize only believers and to be firm pacifists, both customs which had been altered in later centuries, especially once Christianity became the official religion of the Roman Empire. Radical Reformers such as Baptists, however, wished to return to the earliest practice at any cost, and sometimes with little attention paid to the different circumstances in which Christians found themselves in the first and in the sixteenth/tenth century.

Somewhere between the Roman Catholic church and the various churches of the Reformation, what later came to be called the Anglican church, from its base in England, attempted to function on the basis of its being "Reformed Catholicism", a kind of *via media* (middle way) between the two extremes, certainly purifying some of the corrupt practices of the late medieval Papacy and certainly setting aside the supreme authority of the Papacy, but nevertheless also being ready to retain and stress continuity with many of the practices of the medieval church.

More recently in Christian history what some have called a third force has emerged, namely the Evangelical Movement. This has its roots in Protestant Christianity but evolved as a kind of protest against certain developments within Protestantism, especially the emergence of what has been called Protestant Scholasticism, which developed ever more sophisticated statements of Christian doctrine while neglecting the inner spiritual life, and the rather cosy relationship between church and state which had developed in some German states. The roots of the Evangelical Movement can be traced back first to Germany in the seventeenth/eleventh century, with the growth of the Pietist/Moravian movement, but during the next century its principles also became widely-disseminated in the English-speaking world, on both sides of the Atlantic, as a result of the preaching and ministry of John Wesley (d 1791/1205), the founder of the Methodists, and George Whitefield (d 1770/1184). The Evangelical insistence on the need for personal faith, based on the experience of individual conversion or being born again, and on a community of true believers, the invisible church as opposed to the visible church, has become widely accepted among English-speaking Christians, to the extent that over half of the population of the United States of America today claims to have been born again.

It is this Evangelical movement which is primarily responsible for the spectacular growth in the number of different Christian churches and denominations which has taken place during the last two centuries. The distinction drawn between the assembly of true believers and others is an idea which has proved highly amenable to the growth of groups which claim to be the unique and exclusive possessors of Christian truth, so that these groups can justly be called "sects". Recent research has suggested that on a world-wide level today on average five new Christian denominations are created each week, and this figure is clear evidence of the extent to which some parts of the Christian world seem to display no interest at all in even the aspiration towards some kind of unity among Christians.[27]

One group worthy of particular note because of their influence in the so-called Third World is the Pentecostals, who are very numerous in South America and other continents too, and their distinctive conviction is a stress on the Holy Spirit, the third person of the Trinity, and on a particular experience of the Holy Spirit which is sometimes described as being baptized in the spirit or as speaking in other tongues.[28]

In addition to all of these many groups there are also others which, especially in modern times, have evolved beliefs and practices which may have their roots in the Christian tradition but which have been developed in such a way that their links with the main body of Christian opinion have become sufficiently tenuous for them not to be recognised as authentically Christian by many within the Christian community. If the main criterion for membership of the Muslim community has been a proper view of prophecy, on which groups such as the Aḥmadiyya and the Bahā'īs, discussed earlier in this chapter are thought by most Muslims to be wanting, the equivalent criterion for membership of the Christian community has been assent to a Trinitarian view of God, and on this basis groups such as the Unitarians, the Christian Scientists, the Church of Jesus Christ of the Latter Day Saints (Mormons), and many others have not always been recognised by others as being truly Christian.

The Christian world, then, like the Islamic one, has the ideal of a unified community, but history has contributed to the emergence of several deep divisions within that community, as well as the growth of considerable diversity within different branches of the Christian church. Both communities, in other words, have manifestly failed to realise their ideals in practice, and this is perhaps most clearly seen in the fact that even their respective institutions which claim most forcefully to serve as foci of unity have on occasion themselves seen rival claimants emerge. Thus the Muslim community, despite the idea of *khilāfa* (caliphate), the ideal of the whole *umma* being united under one successor to the prophet, at one stage, during the tenth/fourth century, saw three rival caliphs in office, an ʻAbbāsid in Baghdad, a Fāṭimid in Cairo, and an Umayyad in Cordoba; and the Christian world in the early fifteenth/ninth century saw dissension over the Papacy so deep that instead of one Pope in Rome there were at one time three Popes, one in Rome, one in Avignon and one in Pisa.[29] Overall, however, it has to be acknowledged that of the two communities the Muslim community has generally fared better in preserving its unity since the number of sub-groups within it is considerably lower than that within the Christian community.

Ecumenism

In the past century or so, however, embarrassment and concern about this situation have grown up among many Christians, and this has given rise to the emergence of the Ecumenical Movement, one of whose purposes is the re-establishment of a united and unified Christian community.

Originating among Protestant Christians in the nineteenth/thirteenth century, largely as a result of the realisation of the extent of the damage being done to the spread of the Christian church outside Europe by the divisions among Christians, this movement, as represented by the World Council of Churches, also now includes most of the Eastern Orthodox churches, both Chalcedonian and non-Chalcedonian/Oriental, among its members, and in many fields positive working relationships have been established with the Roman Catholic Church, particularly since the establishment of the programme of reform and re-structuring within that church which was established by the Second Vatican Council in 1962/1382.

The World Council of Churches today thus contains some 360 member churches, and regional groupings of churches also contain large numbers of different churches so that, for example, the Council of European Churches includes some 130 members and the Council of Churches of Britain and Ireland has some 30 full members. Many Evangelical Christians, however, regard the Ecumenical Movement as a movement of compromise and a dilution of the true Christian faith which they profess, and so alongside the movement towards reconciliation between Christians there is also an on-going Evangelical movement of protest against this trend, and so even as some ancient divisions within the Christian community are overcome or at least moderated, others emerge, to the extent that some commentators on the state of the Christian world today suggest that there are now in effect two main forms of Christianity in existence, the Ecumenical, which would include not only the established Protestant churches but also the different Orthodox churches and even the Roman Catholic church, and the Evangelical.

In the Muslim community too the past century or so has witnessed some attempts at reconciliation between different groups. In the nineteenth/thirteenth century, confronted with the challenge of the growth of European influence and power within the Muslim world, a thinker such as Jamāl al-dīn al-Afghānī (d 1897/1314) issued a call for Muslim unity in resisting European influence in the Muslim world. al-Afghānī himself put forward a proposal for the reconciliation of Sunnī and Shī'ī Muslims whereby the main body of Shī'īs should be recognised as a fifth school of Islamic Law, on the basis of the fact that the sixth Shī'ī Imam, Ja'far al-Ṣādiq, was a legal scholar who enjoyed a high reputation among Sunnīs as well as among Shī'īs, but his suggestion did not win wide support.[30]

Other attempts have also been made to establish some kind of Muslim unity. Many of these, however, given the traditionally close relationship between religion and the state in the Muslim community, have involved governments rather than religious leaders. Thus the Organisation of the Islamic Conference, set up in 1969/1389, brings together heads of state rather than religious scholars, and although other groups such as the Muslim World League, set up in 1966/1386, attempt to work primarily with religious leaders, the links which many of them have with particular governments in the Muslim world, especially with that of Sa'udi Arabia, inevitably limits their influence.

More recently the growth of Muslim communities outside the Muslim world, especially in western Europe, has contributed to the emergence of further groups which attempt to bring about greater unity among Muslims. To some extent, given that this trend has developed in the context of Muslims finding themselves in a minority and realising how damaging Muslim disunity is to their prospects, this process is similar to the growth of the Ecumenical Movement among Christians as a result of Christian disunity hindering Christian mission in Africa and Asia. But these attempts at co-ordination, yet alone unification, among Muslims in Europe have not always been successful, since in many cases theological as well as political and linguistic differences have resulted in the establishment of alternative co-ordinating groups.[31] In some cases, however, especially on a local level and when confronted with a particular issue or controversy, greater success has been achieved, and one example of this is the work of the Council of Mosques in Bradford in attempting to respond to the controversy caused by the publication of Salman Rushdie's novel "The Satanic Verses".[32]

Some similarities . . . .?

Among both Muslims and Christians, then, the ideal of unity is balanced by the reality of diversity, if not division. Sunnī Muslims differ from Shī'ī Muslims, and Western Christians differ from Eastern ones, and within each of these groups there are further sub-groups which sometimes recognise other sub-groups as Christian or Muslim and sometimes do not. The differences between the various groups are caused by disagreements over a whole range of different factors, but some common factors which have contributed towards division may be discerned in the two communities.

One such factor is disagreement over the question of authority: is the supreme authority scriptural (Sunnī Islam/Protestant Christianity) or personal/institutional (Shī'ī Islam/Roman Catholic and Orthodox Christianity)? To some extent this is an example of a wider tension in many religious communities between a scriptural style of religion and a more personal style of religion, but it is perhaps in the Christian and Muslim communities especially that this tension is most evident. It is also important to note that it cannot be said that the Christian faith is scriptural and the Muslim faith personal or vice versa: both styles can be found within each tradition.

A second is disagreement over particular points of doctrine: this may be more significant in Christianity, given that, as noted earlier, theology is the primary discipline of this tradition, but clearly disagreements over Christology, the person of Christ, were very important in creating some of the divisions which arose within the Christian Church in its early period (the first five centuries), and, even if to a lesser extent, profound theological disagreements emerged in the formative period of Islam too, leading to the creation of a wide range of schools of thought, over such issues as free will and predestination, the attributes of God, and the status of the Qur'ān, especially the question of whether it was created or uncreated. In addition both traditions witnessed long debates about the attitude that should be exhibited towards philosophical knowledge or, to put it another way, about the relationship between revelation and reason.

Thirdly, in more recent times, disagreements have emerged in both traditions over the question of approaches to the reform and reformulation of the faith. In the Christian tradition this was manifested most powerfully at the time of the Protestant Reformation in the sixteenth/tenth century, when there was a widespread feeling of dissatisfaction with the Roman Catholic Church. This gave rise to a widespread conviction of the need to reform it, but there was no agreement about the question of how to reform it, and this resulted in the emergence of a wide range of movements for reform, including some within the Roman Catholic Church itself. Many Protestant denominations spring from the different approaches adopted by different reformers to this question of how to reform the church, though the emergence of others cannot really be explained in isolation from political developments, particularly the growth of nationalism in northern Europe. In Islam the nearest parallel is perhaps the various reform movements already mentioned as having grown up in India in the nineteenth/thirteenth century. Here too, as in late medieval Europe, the conviction was extremely widespread that something was wrong, partly as a result of the growth of British power and influence and the demise of Moghul power; feelings also ran strongly, therefore, that some kind of reform and reformulation was necessary, but there was no agreement as to how that should reform should be brought about, either with respect to the areas which needed to be reformed or with respect to how the reform should be pushed through. It was in this setting, then, that different schools of thought emerged, and because of historical links and the resulting patterns of migration, it is these same schools of thought which have become established in the Muslim community in Britain and which are therefore responsible for some of the disagreements which are evident there.

Conclusion

Some similarities, then, do exist in the causes of division and disunity within the two communities. But given the extent of the diversity which exists within each community, and also some of the passion which is evident in some of the disagreements within both of them, a not impertinent question might be whether in the light of this diversity we should continue to speak at all of Christianity and Islam, or whether we should rather substitute Christianities and Islams.

Notes

1 It could be said, indeed, that this is one area where all religious traditions could be said to have one feature in common, namely that they all have wonderful ideals and then they all fail to live up to them!

2 See Chapter Three above.

3 With respect to terminology, Shīʿī is an adjective or a noun, referring to those who are members of the Shīʿa, which is a collective noun, meaning the party (of ʿAlī). We should therefore speak of Shīʿīs, or Shīʿī Muslims, or the Shīʿa, but not Shīʿa Muslims.

4 See Chapter Four above for further exposition of these terms.

5 For fuller detail on the emergence of Sunnī Islam see W.M. Watt *The formative period of Islamic thought*, Edinburgh U.P., 1973, Part 3 "The triumph of Sunnism".

6 On the background to this see A.A. Sachedina *Islamic Messianism: the idea of the Mahdi in Twelver Shiʿism*, State University of New York Press, 1981.

7 Comparisons are sometimes drawn on this question between Catholic Christianity and Shīʿī Islam on the one hand, with their more hierarchical system of leadership, and Protestant Christianity and Sunnī Islam on the other, which tend to stress scripture as the supreme authority. In other ways, however, particularly with respect to sociological issues, this analogy breaks down as in their respective histories it is Catholic Christianity and Sunnī Islam which have tended to be in positions of dominance and Protestant Christianity and Shīʿī Islam which have tended to be protesting about that situation.

8 An easily accessible account of the ceremony can be found in G.E. von Grunebaum *Muhammadan Festivals*, Curzon Press, 1976, pp 85–94. For more detail on the ceremony in a South Asian context see V.J. Schubel *Religious performance in contemporary Islam*, University of South Carolina Press, 1993.

9 For this reason the ceremony can almost be guaranteed to figure prominently in television documentaries which present a rather alarmist view of Islam as violent, dangerous and threatening. The *taʿziya* seems to illustrate this thesis perfectly, but it needs to be remembered that it is performed by some members of the Shīʿī Muslim community, which is some 10–15% of the Muslim community as a whole, on one day of the year and not, as the documentaries sometimes come perilously close to suggesting, by all Muslims on every day of the year or even five times a day on every day of the year!

10 On the view of suffering in Islam in general see J. Bowker *Problems of suffering in the religions of the world*, Cambridge U.P., 1970, Chapter Three. On the significance of the death of al-Ḥusain in particular, including the possibility of it bearing some kind of redemptive significance, see M.M. Ayoub *Redemptive suffering in Islam*, Mouton, The Hague, 1978.

11 See M. Momen *An introduction to Shiʿi Islam*, Yale University Press, 1985, pp 33 and 236.

12 Opinions on this question on both sides have varied from century to century and from place to place, depending on a whole range of factors, not least the demographic balance between the two groups and the political relationship between them, but as a general statement this can stand. Thus Sunnīs and Shīʿīs share the same text of the Qur'ān, even if they interpret it differently, and pray five times a day in mosques, even if their ritual of prayer differs slightly and opinions differ as to whether or not Sunnīs and Shīʿīs may pray together in the same congregation.

13 The Ḥanbalī has sometimes been viewed with suspicion by adherents of the other schools, but today all four are usually accepted.

14 On new Islamic movements in India see B.D. Metcalf *Islamic revival in British India: Deoband 1860–1900*, Princeton U.P., 1982, and F. Robinson *Varieties of South Asian Islam*, Centre for Research in Ethnic Relations, Warwick, 1988.

15 In this sense too there is an analogy between Protestant Christianity, with its seemingly endless tendency towards the creation of new groups and denominations, and Shīʿī Islam, but the latter can in no way match the former in terms of numbers.

16 The detail of this is that in the tenth/fourth and eleventh/fifth centuries the Ismāʿīlīs came close to dominating the Muslim world through the agency of the Fāṭimid dynasty, a revolutionary movement with its roots first in North Africa and then in Egypt. The Fāṭimids claimed the title of caliph for themselves, but a disputed succession in 1094/487 caused a split in their ranks between Nizār and al-Mustaʿlī. The latter succeeded in his claim to the Fāṭimid caliphate and the followers of him and his descendants became known as the Mustaʿlī or Western Ismāʿīlīs who, after the collapse of the Fāṭimid dynasty in 1171/567 became established in Yemen and India. In 1591/999 a further leadership split occurred, with two groups emerging, the Da'ūdīs and the Sulaimānīs, with the former mainly in India and the latter mainly in the Yemen. Probably the best-known Mustaʿlī community in Britain is the Bohora community, which is made up of Indian Mustaʿlī Ismāʿīlīs. The followers of Nizār after the 1094/487 split became known as the Nizārī or Eastern Ismāʿīlīs who became established in Persia and Syria and later in India. In the medieval period they were best known because of their activities under Ḥasan-i Ṣabbāḥ who from his fortress in Alamut in Persia organised a campaign of the killing of political opponents; this is the origin of the term Assassin, the name given to the group, based on the word Hashishiyin, consumers of hashish, which members of the group were given in order to give them the courage to carry out their killings. In the modern period the Nizārīs are best-known because of the leader of the Indian Nizārī community, the Khojas, who is the Agha Khan. The best analogy in the Christian world for the transition of the Nizārīs from rather wild Assassins to pillar-of-the establishment Khojas is perhaps the Quakers who from their origins in the enthusiastic religious atmosphere of the seventeenth/eleventh century, as illustrated by the name of the group, have subsequently become the more sedate Society of Friends. For fuller detail on the Ismāʿīlīs see F. Deftary *The Ismaʿilis: their history and doctrines*, Cambridge U.P., 1990.

17 See Chapter Three above.

18 See, for example, G.C. Anawati in *Mélanges de l'Institut Dominicain d'études orientales du Caire*, 16 (1983), where in the news section (pp 191–228) he describes the *Takfir wa'l-hijra* group (literally "declaring to be atheist and migration") to be "une résurgence du Kharijisme au XXe siècle".

19 There has been much recent discussion of this in recent years since the current government of Syria, under Hafiz al-Assad, consists largely of Alawis, and the religious authorities in Iran have pronounced the Alawis to be legitimate and authentic Imami Shīʿīs.

20 The fact that the Muslim world is now in the second decade of its fifteenth

century according to its own calendar is perhaps significant here, given that the most spectacular growth in the number of Christian denominations and churches has its beginnings only in the sixteenth century of Christian history.

21 The decisions of all four of the Councils, including Chalcedon, were accepted by Rome, and so in this area the split was definitely within Eastern Christianity and not between East and West.

22 See D. Sahas *John of Damascus on Islam*, Brill, Leiden, 1972.

23 The question of the canon of Scripture was a question which was re-opened as a result of the Reformation, with most Reformers preferring the Hebrew canon for the Old Testament, in other words including only those books which had originally been written in Hebrew, exactly the same choice as had been made by the Jewish community itself at the Council of Jamnia in 90CE, and with other books grouped together separately in the Apocrypha, while the Roman Church retained the traditional selection, based on the Septuagint. More recently, however, the Roman Church has also moved towards recognition of the distinction between the primary books of the Old Testament canon on the one hand and the so-called Deutero-canonical books (which Protestants call the Apocrypha) on the other. See Chapter Two above for further detail of this.

24 One historian of the period, Sir Lewis Namier in Manchester, even went so far as to define religion itself as "a sixteenth century name for nationalism"!

25 Monasticism had its origins in the eastern church, in Egypt, with Anthony (d 356) and Pachomius (d 346), the founders of the anchoritic and eremetic (that is solitary and community-based) traditions of monasticism respectively, but the growth of different monastic orders, with their own structures of authority and their own patterns of worship, is a distinctively western development.

26 Both of these traditions are alike in that in either case the understanding of authority is very much a democratic one, as opposed to the more centralised and hierarchical understanding which is more influential in the Roman Catholic and some other Protestant churches, as well as in the Eastern churches.

27 One example is the First Baptist Church of Berwyn, Pennsylvania, whose constitution affirms: "We disavow the position of the World Council of Churches, the National Council of Churches, the National Association of Evangelicals, and any other association or fellowship that would be in sympathy with them. We stand in opposition to the Ecumenical Movement, New Evangelicalism, Inter-denominationalism, Protestantism, Neo-Orthodoxy and co-operative Evangelistic programs between churches and people not alike of precious faith". See J. Bowker *A year to live*, SPCK, 1991, P 173.

28 See W. Hollenwegger *The Pentecostals*, SCM, 1972. It is worth noting that this "ecstatic" form of religious experience is one which is also found in other religious communities, including among some Sufi orders.

29 There were three Popes only for some six years, but there were rival Popes in Rome and Avignon for over half a century.

30 See A. Hourani *Arabic thought in the liberal age*, Cambridge U.P., 1983, pp 108 and 115–116. For insights into the more negative, polemical, style of relationship between Sunnī and Shī'ī Muslims see H. Enayat *Modern Islamic political thought*, Macmillan, 1982, pp 30–51.

31 See J.S. Nielsen *Muslims in Western Europe*, Edinburgh U.P., 1992, pp 47–48.

32 See P. Lewis *Islamic Britain*, I.B. Tauris, 1994, Chapter Six.

7

SPREAD AND HISTORY

Introduction

The common threads between the two traditions here are obvious: both traditions have a history, and during it both have spread from the lands of their origin. Additionally, in the course of their history and spread both traditions have undergone a certain amount of development. We have already seen, in Chapter One, how an interesting comparison can be drawn between the role of the Apostle Paul in the Christian tradition, largely responsible as he was for the shift in the orientation of the Christian community from the Jews to the Gentiles, and the caliph ‘Umar ibn al-Khaṭṭāb, the second successor to Muḥammad as leader of the Muslim community, the person who launched the community on its career of conquest outside Arabia.

There are also significant differences between the two histories, however, and an early example of this is in the methods used by Paul and ‘Umar in order to bring about the spread of their faiths. St. Paul relied on preaching and persuasion to bring converts into the Christian community; there was no alternative available to him, given that political power rested firmly in the hands of the Roman state rather than in the hands of the Christians. ‘Umar, by contrast, used military force in order to set up an Islamic empire, and at first seems to have displayed little interest in seeing the conquered populations convert to Islam. The process of conversion to Islam among non-Arabs came later, and will be examined in more detail below.

Later in their respective histories, however, both Islam and Christianity moved from the original methods used to secure their spread. In parts of the Indian sub-continent, South-East Asia and Africa Islam spread through peaceful persuasion, through wandering Sufi mystics and through trading merchants. In other parts of the world Christianity spread by force, and this did not simply involve the establishment of Christian rule; it also meant the forced acceptance of the Christian faith through enforced baptism. Charlemagne's conquest of Saxony and the Conquistadors' activities in Latin America are perhaps the most dramatic examples of this. Once again, therefore, a clear contrast cannot be drawn between the two faiths.

The spread of Islam in history

Phase I – 610–750/132

By the time of Muḥammad's death in 632/11 the monotheistic message that he preached, first in Mecca and then in Yathrib (Medina), had been broadly accepted throughout the Arabian Peninsula. The motivations for its acceptance may have been somewhat mixed, in that in some instances a measure of force had been used, while in others diplomatic and political considerations were involved, but there is no denying that most of Arabia had accepted the faith of Islam by the time that he died.

After his death, however, a number of Arab tribes attempted to re-assert their independence, arguing that they had accepted Muḥammad's leadership, but they had not accepted his faith, and now that he had died they therefore were no longer bound by the precepts of Islam. The leaders of the Muslim community in Medina, however, after Muḥammad's death, had selected Abū Bakr as successor, or caliph (*khalīfa*), to lead the community, and his most important action was to crush this rebellion, which in the eyes of the Muslims was an act of apostasy (*ridda*).

Abū Bakr lived for only 2 years after Muḥammad's death, dying in 634/13. It was under his successor, 'Umar ibn al-Khaṭṭāb, who was selected by a very similar process in Medina, that the dramatic period of the expansion of the influence of the Muslim community began. Both of these men were powerful personalities who not only succeeded in holding the nascent Muslim community together but also gave it a keen sense of vocation and purpose even after the death of Muḥammad; their role in the spread of Islam is therefore crucial.

There had been an ancient tradition in Arabia of raids being launched into the surrounding settled, and therefore rich, territories, particularly Syria and Iraq to the North. Under 'Umar this tradition was developed, particularly since the suppression of the tribal rebellion under Abū Bakr had involved the assembling of a larger army than had probably ever been seen in Arabia before. Earlier expeditions had not been intended to lead to permanent settlement, and their aim was thus simply enrichment. There is little evidence to suggest that the raids by the early Muslims were any different in this respect, but there is evidence that in addition to the traditional intentions at least some religious motivation was now involved, since one of the first cities that the Muslim armies headed towards was the holy city of Jerusalem.

What did distinguish the Islamic raids from their predecessors, however, was the complete collapse of the opposing armies of the Byzantine and Sassanian Empires at the battles of the Yarmūk (636/15) and Qādisiyya (637/16) respectively. These armies had hitherto succeeded in repelling Arabian raiders, even if some time had been necessary to assemble their forces, but this time the defending armies crumbled before the Muslim armies, and in quick succession Palestine, Syria, Iraq, Egypt and Persia fell to the Muslims.

After the initial thrust of the conquests in the decade after the death of Muḥammad in 632/11, a similar process of Islamic conquest continued for approximately another century. Muslim armies expanded to both East and West, so that North Africa was conquered later in the seventh/first century and from there Muslim armies reached across the Straits of Gibraltar to conquer Spain in 711/92. In the East, the armies reached into Central Asia and to the borders of China, and also into the Valley of Indus, the area that is now Pakistan.[1]

The end result of this was that within a century of Muḥammad's death, the Muslim community ruled over an Empire which was the largest that had been seen in the history of the world up until that time. Even subsequently, only the Mongol Empire of Genghis Khan and the modern European Empires have exceeded it in size. It is extremely important to remember, however, that within the borders of the Muslim Empire, conquered peoples were generally placed under no pressure to accept the faith of Islam; there was no pressure to convert, in other words, and so in this first period what we see is the spread of an Islamic Empire, in the sense of an empire ruled by Muslims, and not necessarily the spread of the Islamic faith per se.

Phase II – from 750/132

Around the year 750/132 the boundaries of the Islamic Empire stabilized. The process of expansion ceased and the process of consolidation was accelerated. The Islamic faith developed its central disciplines of theology and law, and the study of philosophy and mysticism also became more widespread. From all of this activity the distinctive Islamic civilization of the ʻAbbāsid period, which lasted until 1258/656, emerged.

This does not mean, however, that the Islamic faith did not spread in this period. It spread firstly within the conquered area as the process of the conversion of the conquered population to Islam began.[2] But it also spread, significantly, outside the conquered area, beyond the frontiers of the Islamic Empire, and here, obviously, there was no link at all with conquest and military expansion. Here Islam expanded peacefully and on its own merits completely, and because this process was a gradual one it is impossible to give a date for the termination of the process.

Geographically the two main areas in which this peaceful spread of Islam was significant are Central Asia and Africa south of the Sahara. In Central Asia the key date for the spread of Islam is 956/345, when a number of Turkish tribes accepted Islam. This was a result of two main factors: firstly the activities of Muslim traders who had been active in the area for some time, and through whom some knowledge of the faith of Islam had been spread, and secondly, and more importantly, the missionary activity of a number of Sufi Muslims. One of the areas in which Sufi influence has been greatest in the Islamic world is in the area of the peaceful propagation of the faith, and it was largely through Sufi influence that the Turkish tribes of Central Asia accepted Islam. At first the Islam of these Central Asian tribes was somewhat idiosyncratic, in that they did not abandon all their ancient pre-Islamic practices immediately upon accepting Islam, but their conversion was to be a crucial factor in the later spread of Islam, as will be seen below.

In Africa the process of the peaceful spread of Islam was quite similar, although its subsequent consequences for the spread of the faith were not quite so momentous. In Africa Islam spread through three main routes: firstly across the Sahara from North Africa, via such trading towns as Timbuktu, secondly up the Nile Valley from Egypt into what is now called the Sudan and as far as Uganda, and thirdly across the Red Sea from Arabia into the Horn of Africa, what is now Somalia, and down the coast of East Africa to settlements such as Mombasa and Zanzibar. Again, as in Central Asia, the activities of merchants and Sufi missionaries combined to spread the knowledge of Islam, and the process of conversion to the faith began as early as the mid-eleventh/fifth century. Again as in Central Asia the Islam which was accepted was a flexible and elastic form of the faith, which initially co-existed with traditional African religion and did not seek any particular political role. Only much later did reforming movements arise in Africa which sought to purify the practice of the faith and to give it an explicitly political role.[3]

Phase III – c 1050/c 450–c 1550/c 950

At approximately the same time as the start of the process of conversion to Islam in Africa, the third phase of Islam's spread began. This was a phase which was much closer to the earliest spread of the faith, in which it spread in the wake of military conquest. The prime agents of this third phase of the spread of Islam were the Turks. Even before the conversion of some Turkish tribes to Islam in Central Asia, large numbers of Turks had migrated into the Islamic Empire, where they were employed as soldiers, and where they came to occupy a vital role in the preservation of the authority of the caliph in Baghdad. Increasingly real power came to rest with the Turkish soldiers, and the authority of the Arab caliph became increasingly nominal, although the Turks were always careful to demonstrate their theoretical loyalty to the caliph.

Alongside their increasing importance within the Islamic Empire, the Turks also became extremely important on the frontiers, where a number of Turkish tribes initiated further expansion of the Empire. This was the case in two main areas. Firstly, in Asia Minor, or what is now Turkey, the Seljuk Turks launched a campaign against the Byzantine Empire that was effectively to drive the Byzantines out of Asia Minor with the exception of the coastal areas. A later Turkish group, the Ottoman Turks, was eventually responsible for the extinction of the Byzantine Empire, when its capital, Constantinople, fell to Mehmet II in 1453/857, and much of the Balkans, including what is now Greece, the former Yugoslavia, Bulgaria, Roumania and even Hungary also came under Ottoman Turkish rule.

Secondly, at the other end of the Islamic world, a Turkish dynasty known as the Ghaznavids, because of their capital of Ghazna, now in Afghanistan, initiated a process whereby the frontiers of the world of Islam expanded far into the Indian Sub-Continent. Under another Turkish dynasty, the Moghuls, some three-quarters of the area came under Islamic rule, and thus there came about the situation whereby today there are approximately twice as many Muslims in the Indian Sub-Continent, in India, Pakistan and Bangladesh, as there are in the whole of the Arab World.[4]

In both of these cases it was, as in the years immediately after the death of Muḥammad, a case of Islamic rule being expanded. In other words the conquered population was not compelled to accept the faith of Islam. But whereas in the areas conquered in the first phase of Islamic expansion the process of gradual conversion to Islam has meant that today the vast majority of the population is Muslim, in the areas conquered in the third phase of the spread of Islam, the second wave of expansion in the wake of conquest, the process of conversion has in most cases not gone so far as to establish Islam as the faith of the majority. The exceptions to this statement are Asia Minor and the north-western part of the Indian Sub-Continent, what is now Turkey and Pakistan, but even here the Muslim predominance is partly the result of substantial movements of population after the First World War and Indian independence from Britain in 1947/1366 respectively.

The expansion in this third phase was not at all as dramatic as that in the earliest years of the Islamic Empire, and correspondingly, this third phase was spread over a longer period of time, over some 500 years. And while it was going on it is important to note that in other areas the frontiers of the world of Islam were actually contracting. In particular, Muslim rule was ended in Spain by the process of the Reconquista, culminating in the fall of Granada in 1492/897; and in sharp contrast to its original Islamic conquest, it was not so much as ten years before the Muslim population of Spain were being given the choice of being baptized or expelled from the country by its new Christian rulers.

Phase IV – from c 1450/c 850

The fourth phase of the spread of Islam is again, like the second, one in which the faith spread by peaceful means, and it overlaps to some extent with the third phase. During it commerce and the activities of Sufi missionaries again combined to produce this expansion of the world of Islam, and the particular area in which their activities were most significant is South-East Asia, and in particular what is now Malaysia and Indonesia. Islam came to this area from India, from the thirteenth/seventh century, and its spread was gradual, but after the conversion of the ruler of Malacca to Islam in the fifteenth/ninth century the process greatly accelerated. Only the arrival of the Spanish, indeed, in the Philippines contrived to prevent the further eastward spread of Islam. But one result of the spread that did take place is the existence to-day of the state with the largest Muslim population of any country in the world, namely Indonesia, whose 120 million Muslims are almost as many in number as the Muslim population of all the Arab states put together.[5]

It is true that in Indonesia there are different types of Islam, and some are regarded with some suspicion by Muslims who come from a longer tradition of Islamic thought and culture. This is essentially because some aspects of Indonesian Islam seem closer to the old pre-Islamic Indonesian traditions than they do to the main line of the Islamic tradition elsewhere. But, as we have seen, in other parts of the world too a synthesis has evolved between local culture and 'orthodox' Islam, and so it is not surprising that as a result of a similar interaction Indonesian Islam has developed its own distinctive features.

During this fourth phase of the spread of Islam, which is still continuing, the faith has continued to spread in Africa, and a number of missionary groups have succeeded in establishing a foothold for Islam in almost all the countries of the world. Most recently as a result of migration in search of work, Islam has established a presence in Western Europe and North America. In the former Islam is now the second largest religious community, with, for example, probably around 1,400,000 Muslims in Britain and around 6,000,000 Muslims in Western Europe as a whole, and in the latter there are probably around 3,000,000 Muslims. It should, of course, be stressed that this process is the result of migration rather than conversion, but nevertheless, alongside the migration there has been a trickle of European conversions to Islam, which even if it does not number more than a few hundred, is still roughly equivalent to the number of those who convert from Islam to, say, Christianity, throughout the whole world.

Today, then, Islam is a truly universal faith which has seen four main stages in its spread. The first, lasting approximately a century, saw a dramatic expansion of an Islamic Empire, which even if it did not enforce conversion to Islam nevertheless provided the environment in which over the centuries the majority of the population has converted to Islam. This area is essentially the Arab world of to-day plus Iran. The second phase of the spread of Islam was through peaceful means and took place beyond the frontiers of the Islamic Empire, particularly in Central Asia and in Africa. The third phase was again an expansion in the wake of conquest, this time at the hands of Turkish tribes. Asia Minor, the Balkans, and most of the Indian Sub-Continent came under Islamic rule in this phase. The fourth phase, which still continues, is more like the second phase in its manner. Islam has spread peacefully during it, and the most important area in which it has done so is South-East Asia. But as this phase continues, so Islam has become a truly universal religious faith, in reality as well as in theory, and this process therefore seems likely to continue into the foreseeable future.

The spread of Christianity

In the history of the spread of Christianity as in the spread of Islam, a certain rhythm may be detected, with different phases being evident, and different methods of expansion being used in different periods.

Phase I – the first three centuries

As we have already seen, Jesus lived and worked in Palestine, which happened to be a province of one of the great world states of the time, the Roman Empire. When his disciples came to write down their records of Jesus' life and meaning they did so in the *lingua franca* of the Eastern part of that empire, Greek, and they did so because it was not long before the focus of the Christian community's attention shifted from the pre-occupations of the Jewish community in Palestine to the wider religious preoccupations of the Roman world. The apostle Paul was one of the key architects of this development, and his missionary journeys, described so vividly in the book of Acts, show the results of this shift.

Initially, in many cities, Paul developed contacts with the local Jewish synagogue, to which were often attached groups of proselytes, non-Jews who accepted Jewish teachings and practices, and who were therefore a vehicle of entry into the wider community. In addition Paul also visited cities such as Athens where there was little significant Jewish presence, and entered into discussion with the representatives of the influential schools of philosophy of the day.[6]

This approach was successful in that it attracted people from widely-differing backgrounds and from many different parts of the Roman Empire to the Christian community, but it also resulted in considerable suspicion of the Christians in some quarters and in some cases it led to overt persecution of the Christians by the Roman state. The first three centuries of Christian history therefore see a steady expansion of the Christian church despite its definite status as a numerical minority in the Roman Empire, combined with instances of persecution and harassment of the Christians by the Roman state, which suspected them of disloyalty because of their refusal to bow before statues of the Emperors, and accused them of atheism because of their refusal to recognise the gods of the Roman pantheon.

Some of the worst periods of persecution came in the reigns of Nero (54–68), Domitian (81–96), Decius (249–251), and Diocletian (284–305), but on each occasion attempts to break the Christians failed and eventually, in 311, an edict of toleration for the Christians was issued by Galerius. Large numbers of Christians met their deaths, however, including as victims of gladiatorial contests in the Coliseum in Rome, but such actions often only aroused interest in and admiration for the Christians, and one of the early Christians in North Africa, Tertullian, asserted that "the blood of the martyrs is the seed of the church".

This period came to an end in the year 312 when the Roman Emperor

Constantine, partly out of genuine personal conviction and partly arising from the hope that the Christian faith would serve as a focus of renewed unity in the increasingly diverse and fissiparous empire, was converted to the Christian faith himself, and decreed that that faith was from then on to be the official state religion of the Roman Empire.[7]

Phase II – 312–c 1500/c 900

Constantine's conversion obviously meant a dramatic transformation in the status and position of the Christians in the Empire. From being a vulnerable minority they became closely allied with the state and were thus able to exert considerable influence on the policies of that state so that, for example, Sunday was set aside as a day of rest and even the taxation system began to be used to further the process of conversion to Christianity. This sometimes, however, had unforeseen and even undesirable consequences. Constantine, after all, had had his own reasons, not always spiritual in nature, for accepting Christianity, and it was not long before church leaders began to find it necessary to dissociate themselves from, and even on occasion oppose, state policies.

In general terms, however, this phase of Christian history can be seen as exemplifying two rather different yet nevertheless more or less contemporary methods of bringing about the spread of the Christian faith. On the one hand, where the Christian church was established as the official religion of the state, the increasingly close links between the two developed in such a way that the coercive power of the state began to be used in order to further the interests and influence of the church. Thus in the Byzantine Empire, the successor of the Eastern half of the Roman Empire, in the sixth century, the state began to identify itself quite specifically as a Christian state, and state power was used against any who dared to dissent from this view. Jews, for example, were sometimes forcibly baptised. And in Western Europe, in the centuries after the collapse of the Roman Empire in the West in 476, a number of states which had accepted Christianity did not hesitate to combine political and military expansion with the forcible conversion of conquered peoples to Christianity. Perhaps the best example of this is Charlemagne's campaigns against the Saxons in the late eighth/second century.

On the other hand, the same period also saw the dissemination of the Christian faith by peaceful means beyond the frontiers of those states which had accepted it. This process had begun before 312 as even then some Christians had attempted to spread the message beyond the Roman frontier. One early success involved the conversion of Tiridates (d 342), the king of Armenia, as a result of which Armenians today still claim to be the successors of the first Christian state. Christian communities had also become established in Persia, and, according to some traditions, even as far east as India.[8]

After 312 the process continued. In the fourth century attempts were made to convert the Goths to the north of the Black Sea, and in Western Europe, after the collapse of the Roman Empire in 476, missions were despatched from Rome to the capitals of the new kingdoms which were set up and in due course the Christian faith was accepted in many of them: the Frankish king Clovis was baptised in 496, a century later Pope Gregory sent a mission under Augustine to seek to convert the Anglo-Saxons, and in the first half of the eighth/second century missionaries from England such as Boniface (d 754/137) were largely responsible for large-scale conversion to Christianity in parts of what is now Germany. All of this was accomplished by means of preaching and peaceful persuasion.

In the East too, a similar process unfolded. From Byzantium in the ninth/third century missionaries such as Cyril and Methodius went out into south-eastern Europe to work among the Slav peoples, and achieved great successes. The acceptance of the Christian faith by King Vladimir of Kiev in 988/378 laid the foundation for Christianity to become the official religion of the later state of Russia, and for Moscow to be seen as the "third Rome", after Rome and Constantinople.[9] Further to the East, Nestorian Christians from Persia also spread the Christian message across Asia, reaching as far as China. The Christian message was thus accepted far beyond the frontiers of the Roman state and its successors.

These two avenues by which the Christian message was spread, different as they were in style and method, thus co-existed throughout much of what are often called the Middle Ages. In one instance, however, they to some extent converged, in the movement known as the Crusades. What was involved here was the application of some of the rather coercive methods used in those situations where a close correlation between church and state had developed well beyond the frontiers of Christendom in the world of Islam. It is true that the early generations of Crusaders rarely, if at all, attempted to bring about the conversion of the subjects of the Crusader states to the Christian faith, preferring as they did to bring about Christian control over the Holy Places of Jerusalem, but in the later development of the Crusading movement, in the Reconquista in Spain and in the campaigns of the Teutonic Knights in eastern Europe, conquest and conversion were in effect seen as synonymous. The Inquisition is another example of the view that state power could legitimately be used for the dissemination of Christian faith.

In the medieval period then the spread of the Christian faith took place by two main methods, one, in situations where Christianity was the state religion, often involving a measure of coercion, and the other, where Christians had no political influence, relying on peaceful persuasion.

Phase III – c 1500/c 900–1945/1365

The later years of the fifteenth/ninth century saw the great voyages of discovery of the Portugese and Spanish explorers such as Vasco da Gama and Christopher Columbus, sailing around the Cape of Good Hope and across the Atlantic Ocean respectively. Given the close relationship which existed between church and state in each of those countries, it is not surprising that in their colonial possessions each attempted in different ways to promote and disseminate the Christian faith. Different methods were used in different regions of the world, however, with the Spanish Conquistadors in America at first continuing the Crusading tradition of forced conversion, but some such as Bartholemew Las Casas (d 1566/973) protesting vigorously against this and seeking to use peaceful methods for the dissemination of the Christian message; and in Asia, where the Portugese quickly encountered ancient and well-established religious traditions, "some Christian missionaries began to acquire a new respect for these religions, and a new distaste for the hewing methods as a hindrance to true evangelism".[10] Individuals such as Matthew Ricci in China and Robert de Nobili in India are examples of this more peaceful approach.

At the same time the situation of the church in Western Europe was made more complicated by the movement of the Reformation, which led to division within the Christian community and also to the outbreak of violent conflict between Catholic and Protestant states. Generally speaking the early generations of Protestants displayed little interest in the task of spreading the Christian message outside Europe, and four reasons have been given for this: firstly, the early Protestants thought that the command given by Jesus to his disciples at the end of the Gospel according to St Matthew, to go and preach to the ends of the earth, had actually been fulfilled by the first generation of Christians, in other words the apostles; secondly, the Protestant insistence on the primacy of grace in the matter of salvation led to such a strong belief in the election or predestination of some people that this precluded the need for mission; thirdly, Protestant thinking on the relationship between church and state tended to result in the view that mission was the task of civil rulers rather than of the church independently; and fourthly, the understandable preoccupation with securing the position of Protestantism within Europe led to the conviction that the time for mission in other parts of the world was not ripe anyway.[11]

Protestant involvement in the spread of the Christian church outside Europe therefore had to wait until the late eighteenth/twelfth century when, as a result of the growth of the Pietist and Evangelical Movements, with their insistence on the need for individual conversion and Christian experience, allied with a stress on the existence of an invisible church of true believers as opposed to the visible outward church, a number of missionary societies were established both in the English-speaking world and on the continent of Europe. In the nineteenth/thirteenth century these societies were to contribute towards a period of growth in the Christian church which had probably not been seen since the earliest period of expansion recorded in the book of Acts. One of the consequences of this was that whereas at the end of the seventeenth/eleventh century in the world as a whole Muslims probably exceeded Christians in number, by the start of the First World War that situation was probably reversed, with Christians outnumbering Muslims.[12]

A vexed question of Christian missionary history in this period concerns the extent to which this process was intertwined with, or even explicitly allied with, the growth of European political and economic power which was taking place at the same time, and which resulted in the domination of a large part of the globe by various European empires. Scholarly opinion varies on this, and it can certainly be argued that circumstances varied very much from region to region and with respect to different European powers, but on the whole what seems to have happened is that whereas in the early period of European expansion commercial and religious interests were pursued separately and even on occasion in opposition to each other, as the nineteenth/thirteenth century progressed a greater measure of common interest and co-operation developed and there began to be more reference to "Christian civilization" on the part of both missionaries on the one hand and traders and political agents on the other.[13]

Phase IV – 1945/1365–present

Since the end of the Second World War most parts of the globe which had previously been under European control achieved their political independence, and the heyday of European imperialism thus came to an end. This did not mean, however, that the spread of the Christian church, allied as it had sometimes been with European political influence and control, came to an end. Rather, in many parts of the world at least, that process has accelerated as the Christian church became indigenised and identified itself more fully with local culture and life.

The Christian church in this period has thus witnessed spectacular growth in Africa, and also in some parts of Asia. In the latter, for example, there has for some centuries been one nation in which the majority of the population is Christian, namely the Philippines, whose name derives from that of the Spanish king Philip II, but now there is a second nation in which it seems that Christians may shortly make up the majority of the population, namely South Korea. This development may be explained in part by the particular political circumstances arising from the legacy of the Korean War and the Cold War era, but it is one clear piece of evidence for the assertion that the dismantling of European empires has not resulted in the end of the process of Christian expansion. In addition the emergence of flourishing local traditions of Christian thought testify to the vitality of Christian communities in different continents.[14]

On the other hand, in the part of the world from which the modern expansion of the faith began, namely Western Europe, the Christian church is today witnessing a considerable decline in its influence and power. This is largely as a result of the process of secularisation which can be traced back to the Enlightenment, and certainly in terms of attendance at public worship the various churches of Western Europe have seen a spectacular decline in numbers. On the other hand, in the part of the world which since 1945/1365 has been seen as the leading power of "the West", namely the United States, church attendance continues to flourish, to a far greater extent indeed than in the nineteenth/thirteenth century, and the corrosive effects of secularisation are therefore less obvious and more subtle.

In terms of the world as a whole today, then, the Christian community continues to grow in different ways. It does so, however, with greater effect in some regions than in others, and the global picture may perhaps best be summarised in an aphorism: "today most Christians are not Western, and most Westerners are not Christian". Thus in Christian history as in Muslim history, there are certain phases which can be discerned in the spread of the Christian faith. In its first three centuries the Christian community grew through persuasion in the face of often harsh persecution. In the second phase, after the conversion of Constantine, for over a millennium the Christian faith spread both through its alliance with state power (in Byzantium and in Western Europe) and also through peaceful missionary work beyond the frontiers of Christendom. In the third phase, beginning around 1500/900 the Christian message was then borne to other continents, sometimes in association with European colonial powers but sometimes through peaceful means. And over the past half century the Christian church has continued to grow, but with less dependence on the West and a greater interchange of ideas from one region to another.[15]

It is also important to remember that both the Christian and the Muslim community have also known periods of weakness and also contraction. The expulsion of the Muslims from Spain at the time of the Reconquista has already been referred to, and the memory of this is still vividly alive in the Muslim community worldwide as may be seen from two examples: firstly some elements of the Muslim minority in modern India, which makes up some 10% of the population, are vividly aware of the fate of the Muslims of Andalucia as a possible precedent for their future;[16] and secondly some discussion of the predicament of the Muslim community in Bosnia, which, like Andalucia, finds itself in a vulnerable position in Europe, also interprets current developments in a way which sees Andalucia as a precedent.[17] Conversely, it is also true, of course, that the rise of Islam itself resulted in the loss to the Christian world of many of the parts of the world in which the faith had first taken root, such as Palestine, Syria, Egypt, North Africa and Turkey, though Christian minorities remain in at least some of these regions until today. Muslims sometimes forget that it is the memory of these losses which is largely responsible for the fear of Islam which still exists in the West today, especially when reinforced later by Ottoman Turkish sieges of Vienna in 1529/935 and 1683/1094.[18]

Each community, during the course of its history, has therefore witnessed both the rise and the decline of its influence in certain periods. In some respects this process corresponds to the rhythm of the rise and fall of the two communities' openness to the tradition of Greek philosophical thinking, as examined in Chapter Three above, and this raises interesting questions about the relationship between intellectual curiosity and the spread of the faith. What the future holds, however, by way of the growth or otherwise of the influence of the Christian and Muslim faiths, is not clear, but it will be interesting to see whether competition or co-operation becomes the more widespread model in the relationship between them.

The treatment of subject peoples and minorities

As a result of the spread of the two faiths over the centuries both have encountered members of other faith communities. Sometimes, as in the first phase of the spread of Islam, this has been in the form of Christians (and Jews and others) finding themselves living as subject peoples under Islamic rule but still numerically making up the majority of the population, and at other times, as in the second phase of the spread of the Christian faith, it has been a case of Jews (and others) living as definite minorities within Christian societies. How have the two faiths treated subject peoples and minorities during the course of their history?

One of the most common Western caricatures of Islam is that it spread by means of the sword, in other words that conquered peoples were forced to accept the faith of Islam at risk of their lives if they refused. In reality this is a travesty of the truth, for the Muslim conquerors allowed the majority of those who fell under their rule to retain their ancestral religion. The Muslim Scripture, the Qur'ān, had itself stated that the faith of Jews and Christians was at least to some extent valid, even if substantial criticisms were made of certain of their beliefs and practices. And one verse of the Qur'ān in particular stated that there was to be no "compulsion" (*ikrāh*) in religion, (2:256) so that even if efforts were to be made to persuade non-Muslims of the errors of their ways, force was not to be employed under any circumstances. There are thus a great many appeals to people to accept the faith of Islam, (e.g. 3.64) but the use of force was not countenanced for that purpose. Not all the conquered peoples were Jews or Christians, the two faiths which the Qur'ān specifically spoke of, but even with others the attitude of the early Muslims was quite tolerant. With reference to the people of Persia, the majority of whom were Zoroastrians, who were not mentioned specifically in the Qur'ān, the early Muslims in practice treated them in similar fashion to the Jews and Christians of Syria, Palestine, and Egypt.

Force was used by the early Muslims on one or two small groups. Firstly, idolaters, who did not believe in the existence of only one God, and worshipped idols as a result of their spiritual ignorance, since they had not received a Scripture from God, were, according to the Qur'ān, to be given the choice of accepting Islam or meeting their death; but in reality idolaters were few and far between in the conquered territories, and even those who did exist did not necessarily receive the treatment that was prescribed for them in theory. And secondly, those Arabs who were Christian, in other words those tribes of the Arabian Peninsula who had accepted Christianity before the coming of Islam, were given the choice of accepting Islam or moving out of the Arabian Peninsula. There was thus some kind of link between the faith of Islam and Arab identity in the early period: the early Muslims felt that all Arabs, and that meant all the inhabitants of the Arabian Peninsula as well as those Arabs who found themselves outside that area as a result of the conquests, should be Muslim. On the other hand this meant that there was no need to try and cajole non-Arabs into accepting the faith of Islam.

It is thus not at all correct to say that Islam spread at the point of the sword. Certainly the area of the world ruled by Muslims was increased at the point of the sword, but this process did not involve any enforced conversion to the faith of Islam. Those who found themselves under Islamic rule outside the Arabian peninsula were in general permitted to practise their faith in freedom, although this was to some extent determined by the zeal that they had exhibited in resisting the process of conquest. The more quickly they surrendered, the more generous the terms, so that, for example, a city which surrendered without offering any resistance was permitted to retain all its churches, whereas a city that surrendered after some struggle was likely to have to hand over its main church for conversion into a mosque for Muslim worship.

Non-Muslims were therefore tolerated. A special tax, the *jizya*, was levied on them, and certain careers were closed to them, but they were free to practice, if not to seek to spread, their faith, and initially at least the Muslim conquerors were actually welcomed by many of the Christian population because of their willingness to allow this freedom of worship. Some time later, beginning in the eighth/second and accelerating rapidly in the ninth/third century, the process of conversion among the subject peoples did begin, encouraged in part by their becoming increasingly second-class citizens in the Islamic world, but in most cases it was only centuries later that Muslims came to make up the majority of the population in conquered areas such as Syria and Egypt, and so conversion was still not brought about by force.[19]

In the Christian world, by contrast, there is a widespread conviction that the spread of the Christian faith has always been achieved by peaceful means, that is by persuasion rather than by the use of any kind of force. This is a view which it is just possible to sustain if only certain periods of Christian history are examined, especially the first and fourth of the four phases outlined earlier in this chapter, but if the whole of Christian history is examined it is clear that this is certainly not the whole truth, for if the second and third phases are also considered it is clear that in some areas of the world the spread of the Christian faith has been achieved in a manner which is very closely linked with the use of force. In particular in those periods in which some states identified themselves openly and specifically as "Christian states" the power of the state was very often used in order to support the promotion of the Christian faith, or sometimes even one particular expression of that faith.

The ideals contained in the teaching of Jesus and the example of the early apostles have not always been adhered to, therefore, in later Christian history. Indeed in some instances these things have been interpreted in ways which to modern Christians seem extremely puzzling. Thus the words of Jesus in one of his parables "Compel them to come in" (Luke 14:23) have been interpreted, for example by Saint Augustine, as justifying the Christian use of coercion, in his case with reference to Donatist heretics in North Africa, and it is hard to reconcile the exhortation of Jesus to "love your enemies and pray for those who persecute you" (Matthew 5:44) with such things as the Crusades in Christian history. But in many cases it was other parts of the Christian scriptures which were used in order to justify these movements, especially some parts of the Old Testament which drew a sharp line of distinction and antipathy between the people of God and their enemies, and if the Christian community laid a lot of stress on its identity as the new people of God it was not difficult for the use of force against its enemies to be legitimated.

In the medieval period, then, it was probably better to be a Christian (or a Jew) in the Islamic Empire, than to be a Jew (or anything else) in Western Europe. Perhaps the best evidence for this is the migration of many Jews from Spain to the Islamic World after the Christian Reconquista, as their prospects were much better there.

In more recent times, however, this situation has to some extent changed, and today the situation is perhaps less clear. It is at the moment perhaps better to be Muslim in Western Europe than a Christian in Iran, but the same would probably not be true in other parts of the world. In the Christian majority Philippines or South Africa, Muslims have not always been treated with great tolerance, and it is interesting to see how in the latter Muslims until recently have been more "liberal" with respect to breaking down barriers than many Christians. Moreover in Western Europe, as in Iran, circumstances are always changing, and the position of all minorities in Western Europe is perhaps increasingly vulnerable in the light of the rise of extreme right-wing parties, with some such as those in France interlacing their racist rhetoric with large doses of talk of "Christian values". And in Eastern Europe, especially in Bosnia, the situation of Muslims has become increasingly vulnerable during the

1990's/1410's, with some Muslim commentators even talking of plans being made by the Serbs for a genocide of Muslims.[20] In this context, then, it is the (mainly Muslim) government of Bosnia-Herzegovina which is "liberal", in that it seeks to preserve a tolerant multi-cultural society, while it is the (traditionally Christian) Bosnian Serbs (and to a lesser extent Croats) who seek to establish mono-cultural and mono-religious statelets. Thus in the Bosnian government armed forces, some of the commanders are Serb, a situation which it is hard to envisage being mirrored in the armed forces of Bosnian Serbs or Croats.[21]

It may, therefore, be the case that in some parts of the world it is perhaps better to be a member of a Muslim minority in a traditionally Christian society than a member of a Christian minority in a majority Muslim society, but this is not to say that this is the case in all parts of the world. And even in those regions where this may be true, it may be due not so much to Christian teaching specifically as to the growth of liberal traditions of tolerance associated with secularisation and in some cases in the face of considerable opposition from Christian thinkers and churches.[22] The real question, therefore, is what makes some societies tolerant of minorities and other less so? In answer, it may well be the case that even if religion is used by some political leaders to arouse passions on the subject, it is not always in fact religion which is the key cause of hostility to minorities. Other factors such as economic ones like unemployment, and general feelings of uncertainty and insecurity may well be much more significant.[23] Minorities often serve simply as convenient scapegoats in these circumstances.[24]

Conclusion

However these questions are answered it is clear that in the twentieth/fourteenth century and even more so in the twenty-first/fifteenth, there is, in the relationship between Christianity and Islam, now a certain reciprocity with respect to the treatment of minorities, for with a new Muslim presence in Western Europe to balance the ancient Christian presence in the Muslim world, if Muslims in the West are discriminated against the people who will suffer for it in the long term are Christians in the Muslim world, and equally if Christians in the Muslim world are made to suffer, then the consequences will rebound on the heads of Muslims in the West. This is one of the challenges which will confront the members of both faiths in the future as they live together on the same planet.

Notes

1 The most convenient book tracing the course of the early Islamic conquests is F.Gabrieli *Muhammad and the conquests of Islam*, Weidenfeld and Nicolson, 1968.

2 See later sections of this chapter and also the Conclusion below for further detail on the process of conversion.

3 On the spread of Islam in Central Asia see V.V. Barthold *Turkestan down to the Mongol invasion*, (4th ed), Luzac, 1977, and *Histoire des Turcs d'Asie centrale*, Adrien-Maisonneuve, Paris, 1945; and on Africa see J.S. Trimingham *The influence of Islam upon Africa*, (2nd ed), Longmans, 1980, and I.M. Lewis (ed) *Islam in Tropical Africa*, (2nd ed), Hutchinson, 1980.

4 On the expansion of the Turks into Asia Minor and the Balkans see C. Cahen *Pre-Ottoman Turkey*, Sidgwick and Jackson, 1968, and H. Inalcik *The Ottoman Empire*, Weidenfeld and Nicolson, 1973; on the Ghaznavids see C.E. Bosworth *The Ghaznavids*, Edinburgh U.P., 1963, and *The Later Ghaznavids*, Edinburgh U.P., 1977.

5 On the spread of Islam in South-East Asia, see M.B. Hooker (ed) *Islam in South-East Asia*, Leiden, Brill, 1983, and the three chapters which make up Part VI of B. Lewis, P.M. Holt and A.K.S. Lambton (eds) *The Cambridge History of Islam*, Cambridge U.P., Vol II, 1970.

6 See Acts 17:16–34.

7 See A.H.M. Jones *Constantine and the conversion of Europe*, Penguin, 1962. One of the leading historians of this dramatic change, Eusebius of Caesarea, was convinced that the Kingdom of God had come when he saw the Emperor publicly receiving the leaders of the Christian church, who had until recently been persecuted as enemies of the state, at a banquet. See K. Ware *The Orthodox Church*, Pelican, 1963, p 27.

8 See W.G. Young *Handbook of source materials for students of church history*, Christian Literature Society, Madras, 1969, pp 11–40.

9 There is a story, probably apocryphal, that Vladimir had also considered the possibility of converting to Islam rather than Christianity. When he discovered, however, that Islam, while allowing polygamy, prohibited alcohol, he opted for the Christian faith which might have prohibited polygamy, but did not forbid alcohol!

10 O. Chadwick *The Reformation*, Penguin, 3rd ed., 1972, p 337. The whole of Chapter Nine of this book is a good survey of the different attitudes towards spreading the Christian faith in this period.

11 See L.L Vander Werff *Christian mission to Muslims*, William Carey Library, 1977, p 19.

12 See S.C. Neill *A history of Christian missions*, Penguin, 1964, pp 243–260 on the broad trends during this period.

13 See, for example, A.A. Powell *Muslims and missionaries in pre-Mutiny India*, Curzon Press, 1993, and C. Bennett *Victorian images of Islam*, Grey Seal, 1992.

14 See, for example, R. Gibbelini *Patterns of African theology*, Orbis, Maryknoll, 1994, and R. Sugirtharajah *Asian faces of Jesus*, SCM, 1993.

15 The title of one recent book on Christian mission is thus *From everywhere to everywhere*, by Michael Nazir-Ali, Collins, 1990.

16 See A.S. Ahmed *Discovering Islam*, Routledge, 1988, pp 158–171, where the author discusses what he calls "The Andalus syndrome" particularly with reference to the state of Hyderabad in South India.

17 See, for example, Khalid Duran "Bosnia: the other Andalusia" in S.Z. Abedin and Z. Sardar (eds.) *Muslim minorities in the West*, Grey Seal, 1995, pp 25–36.

18 On the early Western European reactions to the coming of Islam see R.W. Southern *Western views of Islam in the Middle Ages*, Harvard U.P., 1962 and N. Daniel *Islam and the West: the making of an image*, 2nd ed., One World, Oxford, 1993; and on later European perceptions of Islam see N. Daniel *Islam, Europe and Empire*, Edinburgh U.P., 1966.

19 On this process of conversion see especially R.W. Bulliet *Conversion to Islam in the Medieval period*, Harvard U.P., 1979, and N. Levtzion (ed.) *Conversion to Islam*, Holmes and Meier, New York, 1979.

20 Some of the Muslim commentary on events in Bosnia-Herzegovina, which has suggested the existence of a western Christian-inspired conspiracy against the Muslims of that republic, does seem to be an example of over-heated imagination rather than cool examination of reality. In particular one obvious question might be asked: if the orchestrators of the campaign against the Muslims are western Christian powers, how is it that the leading campaigner for the ending of the United Nations arms embargo is the government of the United States of America?

21 Outside Bosnia, however, some Christian leaders have been conspicuous in attempts to draw attention to the predicament of the Bosnian Muslims and the misdeeds of their Christian co-religionists. In a British context Professor Adrian Hastings of the University of Leeds should be mentioned particularly. See his "SOS Bosnia" in *Theology*, No. 778, July/August 1994, pp 242–244.

22 The growth of the idea of "natural law", for example, as outlined by the Dutch thinker, Hugo Grotius (d 1645/1055), was explicitly caused by a reaction to the savage Wars of Religion which were being waged between different Christian churches in Europe at the time.

23 A number of examples could be given from medieval Spain to illustrate this, with reference to both Christian and Muslim rulers: when they felt politically secure they were generally ready to be tolerant of religious minorities, but this situation was generally reversed as and when the other community was felt to be a political threat. See F. de B. de Medina "Islam and Christian spirituality in Spain: contacts, influences, similarities" in *Islamochristiana*, 18 (1992), pp 87–108, especially pp 87–96, where the author points to some interesting contrasts between the attitudes reflected in the epitaphs of the Ferdinand III (in the thirteenth/seventh century) and the more famous Ferdinand and Isabella (at the end of the fifteenth/ninth century). The former was written in four languages, Latin, Castilian, Hebrew and Arabic, with the date of Ferdinand's death being given according to each tradition's own calendar and the wording being according to the customary formulation of each tradition. Thus the Arabic epitaph includes the phrase "May Allāh have mercy on him". The latter, by contrast, written only in Latin, includes the phrase "the 'prostrators' of the Muhammadan sect and the 'extinguishers' of the stubborn heresy (i.e. Judaism)". The

difference between the attitudes reflected in the two epitaphs, the author suggests, can be explained in part by the transition within the Muslim community from the relatively tolerant attitudes of the early period of Islamic rule to the more assertive and intolerant policies of the Almoravid and Almohad dynasties.

24 There may be some correlation between a religious community's openness to external sources of knowledge (as outlined above in Chapter Three) and its attitude towards minorities, since the relatively positive attitude towards minorities on the part of both Muslims and Christians has historically coincided with relative openness towards the Greek philosophical tradition, but this does not mean that the two are necessarily correlated, since knowledge does not always lead to tolerance.

8

MODERN DEVELOPMENTS

Introduction

In the modern period as in all others certain similarities may be discerned in developments within the Christian community and those within the Muslim community, yet alongside these each tradition has also concentrated on a number of its own particular issues and witnessed the growth of its own distinctive trends of thought.

The phenomenon of modernity

The term "modernity" is a convenient short-hand term for a number of trends and developments which have unfolded, roughly-speaking, over the past two centuries. Thus in political terms the American Declaration of Independence of 1776/1190 and the French Revolution of 1789/1203 have had considerable effects on thinking about how societies should be governed, with republics being set up in all continents and, in many cases, constitutions enshrining clear separation between religion and the state. The modern state has also become far more comprehensive in its spheres of operation, becoming involved in every area of life, including such things as health and education, as well as its traditional role in matters of law, foreign policy and taxation.

Intellectually, building on the legacy of Descartes, the Enlightenment proclaimed the supremacy of reason and of empirical investigation, thereby contributing to the growth of secularisation and the decline of public religious observance, especially in Western Europe. Confidence in reason gave rise to the critical study of history, religion, and even what had traditionally been taken to be sacred texts. And the application of reason in the field of science gave rise on the one hand to huge advances in medicine and other human sciences, and on the other to great leaps forward in the area of industrial technology. The Industrial Revolution and the development of this scientific culture brought about huge changes in communications, for example, with the telegraph, the telephone, the radio, the television, the fax machine and the personal computer on the one hand, and the steamship, the motor car and the aeroplane on the other.

These changes also had a considerable effect on the balance of power in the world as a whole, with the western European countries which had first experienced them projecting their power, initially through commerce and later through force of arms, across all continents. The Muslim world was on the receiving end of this process, with first India witnessing the expansion of British influence, especially after the battle of Plassey in 1757/1170 and then the Middle East experiencing European intervention in the form of Napoleon Bonaparte's invasion of Egypt in 1798/1212. In the heyday of European imperialism between the two World Wars only three parts of the Muslim world had succeeded in not coming under some kind of European administration, namely Turkey, Afghanistan and Sa'udi Arabia.

Even when direct European political influence was pushed back, with most Muslim nations achieving their independence in the years after 1945/1365, the influence of the West in the broader sense, that is including the United States of America, remained considerable, especially in the fields of economics and culture. Increasingly, therefore, all regions of the world became subject to the process of globalisation, with information, ideas and industrial products being disseminated ever more quickly across all segments of the globe. Not for nothing has it been said that the world, in the sense of being something that it is widely possible both to know about and to experience, only came into existence in the twentieth/fourteenth century.

Reactions to all of these developments have been mixed. Some have been broadly positive, seeing them as bringing opportunities and increasing the potential for happiness and prosperity. Others, by contrast, have been more negative, viewing modernity as a threat and a danger, undermining the contentment and security of traditional communities and bringing about the real possibility of nothing less than global destruction. To some extent the difference between these two views can be explained by the different views of history held by their proponents: does the peak or apogee of human history lie in the past, so that all later developments are necessarily a decline from that point, a view which is bound to produce pessimism about the new trends of modernity, or alternatively is history progressing or evolving from past imperfection towards future improvement or even perfection, in which case optimism about modernity is appropriate?[1]

Within the Christian and Muslim communities the developments associated with modernity have resulted in a concentration on rather different issues, not least because it was in the part of the world in which the Christian faith was dominant that most of these modern ideas grew up, and so Christians were compelled by local circumstance to react to them, whereas in the Muslim world the different aspects of modernity tended to arrive as imports, usually in association with some European political power, and the Muslim reaction to them was therefore made more complex by their foreignness.

Thus in the Christian world over the past two centuries or so some of the important issues which have attracted much attention are these. Firstly there has been considerable discussion of the relationship between science and religion, stimulated on the one hand by the evolutionary theories of Charles Darwin and on the other by discoveries in the fields of geology and physics which seemed to challenge traditional Christian understandings of the creation of the universe. Some famous nineteenth/thirteenth century controversies such as the debate between Samuel Wilberforce and Thomas Huxley in Oxford in 1860/1276 led to the emergence of a widespread view that there was an inevitable conflict between science and religion, a view which is still found today in the thinking of Richard Dawkins, a Reader in Zoology in Oxford, who has suggested that Theology is not a proper subject for study in a university, since its statements are not amenable to empirical observation. But there are many other scholars, some of whom, for example Arthur Peacocke, have been trained both in Theology and in scientific disciplines, who suggest that there is no inherent conflict between the two disciplines.

Secondly considerable attention has been devoted in modern Christian thinking to the question of the relationship between myth and history. This was in part stimulated by the science-religion debate, which raised the question of how the accounts of creation in the book of Genesis were to be understood: should they be seen as scientific accounts, or rather as mythical statements, whose purpose was primarily theological, that is to affirm the divine origin of creation? It was also furthered by other developments in biblical study, especially the so-called quest for the historical Jesus, which investigated the question of the extent to which the gospel-accounts of Jesus' life at the start of the New Testament were to be understood as history or biography and the extent to which they too were to be understood primarily as theological statements from the pens of those who were already committed to a particular interpretation of what was being described. Were New Testament accounts of, for example, the resurrection of Jesus from the dead thus to be understood as being historical, physical fact, or rather as mythical, asserting that despite Jesus' crucifixion God had nevertheless brought about spiritual victory over death and the grave?[2]

A third focus of discussion in the Christian community has been the relationship between church and society. In part this involved attention being paid to how Christians should respond to the social changes which occurred in the wake of the Industrial Revolution, with rapid migration from the countryside to the cities and the growth of slums, with appalling living conditions, in those cities. Urgent attention was therefore given to the construction of church buildings in industrial areas and, based upon them, to the pastoral tasks confronting Christian ministers there. Political action in order to counteract, or at least minimise, some of the worst effects of social change, was also regarded as necessary by some Christians and in England in the nineteenth/thirteenth century the movement of Christian Socialism grew up in order to campaign for social and economic justice. There was also much debate concerning relationships between the church and the state, stimulated by the concerns of the American and French Revolutions to introduce a formal separation between the two and also by the concerns of some Christians to challenge the privileges enjoyed in some European countries by state, or established, churches. In the twentieth/fourteenth century the Russian Revolution in 1917/1336 and the later establishment of Communist governments in many Eastern European countries also necessitated much reflection on the nature of the link between church and state.

Attention. has also been devoted, especially in the twentieth/fourteenth century, to new styles of worship and ministry, with a process of revision of formal Christian liturgical worship being undertaken in many Western Christian churches, including the Roman Catholic Church which at the Second Vatican Council in 1962/1382 permitted the use of local languages in worship in place of Latin. Questions of ministry have also been widely discussed, with one of the most controversial and acrimonious debates taking place concerning the possibility of women serving as leaders of worship and celebrants at the central acts of Holy Communion/the Mass/the Eucharist. On this question it has generally been Protestant churches which have been most positive in their view of women's ministry, with the Roman Catholic and Orthodox churches generally opposed and the Anglican church, in England at least, witnessing potential di- vision over the issue.[3]

Finally, ethical questions have also been prominent in modern Christian discussion, partly with reference to human sexuality and partly with reference to issues raised by the achievements of modern science. Thus there has been much discussion, especially in western Christian churches, of the permissibility or otherwise of contraception and abortion, with Protestant churches displaying a greater readiness to view them favourably, under certain circumstances, at least, and the Roman Catholic Church generally far more negative.[4] And attention has also been devoted to the legitimacy or otherwise of nuclear weapons and to scientific developments in such fields as genetic engineering, including the permissibility of using human embryos for research. No clear consensus has arisen on these issues, but the importance of continuing discussion with reference to them is obvious.[5]

In the Muslim community discussion in the modern period has generally focused on rather different issues, and this needs to be seen in the context of the relative powerlessness of the Muslim world as compared with the various European powers of the day. It was this fact which explains firstly why in some respects much modern Islamic thought is reactive rather than proactive and secondly why the preoccupations of some recent Muslim thinkers may appear to be rather introverted.

The first prominent theme in modern Islamic thinking is that of renewal, *tajdīd*. Given the relative decline in power and influence of the Muslim world vis-a-vis Europe, many Muslim thinkers were preoccupied with the issues of what had caused this decline and how it might be reversed. One possible solution was the renewal of devotion and practice of the faith within the Muslim community, and a precedent for this in Islamic history could easily be found in the tradition that at the start of each new Islamic century a renewer, *mujaddid*, of Islam would arise and bring about such a renewal.[6] Many Muslim thinkers, including the important nineteenth/thirteenth century figure Jamāl al-dīn al-Afghānī (d 1897/1314), were insistent on the need for such a renewal if the political and military fortunes of the world of Islam were to be restored to the glories which they had witnessed in the early centuries of the community. Among his suggestions as to how this might be achieved was his call for renewed stress on the proper observance of the Sharī'a (Islamic Law), and the liberation of the study of the Sharī'a from the dead weight of tradition by the fresh use of *ijtihād* (independent reasoning) based on only the first two sources of Law, namely the Qur'ān and the Ḥadīth (Tradition).[7]

Closely related to the theme of *tajdīd* is the theme of *iṣlāḥ*. This is sometimes translated as reform, but given that there is a prominent intellectual element to such reform the term reformulation is perhaps a better equivalent. Involved here are questions such as the extent, if any, to which Islamic teaching and practice may need some kind of reconsideration or revision in order to take some account of the discoveries of modern science and the development of modern knowledge in general. Some nineteenth/thirteenth century Muslims, such as Sayyid Aḥmad Khān in India (d 1898/1316), were prepared to consider a considerable measure of reformulation so that, for example, the Ḥadīth should be recognised to be inauthentic and therefore no longer be considered as authoritative, and the Qur'ān itself should be seen as being in some way the word of Muḥammad as well as the word of Allāh. Some recognition of the role of the human personality of the prophet in the composition of the sacred text should therefore be given, according to Sayyid Aḥmad Khān, and for this reason, he suggested, it was important to interpret the Qur'ān in its original historical context and thus recognise the distinction between what he called the principles of the Qur'ān's teaching, which he considered to be eternally binding, and the details, which he reckoned to be relevant only to the time of Muḥammad himself. The Qur'ān's statements about such things as polygamy and slavery did not thus need to be heeded by later generations of Muslims.

The views of such "modernists" were not widely held within the Muslim community in the nineteenth/thirteenth century and this broadly-speaking remains the case in the twentieth/fourteenth century too. Far more widespread was the view that any reformulation should be in the direction of returning to the earliest sources of Islam, going back to, in other words, rather than on from, the Qur'ān and the Ḥadīth. According to this view there was little if any need to take account of modern thinking, and the primary task was to excise and shed medieval thinking, the accretions which had developed in the classical period of Islamic thought, in order to return to the pristine purity of the earliest Muslim community. Then, shorn of the baggage of the medieval period, it would be possible to undertake fresh thinking on the basis of the two earliest sources of Islamic teaching.

The third theme which has exercised Muslim minds over the last two centuries is, not surprisingly, the relationship between Islam and the West. The dilemma here was simple: on the one hand the West was perceived as a threat and a danger to the world of Islam, not least as various of its members firstly encroached upon and secondly began to establish their control over different parts of the Islamic world. On the other hand the power and knowledge which made this process possible was also an object of admiration and even wonder for many Muslims, who therefore wished to learn the secrets of such power and emulate

European patterns of thought and ways of doing things in the Muslim world. Consideration of the two nineteenth/thirteenth century Muslim thinkers whom we have already discussed, Jamāl al-dīn al-Afghānī and Sayyid Aḥmad Khān, will reveal that on this question they adopted diametrically opposite points-of-view, with the former speaking and writing of Islam as being in danger from the West, with the British in particular as the main threat, while the latter was extolling the virtues of British government, education and culture and seeking to persuade the Muslims of British India to establish their loyalty to their British rulers and learn what they could from them.

Finally, and here there is perhaps most common ground between the issues which have preoccupied Christians and Muslims in the modern period, there has been considerable Muslim debate concerning the relationship between religion and the state. The reasons for this issue acquiring such significance in the Muslim world, however, are rather different from those which propelled it to the forefront of Christian thinking. In an Islamic context the question of the relationship between religion and the state has been related to the question of what caused the decline and weakness of the Muslim world. One suggestion on the part of some recent Muslim thinkers has been that it was particularly because of the failure of Muslim governments to take seriously the teachings of Islam in the formulation and implementation of their policies, especially in the area of law, which led to the weakening of Islamic societies. The solution, it is therefore argued, is for governments once more to take the faith more seriously, particularly with respect to their duty to enforce and implement the Sharī'a, Islamic Law. If this is done, argue some modern Muslim thinkers, then the fortunes of the Muslim world will be rapidly restored.

Other thinkers, however, of whom perhaps the most celebrated is the Egyptian thinker 'Alī 'Abd al-Rāziq (d 1966/1386) argued in a diametrically opposed way. In their view the historically close links between religion and the state which had existed in Islamic history, going back to the time and example of the prophet in Medina, were not an essential part of the core teaching of Islam but rather a response by the prophet to the particular circumstances of his time. On this basis 'Abd al-Rāziq suggested that the way forward for the Muslim community was to look not so much to the prophet's career in Medina as to his earlier career in Mecca, where he had been the proclaimer of a message, a warner to Meccan society, and to seek to communicate this more spiritual message to the world. Building on this view it was also suggested that for the Muslim world the way forward was to move towards an explicit separation of religion from the state, which should be seen not as the abandonment of classical Islamic models but rather a return to the earliest practice of the prophet himself. This view has not become widely-accepted, but some more recent thinkers, such as Maḥmūd Ṭāhā and the Republican Brothers in the Sudan, have espoused a similar view, and the governments of some Muslim countries, most notably Turkey, have included a specific clause in their constitutions concerning the separation of religion and the state.[8]

Different issues have therefore preoccupied the Christian and Muslim communities over the past two centuries, largely because of the differing circumstances in which they encountered the issues raised by the phenomenon of modernity. Some similarities may be discerned, however, in a broad sense, in the reactions of the two traditions to the idea of change.

One reaction – "fundamentalism"

One of the most obvious, as well as one of the most confusing, trends in each community is the emergence of what is often called "fundamentalism" (in inverted commas until a definition is given, since the term is now very widely-used with respect to Jewish, Christian and Muslim (and other) "fundamentalism", yet it is used to mean so many different things that unless tightly defined it may be less than helpful). A whole spate of recent studies has been produced on this subject.[9]

"Fundamentalism", I suggest, is used in essentially five different senses. The first is in a theological sense, referring especially to a particular view of scripture and of how it came into being. With respect to Christians and the Bible, this might mean describing the Bible as "infallible" because of its having been dictated by God; with respect to Muslims this might mean viewing the Qur'ān as uncreated. There is immediately an important difference between these two views, however, since in today's world the view that the Bible was dictated by God is probably a minority view in the Christian community as a whole, and the use of the word "infallible" with reference to the Bible is certainly a relatively recent innovation in Christian history; it goes back no further than the emergence of Protestant Scholasticism in the seventeenth/eleventh century and has acquired particular prominence in more recent Christian history in North America through the activities of a group of Christians who gave rise to the coining of the term "fundamentalism" in the second decade of the twentieth century/the 1330's by publishing a series of pamphlets which were simply called "The fundamentals". One of these pamphlets insisted on viewing the Bible as infallible.[10] In the

Muslim community, however, the view that the Qur'ān is uncreated is historically the majority view, at least among Sunnī Muslims, and so it should justifiably be seen as a mainstream rather than a peripheral opinion.

Secondly, "fundamentalism" is used in a philosophical sense, referring here in particular to an attitude of hostility to the use of critical method in approaching the study of the scriptures. In both communities there is a wide spectrum of opinion on this question, with ferocious debates taking place in some Christian circles on the question of whether or not Biblical criticism somehow undermines the status and authority of the Bible. A negative answer to the question seems to be gaining ground in many places, although the critical study of the Bible is well-established in main-line Protestant churches. In Islam there is something of a contrast to this situation because the application of critical methods to the study of the Qur'ān does not have a long history and is suspect to many Muslims by virtue of being seen as something that non-Muslims have done to the Qur'ān, with the intention of undermining it, rather than something which Muslims should do because the text demands it or because it is necessary in order to understand it properly. But in some circles at least, as awareness of literary critical theory becomes greater as a result of its application to other areas, not least Arabic literature, there is the beginning of a debate as to the legitimacy of critical study of the Qur'ān.[11] This is clearly more difficult for Muslims than for Christians since, as observed above, the Qur'ān occupies a rather different place within Islam from that of the Bible within Christianity, since in Islam the scripture is itself the main locus of revelation, whereas in Christianity the scripture is the testimony to the main revelation, Jesus Christ, rather than the revelation itself, but even so given that the Qur'ān is a book, a text, it may be hard to sustain a view that considers it immune from the application of textual criticism for ever.[12]

A third aspect of "fundamentalism" is a sociological one, relating to the phenomenon of sectarianism or membership of a group which considers that those outside the group are not "true" believers. Generally this line of thinking has a stronger influence in Christianity than in Islam, partly because in its early history the Christian church was essentially a sect, and partly because of the great extent of diversity within the Christian community, as outlined in Chapter Six above. This has resulted in the emergence of many small groups insisting that they alone are the "true" believers and that others claiming to be Christians have in fact gone astray. But in modern Islam, partly due to political pressures, the emergence of reform schools seeking to address the contemporary problems of the Muslim world has contributed to the emergence of groups which insist that non-members may call themselves Muslim but they are in fact unbelievers, and on the basis of this view these groups may legitimately be called sectarian.

Fourthly, "fundamentalism" is used in a historical sense, meaning "religiously conservative" or seeking to return to the origins of a faith: "back to the foundations" (or fundamentals) is thus a prominent cry. There is thus a certain suspicion of modernity evidenced by those holding this view, and this is parallelled by a certain idealism concerning the origins of the community. For some Christians, therefore, the early church is the ideal, a paradigm of perfect Christian faith and love, a view which seems blind to the fact that if that were really the case there would have been no need for Paul or any other of Jesus' apostles to have written any of their letters, the whole point of which was to try to resolve problems and issues which had arisen in the early Christian communities. And equally some Muslims look back longingly to the age of the first four caliphs, the "rightly-guided caliphs" as a kind of utopia when all in the Muslim community was sweetness and light and the process of corruption had not set in; such a view, however, completely ignores the fact that only one of those four caliphs died in his bed – the first, Abū Bakr. The other three were all assassinated, by a Persian Christian, rebellious Muslim mutineers from Egypt, and a disillusioned former supporter in his struggle for the leadership succession who had joined the Khawārij respectively.

And, last but by no means least, "fundamentalism" is frequently used in a political sense, to refer to attempts to bring about revolution in the name of religion.[13] The irony here is that the use of the word to refer to political movements takes almost no account of the total package of views of these movements: the sole criterion is usually their usefulness or otherwise to the West. This is very significant with reference to popular and media use of the term "fundamentalist". Here, if a group opposes an anti-Western government it will not usually be described as "fundamentalist". Thus Western commentators in particular rarely referred to the Mujahidin in Afghanistan as "fundamentalists" as long as they were fighting against the Russian occupation of their country, yet after the Soviet withdrawal, when the Mujahidin took over power and formed a government, they quickly began to be described as "fundamentalist", because of such things as their generally conservative attitudes towards, for example, women. And governments which are very similar in their attempts to identify themselves and form their policies according to

Islamic principles will find that it is their foreign policy which determines whether or not they will be described as "fundamentalist" in the Western media. Thus after 1979/1400 and the Islamic Revolution in Iran, Ayatollah Khomeini, with his fierce anti-Western rhetoric, was routinely described as a "fundamentalist" during the 1980's/1400's, and yet in the early 1990's/1410's, during the Gulf War the Sa'udi Arabian government, crucial to the western economic system and pro-western in its foreign policy, was rarely described as "fundamentalist", despite the fact that both regimes lay great stress on the Islamic focus of their identity and devote much attention to implementing the principles of the Sharī'a (even if they do not share the same interpretation of it), not least with reference to women. With respect to many of the aspects of "fundamentalism" discussed above, both would have to be described as "fundamentalist".

Other groups, however, which share many of the views of the Afghan Mujahidin and the Sa'udis in other areas of the Muslim world, are quickly labelled as "fundamentalist" if they challenge secular or pro-Western governments, such as that in Algeria, despite the fact that they may well receive moral and even financial support from Sa'udi Arabia, while those who challenge the Sa'udi government, alleging it to be hypocritical in its claim to represent and practice Islam, are certainly described as "fundamentalists" in the Western press. In this latter case the description does at least fit many of the groups' opinions – they could even be described as "arch-fundamentalists" – but the view of most Western commentators is influenced more by the fact that they are opposing a pro-western government than by an appreciation of all the elements of their thinking. Special care is therefore necessary with respect to the use of the word "fundamentalist" in a political context.

"Fundamentalism" is thus a word used in a great variety of ways, and some idea of the sense in which it is being used in a particular context needs to be given if the word is to be of any use. Often it is simply a kind of short-hand for obscurantist/authoritarian, unthinking/bigoted, arrogant/exclusive, backward-looking/nostalgic, and subversive or reactionary (depending on your point-of-view), corresponding to the five different aspects which I have outlined.

Careful definition is therefore necessary concerning the sense of which dimension is being referred to before the word "fundamentalism" can be used of Christianity or Islam. In the first sense, mainstream Sunnī Islam may be "fundamentalist" since it holds to the idea of the uncreated Qur'ān. But that does not mean that it is "fundamentalist" in the other senses too. Early Sunnī commentators on the Qur'ān were in many respects good models of serious critical study of the text, determined as they were to locate particular chapters and verses in their original context within the career of Muḥammad and recount how earlier generations of Muslims had understood them, rather than simply leaping to their own conclusions. Mainstream Sunnī Islam is certainly not sectarian, since its whole tradition has been to be inclusive – to count in as Muslim anyone who says that he/she is Muslim. Neither is it necessarily looking back to the first four caliphs as its model, since the whole classical period of Islam at least is usually seen as significant so that, for example, the consensus of opinion (*ijmāʿ*) of the classical period in matters of law has traditionally been taken as a third source of guidance on matters of law. And it is not usually revolutionary in a political sense, since Sunnī Islam has usually enjoyed the status of being a kind of state religion.

But some Muslims from a Sunnī background may be "fundamentalist" in these other senses: they may explicitly condemn critical study of the Qur'ān, condemning it as an Orientalist plot to subvert Islam; they may dismiss the claims of anyone other than themselves to be authentically Muslim; they may want to go back to the foundations of Islam, in the sense of Qur'ān and Sunna; and they may be politically assertive, seeking to overthrow an existing nominally Muslim government. But they may not hold to all of these things, so care does need to be exercised.

Equally in a Christian context, some groups may conform to the necessary characteristics with respect to some of the areas which have been outlined, but it needs to be made clear in which particular aspect they are being referred to as "fundamentalist" before they are assumed to be so in every respect. Some Roman Catholic Christians may be respectful of the Christian scriptures but not describe them as being "infallible", cautious in their attitude towards biblical criticism, inclusive rather than exclusive in their understanding of membership of the Christian community, have a high sense of the value of tradition so that they do not generally wish to "go back to" the early foundations of the Christian faith, but be passionately committed to political action in order to increase their influence in the societies in which they live. Should they therefore be described as "fundamentalist"?

Other Christians, by contrast, may hold to the infallibility of the Christian scriptures, abhor the critical study of them as historical documents (which may be dismissed as reductionist), be convinced that they alone are the true Christian believers, call passionately for a constant vigilance in the task of restoring the faith and practice of the first generation of Christians, and hold themselves utterly aloof from any kind of involvement in political matters at all, since the whole political sphere is understood as being "worldly", so that true believers should seek to keep themselves unpolluted from it. They are thus not "fundamentalist" in every sense of the word as we have discussed it.

What is clear, therefore, is that it is extremely important to define the word "fundamentalism" carefully and to indicate especially the sense in which the word is being used. On the other hand the word is sometimes a useful shorthand term for a particular set of opinions and attitudes, on two conditions: firstly that it is recognised that these opinions are not confined to any one religious community;[14] and secondly that these opinions are not necessarily held by all members of that community. Some Muslims may be "fundamentalist" in one sense or another (but not necessarily in every sense), but that does not mean that all Muslims are "fundamentalist". Equally, some Christians may be "fundamentalist" (in one or more senses), but that does not make all Christians "fundamentalist".[15]

Another reaction – liberalism

At the other end of the spectrum of religious thought, at least as a convenient shorthand term, is liberalism, understood as a tendency to seek to move on from, or be liberated from, traditional understandings. As with "fundamentalism" there are differing degrees and different aspects of liberalism, but since it is a longer-established term there is perhaps a greater degree of consensus as to its meaning and content, and so there is no need to use inverted commas around the word. In addition liberalism in most cases does not bear the pejorative implications of "fundamentalism"; whereas the word "fundamentalist" is not one people usually use to describe themselves but rather to describe other people, the use of the word "liberal" would not normally be resisted or opposed by those thinkers of whom it is used.[16]

Within the Christian community nineteenth/thirteenth century Christian thought was perhaps dominated by Liberal Theology, with its foundations laid by Friedrich Schleiermacher (d 1834/1249) in Germany, who sought to base the Christian faith on the foundation of "the feeling of absolute dependence", thus suggesting that at the core of religion and piety lay experience.[17] The growth of biblical criticism, with its pressure for the biblical accounts of, say, creation in the Old Testament and the miracles of Jesus in the New to be understood as myths, metaphorical or theological statements, rather than scientific ones, also encouraged the development of Liberal Theology; the meaning that these things represented was thus seen as being more significant for later generations than the course of events as described in the biblical texts. Liberal Theology also tended to be generally optimistic about human nature and the course of human history, suggesting that humankind was progressing towards a better future, and liberal theologians tended to take the view that as new knowledge became available as a result of this progress so the traditional formulations of the Christian faith needed to be revised in order to take account of it.

The origins of Liberal Theology were to be found originally in Protestant Christianity, but many of the points it raised have become more widely-accepted in the Christian community, so that today Roman Catholic scholars, especially since the Second Vatican Council in 1962/1382, have accepted and developed the methods of biblical criticism. Twentieth/fourteenth century Protestantism, by contrast, has seen a vigorous reaction against Liberal Theology, partly as a result of the shattering of some of its optimistic assumptions about human progress by two World Wars. Theologians such as Karl Barth (d 1968/1388) and Emil Brunner (d 1966/1385) argued for a new emphasis on the givenness of revelation and of salvation, so that human beings needed rather to hear and to receive, than to experience and to work for knowledge of God.

In the Muslim community, as mentioned above, some thinkers in the nineteenth/thirteenth century also sought to develop and outline a new formulation of the Islamic faith. Figures such as Sayyid Aḥmad Khān (d 1898/1316) in India and Muḥammad ʻAbduh (d 1905/1323) in Egypt were among those who sought to promote *iṣlāḥ* (reformulation), and they are sometimes described as "modernists" because of their insistence that Islam needed to be rendered comprehensible in terms of modern scientific knowledge. "Modernism", interestingly, was a term originally used for a movement in the Roman Catholic Church at the beginning of the twentieth/fourteenth century which sought to reinterpret traditional Christian teachings and which was condemned by a Papal encyclical in 1907/1325. The word was then taken over and used of Muslim thinkers such as Muḥammad ʻAbduh by Western scholars such as C.C. Adams and H.A.R. Gibb.[18]

In the twentieth/fourteenth century, however, in the Muslim world as a whole there has been an appreciable reaction against the ideas of modernist or liberal thinkers, and increasing influence has been won by thinkers of a more conservative bent whose hopes for the future of the Muslim community involve not so much a reformulation of Islamic teaching as a reconstruction of the patterns of earlier centuries. Probably the most widely-read Muslim thinkers of this century are Abū'l-A'lā Mawdūdī (d 1979/1399), whose influence has spread far beyond his home in South Asia, and the Egyptian Sayyid Quṭb (d 1966/1386), and the movements with which they were associated, the Jamā'at-i Islāmī (literally "Islamic Group") and the Ikhwān al-muslimūn (Muslim Brethren) respectively continue to enjoy widespread support in different parts of the Muslim world.[19]

No more in the Muslim than in the Christian community, then, was liberalism universally accepted. Something of the polarisation between different trends of thought in the Muslim community can be discerned in the fact that modernists are sometimes described as apostates or unbelievers and the modernists sometimes reply that their opponents are obscurantists and reactionaries, and within the Christian community, even if generally not in quite such strident terms, similar tensions are evident. What is really at issue here, therefore, is the question of how religious communities respond to change and the issue of the extent of tolerance which should be given to dissent and non-conformity, and to that we now turn.

Tolerance and dissent

In the history of both the Christian and Muslim communities there have been a number of instances of rather harsh treatment being meted out to anyone who dissents from what is seen at any particular time as being the truth. Thus in medieval and early modern times both the philosopher Ibn Rushd (Averroes) (d 1198/595) in the Muslim community and the astronomer Galileo (d 1642/1051) in the Christian world were accused of deviance from the straight path of orthodoxy and threats were issued against them if they did not retract or desist from disseminating their views. Ibn Rushd was accused of espousing the view that there were two truths, one for intellectuals and philosophers and one for the ordinary mass of people, and his books were burnt. Galileo was accused of believing that the sun went round the earth rather than the other way round, and was threatened with death, but his recantation before the Inquisition saved him from that fate, though he did have to spend the last eight years of his life under house arrest.[20]

In the modern period too debates have arisen in academic circles in both communities concerning the boundaries of what were considered to be acceptable opinion. In the nineteenth/thirteenth centuries figures such as William Robertson Smith and F.D. Maurice in Britain both fell foul of conservative Christian opinion and were obliged to resign from academic positions as a result. Smith was the Professor of the Old Testament at the Free Church College in Aberdeen. In 1875/1292, in an article on the Bible which he contributed to the Encyclopaedia Britannica, he gave support to the view that the Pentateuch, the first five books of the Old Testament, was made up of a number of different strands which had been amalgamated by a later editor (or editors). He was put on trial in the church courts and after five years of controversy he was deposed from his chair in 1881/1298, though shortly afterwards he found another post as Professor of Arabic in Cambridge. F.D. Maurice was Professor of Theology at King's College in London, and he was expelled from the College in 1853/1270 as a result of a clamour of protest against the views expressed in an essay on Eternal Life and Eternal Death, in which Maurice rejected the idea of the eternal punishment after death of the wicked and those who did not believe. He too was later (but after some years) appointed to a Chair of Moral Theology and Philosophy in Cambridge.

Similar discussions have taken place in the Muslim world in the twentieth/fourteenth century over the views of such figures as Ṭāhā Ḥusain (d 1973/1393) in Egypt and Fazlur Rahman (d 1988/1408) in Pakistan. Ḥusain was a lecturer in the Department of Arabic Literature in Cairo University when he published a book on pre-Islamic poetry in 1926/1344. This caused a furore, and resulted in accusations of apostasy against the author, because in it he argued that what had traditionally been called pre-Islamic poetry was not in fact pre-Islamic at all but had rather been produced after the time of Muḥammad and the Qur'ān. This was controversial not so much because of the dating itself but because it seemed to undermine one of the traditional arguments for the divine authorship of the Qur'ān, namely its clear literary superiority to the (so-called) pre-Islamic poetry. Ḥusain was tried, and acquitted, but five years later he was dismissed from his university post by the Prime Minister. Rahman was forced to resign from his post as Director of the Central Institute of Islamic Research in Karachi in 1968/1388 as a result of the strength of public feeling against some of his views concerning the authorship of the Qur'ān, particularly the idea that the Qur'ān should be seen as being in some way a product of Muḥammad's own personality, as well as being, in its entirety, the word of God. These views had been expressed in his book *Islam*.[21]

Both the Christian and Muslim communities have thus witnessed controversy over the issue of academic freedom in the past two centuries, though the Islamic community has seen greater involvement of political authorities in those controversies.[22] Recent times have seen many other examples of sanctions being employed against dissenting views. Thus Hans Küng was deprived of official recognition as a Roman Catholic theologian in 1979/1400, and more recently, in 1994/1415 a parish priest, Anthony Freeman, was dismissed from his post in the Anglican Church in England because of his support for the "Sea of Faith" movement, which is associated with the radical Cambridge theologian, Don Cupitt. In the Muslim community dissenting voices have had their lives threatened, the most celebrated case being, of course, Salman Rushdie, and in some cases been physically attacked, for example Mushirul Hasan, a University professor in Delhi (in 1992/1413) and the Egyptian Nobel-prize-winning novelist Naguib Maḥfūẓ (in 1994/1415).

It also needs to be remembered, however, that such threats and attacks are not limited to the Muslim community for within the Christian community, on a rather different issue, the ethical one of abortion, hostility has been sufficiently strong in some parts of the world for surgeons who have carried out abortions to be murdered: this happened to Dr David Gunn in 1993/1413 and Dr John Bayard Britton in 1994/1415, both in Florida. It seems, therefore, that in the Christian community the critical analysis of religious practices and history, of theology and doctrine, and of scripture and the teaching of Jesus is generally acceptable, but questioning traditional theism (as in the "Sea of Faith" movement) or carrying out abortions are less acceptable and run the risk of certain penalties being applied. In the Islamic community, by contrast, the critical analysis of religious practices and history and of certain aspects of theology and doctrine may be acceptable, but any such analysis of the Qur'ān or of the person of Muḥammad is generally not acceptable and questioning traditional theism is hardly considered at all, so the boundaries of where academic enquiry may freely range are set differently in the two traditions. The debates continue.

Conclusion

Modernity has thus brought many challenges to both Christians and Muslims. Some of these have taken different forms for each community, so that, for example, the Muslim need to react to Western power and influence has given political questions a far greater prominence in Muslim thinking than in Christian. But issues arising from modern knowledge in different spheres confront both communities equally, and in each of them reactions to change stretch from the aggressively antagonistic to the broadly welcoming, with "fundamentalists" and liberals usually taking diametrically opposed views.

Notes

1 An appropriate analogy here may be that of a glass, 50% of which contains some substance. The optimist will probably describe it as being half full, and the pessimist as half empty. Or as a witty aphorism has it: the optimist believes that we live in the best of all possible worlds; the pessimist fears that it is so!

2 See Chapter One above for discussion of these issues.

3 See Chapter Four above for further detail of discussion of this question.

4 At the Cairo conference on world population in the autumn of 1994/1415 an interesting example of divisions on these questions transcending the boundaries of religious communities was the co-operation between the Vatican delegation and some Muslim representatives in seeking to limit the availability of contraception and to restrict the possibility of abortions being carried out.

5 See, for example, *The church and the bomb*, Hodder and Stoughton, 1982, a report of a committee of the Anglican church in England on the ethics of nuclear warfare.

6 Thus at the start of the sixth Islamic century (1105CE) many Muslims had thought of the great theologian and mystic al-Ghazālī (d1111), the author of the *iḥyā' 'ulūm al-dīn* (the revival of the religious sciences) as the *mujaddid* for the new century, and more recently at the start of the fifteenth Islamic century (1979CE) some Muslim opinion suggested that Ayatollah Khomeini should be seen as the *mujaddid*.

7 It is particularly because of the theme of renewal that comparisons are sometimes drawn between much modern Islamic thought and some prominent Christian thinking at the time of the Reformation in the sixteenth/tenth century, when a major preoccupation of thinkers such as Martin Luther and John Calvin was their conviction that the Christian church had erred during the course of its history and that the major task before them was firstly to purge it and secondly to revive it through reforming its beliefs and practices with reference to its earliest custom. G.J. Jansen's *Militant Islam*, 1979, makes particular use of the Christian Reformation as an analogy for contemporary developments in the Islamic world.

8 Maḥmūd Ṭahā was executed in 1985/1405. On Turkey see F. Ahmad *The making of modern Turkey*, Routledge, 1993, especially Chapter Four.

9 See, for example, The Fundamentalisms Project in the United States, which has so far resulted in the publication of three volumes edited by M.E. Marty and R.S. Appleby: Vol I, *Fundamentalisms observed*, University of Chicago Press, 1991, Vol II, *Fundamentalisms and society*, University of Chicago Press, 1993, and Vol III *Fundamentalisms and the state*, University of Chicago Press, 1993. For comparisons involving the three monotheistic traditions see R.T. Antoun and M.E. Hegland (eds.) *Religious resurgence – contemporary cases in Islam, Christianity and Judaism*, Syracuse U.P., 1987, L. Caplan (ed.) *Studies in religious fundamentalism*, State University of New York Press, 1987, N. Biggar et al (eds.) *Cities of gods: faith, politics and pluralism in Judaism, Christianity and Islam*, Greenwood Press, 1986, B.B. Lawrence *Defenders of God: the fundamentalist revolt against the modern age*, I.B. Tauris, 1990, and L. Kaplan *Fundamentalism in*

comparative perspective, University of Massachusetts Press, 1992; and for comparisons involving Christianity and Islam in particular see M. Riesebrodt *Pious passion: the emergence of modern fundamentalism in the United States and Iran*, University of California Press, 1993, W. Shepard "'Fundamentalism' Christian and Islamic" in *Religion*, 17 (1987), pp 355–378, with critique by B.B. Lawrence in *Religion*, 19 (1989), pp 275–280, with further contributions from each in *Religion*, 22 (1992), pp 279–283 and 284–286 respectively, and H. Zirker "Revelation in history and claims to finality: assumptions underlying fundamentalism in Christianity and Islam" in *Islam and Christian-Muslim relations*, 3 (1992), pp 211–225.

10 On the development of the term "fundamentalism" in general and on the activities of the group which sponsored the publication of "The fundamentals" in particular, see J. Barr *Fundamentalism*, 2nd ed., SCM, 1981. See also R. Gill *Competing convictions*, SCM, 1989, especially Chapters Two and Three.

11 See, for example, the works of the Egyptian scholars Ṭāhā Ḥusain (d 1973/1393), Amīn al-Khūlī (d 1966/1386), Muḥammad Abū Zaid, and Muḥammad Khalafallāh, some of whose works are discussed in A. Rippin *Muslims: their religious beliefs and practices*, Vol II, Routledge, 1993, especially in Chapter Six.

12 A very interesting example of these issues being tackled by Christians and Muslims together may be found in the report of the Muslim-Christian Research Group *The challenge of the scriptures – Bible and Qur'ān*, Orbis, Maryknoll, 1989. See Chapter Two above for further detail on questions concerning the status of the scriptures within the two traditions.

13 In modern times this more politically radical tradition, which can be traced back to Ibn Taimiyya (d 1328/728), has enjoyed something of a resurgence in many regions of the Islamic world. See E. Sivan "Ibn Taimiyya: father of the Islamic Revolution" in *Encounter*, Vol 60, No 5 (May 1983), pp 41–50. An interesting comparison could be made between the views of Ibn Taimiyya on the one hand and the views of the sixteenth/tenth century Scottish church leader, John Knox. See his *On rebellion*, (ed. R.A. Mason), Cambridge U.P., 1994.

14 Further examples of this might be the existence in both communities of groups whose names indicate that their members see themselves as somehow acting on behalf of God: thus there is a suggestive parallel between the Shī'ī group in the Lebanon, Ḥizballāh (the party of God), and the controversial Roman Catholic group Opus Dei (the work of God). Nor is it only Muslims who use the language of God concerning their actions in the political sphere, for it is only necessary to recall those Protestant paramilitary groups in Northern Ireland whose motto is "For God and Ulster" and the statement of President Bush in his State of the Union address in 1992/1412: "by the grace of God we won the Cold War". See also note 37 of Chapter Five above.

15 It is also possible, for example, to have "secular fundamentalists" in the sense of those who crusade actively for various causes in the political arena and are totally uncritical of their perspective, which is held to be self-evidently true and therefore beyond criticism. See G. D'Costa "Secular discourse and the clash of faiths: 'The Satanic Verses' in British society" in

New Blackfriars, October 1990, pp 418–432. And with reference to other religious communities, newspaper reports of Buddhist monks in Thailand taking to the streets and participating actively in anti-government demonstrations suggests that in one sense at least it is even possible to have Buddhist "fundamentalists"!

16 On the other hand, if "fundamentalism" is sometimes referred to as "the f word", in order to express distaste for it, as in a recent study-pack produced by the Student Christian Movement in Britain, liberalism is sometimes referred to as "the l word" in a similar spirit, as, for example, by President Bush in the 1992/1413 U.S. elections.

17 It is worth noting that *tawakkul*, usually translated as trust or dependence, is also extremely significant for many Sufi Muslims.

18 See respectively *Islam and modernism in Egypt*, Oxford U.P., 1933, and *Modern trends in Islam*, University of Chicago Press, 1947, especially Chapter Three. See also A.Ahmad *Islamic modernism in India and Pakistan, 1857–1964*, Oxford U.P., 1967 and A. Hourani *Arabic thought in the liberal age*, Cambridge U.P., 1983.

19 On Mawdūdī and Quṭb respectively see Chapters Five and Four of J.L. Esposito (ed.) *Voices of resurgent Islam*, Oxford U.P., 1983, and Chapters Five and Seven of A. Rahnema (ed.) *Pioneers of Islamic revival*, Zed, 1994. On the organisations with which they were linked see S.V.R. Nasr *The vanguard of the Islamic Revolution*, I.B. Tauris, 1994, and R.P. Mitchell *The society of the Muslim Brothers*, 2nd ed., Oxford U.P., 1993.

20 Others were not so lucky: the Sufi mystic al-Ḥallāj was crucified in Baghdad in 922/309 for having said "I am the truth", which was taken by his contemporaries as being a blasphemous claim, and Michael Servetus was burnt to death in Geneva in 1553/960 for attacking the doctrine of the Trinity.

21 Published by Weidenfeld and Nicolson in 1966, with a second edition published by the University of Chicago Press in 1979. For Rahman's own account of his resignation see "Some Islamic issues in the Ayyūb Khān era" in D.P. Little (ed.) *Essays on Islamic civilization presented to Niyazi Berkes*, Brill, Leiden, 1976, pp 284–302. It is important to remember the political dimension of this whole debate, especially the tension between the government and the Jamā'at-i islāmī of A.A. Mawdūdī, on which see S.V.R. Nasr *The vanguard of the Islamic revolution*, I.B. Tauris, 1994, pp 158–159 (where Nasr says that Rahman was dismissed). For a general appreciation of Rahman see the comments of F.M. Denny in "Fazlur Rahman: Muslim intellectual" in *Muslim World*, 79 (1989), pp 91–101, and "The legacy of Fazlur Rahman" in Y.Y. Haddad (ed.) *The Muslims of America*, Oxford U.P., 1991, pp 96–108.

22 It is partly for this reason that many creative Islamic thinkers have taught and published outside the Islamic world. Thus Fazlur Rahman, after leaving Pakistan, spent most of the rest of his life as Professor of Islamic Thought at the University of Chicago, and a Muslim intellectual such as Muhammad Arkoun has seen many of his works published in the West. See especially his *Rethinking Islam: common questions, uncommon answers*, Westview Press, Colorado, 1994.

CONCLUSION

Introduction

In any attempt to describe and evaluate two religious traditions, the role of converts between them, in both directions, may provide some useful insights into the nature of both. Conversion to Islam from a Christian background and to Christianity from a Muslim background are phenomena which have occurred to a different extent in different contexts of time and place, but conversion has, and does, take place in both directions, and the insights provided by such converts may provide useful material for evaluating the important features of both traditions.

Conversion between the two traditions

Two recent studies of conversion, S. Syrjänen *In search of meaning and identity*[1] and L. Poston *Islamic Da'wah in the West*[2] (especially Part IV, on conversion), look respectively at conversion to Christianity in a Pakistani context and conversion to Islam in a Western context. Syrjänen analysed 36 conversion stories which were based mainly on interviews and 3 other stories which were based on published material, without interview, and Poston looked at 72 conversion accounts, of which 12 were based on replies to a postal questionnaire and 60 were based on published accounts, found either in newsletters or in autobiographies.[3] On the basis of these admittedly small samples, the following points seem to emerge.

Firstly, an important factor in all conversion, either way, seems to have been a negative experience within the convert's original religious community. Such experiences are not difficult to come by in any religious community! But in the midst of disillusionment, an encounter with a member of a different religious community, who effectively presented the ideals of that community's message, seems to have led to an irresistible attraction to that other community. This is true even if the positive features of that message do not seem widely different to an outside observer, with converts to Christianity speaking of the attraction of the idea of the love of God and converts to Islam enthusing about the idea of the mercy of God. What probably lies behind this paradox is that for someone who has experienced a lack of love within the Christian community or a lack of mercy within the Muslim community, the other community's ideal may appear highly attractive, and a common pattern in the later experience of converts either way is a measure of disillusionment when it becomes clear that not only the community which they have left but also the community which they have joined fails to live up to its ideals, especially if the notoriously lukewarm welcome which converts sometimes receive underlines this point particularly powerfully.[4] What the converts' experience in this respect thus seems to show is the importance of seeing conversion as a social process: in other words, it is not necessarily the message itself that encourages conversion but rather the social milieu in which someone moves.[5]

Secondly many of the converts speak or write of the importance of the practical guidance offered by the faith to which they converted in persuading them to move. In particular issues of freedom and discipline occur frequently, with many of those coming from a Muslim background finding Christian freedom attractive, in the sense both of the absence of binding rules and in the sense of the freedom to question and criticise, while many of those coming to Islam speak of the attraction of its discipline and guidance, so that the fact that Islam provides a focus and framework for living, rather than needing to work everything out for oneself, was a major attraction. Several Western women in particular have stressed the importance of this factor in their decision to convert.

Thirdly a common theme in the accounts of many converts is the contrast between the spiritual and other-worldly preoccupations of the Christian faith, attractive to many converts from Islam, and the practical and this-worldly focus of Islam, which attracted disillusioned westerners who came to regard the Christian faith as too idealistic and impractical.[6] Thus the Christian message of the gift of salvation, as encapsulated in a scriptural verse such as Matthew 11:28 "Come to me all who labour and are heavy-laden and I will give you rest", pointing to salvation as a gift, proved very attractive to converts to the Christian faith, whereas Poston states that the five most attractive features of Islam for the converts he investigated were its simplicity (mentioned by 20%), its rationality (21%), its stress on the brotherhood of man (19%), its this-worldly focus (19%), and its lack of a priesthood or medial agent (10%).[7]

There are a number of other interesting contrasts between the two groups of converts as well. For example with respect to the age at which people converted almost two thirds (23 out of 36) who converted to the Christian faith did so between the ages of 16 and 25, whereas the average age at which those who converted to Islam did so was 31.4. With respect to the mechanics of the conversions almost a half of those who joined the Christian community (15 out of 36) referred to some kind of supernatural event, a dream, a vision, or hearing a voice, as having an important role in their conversion, whereas only 3 of the 72 western converts to Islam made any reference to such an experience, with 2 mentioning a dream and 1 a vision. And in describing their conversions there is tendency for converts from Islam to describe their conversion as being a rather sudden event, whereas converts to Islam see it rather as a process, speaking of it in such terms as "slipping effortlessly" into Islam, through some kind of gradual transition.

What the converts reacted against, it might therefore be said, was respectively legalism and apparent neglect of the spiritual arena on the one hand, and antinomianism and neglect of the affairs of this world on the other, and what they found was respectively spiritual release and practical guidance.[8] The accounts of these converts thus help us to locate some of the key differences in emphasis between Christianity and Islam. As a summary, we could therefore do a lot worse than to refer to the old statement of the Dutch phenomenologist of religion G. Van Der Leeuw, who described Islam as a religion of majesty and humility, and Christianity as a religion of love.[9] Perhaps, though, in the light of more recent trends in the two communities, one additional element should be added to that analysis, namely that in today's terms at least, in some areas such as that of morality and the question of the relationship between religion and the state, Islam as a whole may simply be more "right-wing" than Christianity.[10]

How to picture the relationship between the two traditions

One thing which should have become clear to a reader of earlier chapters of this book is that within both the Christian and the Muslim communities there is a considerable spectrum of opinion on most issues. On some issues, indeed, the bewildering variety of opinion within each community has given rise to the suggestion that perhaps we should no longer speak of Islam and Christianity but rather of Islams and of

Christianities.[11] Each faith may therefore be represented diagrammatically as a spectrum:

[---------------]

Thus, in the Christian community, a wide range of opinion may be found on the following issues, to name only a few: about scripture (dictated by God or involving a measure of human participation in its composition through the personality of the author), the value to be attached to other sources of knowledge such as the philosophical (useful and beneficial, and therefore to be keenly studied, or of little or no value, and therefore to be keenly distrusted or utterly avoided), the position of women in society (full public participation, even to the extent of holding official religious office, or separate and distinct role, especially in the domestic sphere), the question of religion and the state (as close a relationship as possible desirable or the evolution of clear separation between the two spheres), or approaches to the contemporary issues facing members of the community ("back to" the foundations of the faith or "on from" those foundations to respond positively to new thinking and new discoveries). A wide range of opinion may also be found with reference to even more fundamental questions such as the nature of God (sovereign and utterly transcendent, hardly knowable in a personal way (as in some forms of high Calvinism), or immanent, personally knowable, and intimately involved with human beings and in the affairs of the world (as in some forms of Evangelicalism and Pentecostalism)), and the person of Jesus (uncreated cosmic Christ, with a central role in the creation of the whole universe, or wise prophetic teacher, sharing human limitations to the full).

Within the Muslim community, a similar range of opinion may also then be found as follows: is the Qur'ān uncreated and dictated by God or does its composition involve a measure of human participation through the personality of the prophet Muḥammad? What is the value to be attached to other sources of knowledge such as the philosophical? Are they useful and beneficial, and therefore to be keenly studied, or of little or no value, and therefore to be distrusted or avoided? What about the position of women in society: are they to be allowed full public participation, even to the extent of holding official religious office, or should they rather have a separate and distinct role, especially in the domestic sphere? On the question of religion and the state, should the relationship between them be as close as possible, leading to the formation of Islamic states, or alternatively is the evolution of clear separation between the two spheres preferable? And what about the question of how the Muslim community should respond to the contemporary issues facing its members? Should the aim be to get "back to" the foundations of the faith, or rather to go "on from" those foundations to respond positively to new thinking and new discoveries? With reference to even more fundamental questions, too, a range of opinion may be discerned: is God essentially utterly transcendent and great, hardly knowable in a personal way, or is God rather immanent, "closer to human beings than their jugular veins" (Qur'ān 50:16), and intimately involved with human beings and in the affairs of the world? And is Muḥammad an ordinary human prophet and messenger, or rather the pre-existent perfect man, sinless and emanation of the divine light? Within each faith, then, a spectrum of opinion may be found.

If we turn now to the question of the relationship between the two faiths, the suggestion may be made that each faith may be represented as a spectrum on one diagram.

```
Christian faith     [--------------]
                                        [--------------]     Muslim faith
```

The further suggestion may then be made that at least to some extent the two spectrums cross, to represent an area of common ground between at least some members of each community.

```
Christian faith               [--------------]
                                        [--------------]     Muslim faith
```

The more difficult question, however, is to what extent do the two spectrums cross? Are the two spectrums basically distinct but nevertheless cross to a very small extent?

```
Christian faith            [--------------]
                                         [--------------]    Muslim faith
```

Or do they basically cover much the same range of opinion with only small differences of emphasis, so that the spectrums should be drawn with only a small range which does not overlap?

```
Christian faith                [--------------]
                                 [--------------]            Muslim faith
```

Or is the position somewhere between these two extremes?

```
Christian faith               [--------------]
                                        [--------------]     Muslim faith[12]
```

In practice different diagrams will probably need to be drawn with respect to different issues, and there will be variation between different geographical areas and different historical periods, as well as with reference to individual Christian or Muslim thinkers. For example, on the question of human nature, some Christians at some stages of Christian history have overwhelmingly emphasised humankind's fallenness because of "original sin", while at other stages an emphasis on the creation of humankind in the image of God has given rise to a more optimistic assessment of human value and potential. Muslim opinion over time has been similarly divided, with Sufis and philosophers generally accepting that humankind is in God's form or image but the main body of theological opinion rejecting that view.[13] When the spectrums representing opinion in the two faiths on this question are put together, therefore, it would certainly quickly become clear that the central points of each spectrum would not match precisely: the central point of the Christian spectrum, that is the opinion which has been most widely-accepted over the centuries, would lay more emphasis on a pessimistic, fallen, view of human nature, whereas the central point of the Muslim spectrum would testify to a more optimistic view of human nature. It would be very difficult, however, to deny altogether that on this issue there is at least some common ground between some Christians and some Muslims, and a similar situation exists with reference to most other issues.[14]

In each tradition, of course, some issues are more important than others: in each there are certain points which are shared by almost all members of the community, and these should be seen as being central to the faith and thus what might be called core convictions, and then around and on the basis of these essential affirmations other beliefs and other practices have developed in each tradition, but these are relatively less significant and should therefore be seen as secondary issues. The model of the two spectrums works with respect to most of these secondary issues and a great many of the core convictions too, not least the nature of God, since both the Christian and Muslim faiths insist on the centrality and importance of the worship of the one true God (even if Christians and Muslims then differ over how that one true God is described). With respect to some other areas, however, the affirmations which serve as the central focus of each faith are, surely, the significance of the person of Jesus and of the Christian scriptures for Christians and the significance of the message of the Qur'ān and the person of Muḥammad for Muslims,[15] and on these questions the model of the two spectrums works less well.

It is true that in recent years the re-examination by Muslims of the traditionally negative Muslim views of Christian convictions about Jesus and the New Testament and Christian re-evaluation of the traditionally negative Christian views of Muḥammad and the Qur'ān have led to some convergence even on these questions: thus a Christian who is prepared to affirm Muḥammad as a prophet may come close to sharing the opinion of a Muslim who sees Muḥammad as a mortal being who simply brought a message, rather than a pre-existent being of any kind, and a Muslim who attributes positive significance to the person as well as the message of Jesus may come close to the view of a Christian who stresses the full humanity of Jesus, rather than his identity as the cosmic Christ, but even in these cases the spectrums are probably only just beginning to cross. At the end of our review of the two faiths, therefore, these are the two fundamental options which need to be considered – the person of Jesus and the Christian scriptures on the one hand, and the message of the Qur'ān and the person of Muḥammad on the other – and we are therefore ultimately confronted with the need to make a choice. The question which remains before us at the end of our review of the two faiths is thus very simple yet also very complex: which of these two should be seen and accepted as supreme exemplar and source of guidance?[16]

Notes

1 Subtitled "Conversion to Christianity in Pakistani Muslim culture" and published by the Finnish Society for Missiology and Ecumenics, Helsinki, 1984.

2 Subtitled "Muslim missionary activity and the dynamics of conversion to Islam" and published by Oxford University Press, 1992.

3 In more detail, 34 of Syrjänen's interviewees were male and 2 female, 35 from a Sunnī background and 1 from a Shi'ī background; they came from different provinces of Pakistan, and all had converted to Protestant Christianity. Of the converts investigated by Poston, 50 were male and 22 female; they included 34 Americans and 38 Europeans, of whom 22 were British; they came from different religious backgrounds, with 41 mentioning a Christian background (10 Roman Catholic, 8 Protestant and 23 unspecific), 5 a Jewish background, 1 a Hindu, 2 agnostic and 23 unspecific, and there is no indication in Poston's analysis of which part of the Muslim community they have joined.

4 Only 3 of the 36 converts interviewed by Syrjänen felt that they had been warmly received within the Christian community, with the majority quickly proceeding to make unfavourable comparisons between the Christian and Muslim communities, and a number of them therefore found it necessary to experiment with a number of different Christian denominations before becoming settled as a member of the Christian community.

5 A recent anthropological study of conversion to Christianity in a wider context makes this point very powerfully: see R.W. Hefner (ed) *Conversion*

to Christianity: historical and anthropological perspectives on a great transformation, University of California Press, 1993.

6 This is reminiscent of one of the clearest simple outlines of the essential differences between the Christian and Muslim faiths as given by S.H. Nasr in his *Ideals and realities of Islam*, 2nd ed., George Allen and Unwin, 1975, pp 21–22, namely that Christianity is a religion of mystery, whereas Islam is a simple religion.

7 As an illustration of the partial understanding of their new faith exhibited by some new converts, one European convert to Islam discussed by Poston described how "the concept of human brotherhood under the all-encompassing *fatherhood* of God is much stressed in Islam", which is not language traditionally used of God in Islam, and is also the main reason for one of the individuals discussed by Syrjänen choosing to convert to Christianity! See Bilquis Sheikh *I dared to call him father*, Kingsway, 1978.

8 It is worth adding that similar things have been said by some who have converted within the two traditions, that is from one variant to another, such as from Roman Catholicism to Protestantism or vice versa. Recent examples of this intra-Christian conversion include a number of liberal Roman Catholics such as the American theologian Matthew Fox, a pioneer of theological interest in ecological questions and creation spirituality, and a Belgian Professor of the Sociology of Religion, Karel Dobbelaere, who was angered by the Papal veto of further discussion of the ordination of women; they converted to Anglicanism, while several traditionalist Anglicans, such as the former Bishop of London, Graham Leonard, and the Duchess of Kent, who were unhappy about the Church of England ordaining women and other recent developments in Anglicanism, have joined the Roman Catholic church. Some intra-Muslim conversion does also take place: see, for example, Muḥammad al-Tijānī al-Samāwī *Then I was guided*, Ansariyan Publications, Qum, Iran, where the Tunisian author explains how he found enlightenment in Shī'ī Islam.

9 See his *Religion in essence and manifestation*, George Allen and Unwin, 1938, Chapters Ninety-nine and One hundred.

10 One of the individuals referred to by Syrjänen, Daud Rahbar, draws a contrast between the Christian and Muslim traditions in terms of the difference between unconditional and conditional divine love: "unqualified divine love for mankind is an idea completely alien to the Qur'ān. In fact 'to love' is too strong a phrase to convey the idea . . ." See his *God of justice*, Brill, Leiden, 1960, especially Book IV, and his autobiography *Memories and meanings*, privately published in 1985.

11 See especially Chapter Six on this theme.

12 Another way of representing this diagrammatically would be to use a circle to represent each faith, since within a circle a number of different positions or views are possible. The question would then concern what happens when the two circles representing the two faiths are put alongside each other: is only a small area of overlap held in common between them? Or, by contrast, do the two circles more or less coincide, with only a small area of each remaining outside the area of common ground? Or is the position somewhere between these two extremes?

13 See W.M. Watt "Created in his image: a study in Islamic theology" in *Early Islam*, Edinburgh U.P., 1990, pp 94–100.

14 It is this fact which has made possible, for example, co-operation between some Christians and some Muslims over the issues raised by the United Nations Population Conference in Cairo in late 1994.

15 The order in which these features are listed is, of course, extremely significant. See the Conclusion of Chapter Two above.

16 This is the choice often outlined by perceptive Roman Catholic theologians. See, for example, T. Michel "The fundamental option of Jesus or Muḥammad" in *Salaam*, New Delhi, 10 (1989), pp 71–74, and the report of a group of Jesuit Islamic scholars "Food for thought" in *Salaam*, 10 (1989), pp 139–144.

BIBLIOGRAPHY

The works listed here include both some of those which have been referred to in the main part of the book and those which are useful for further reading on particular subjects.

Introduction

a) Examples of the approach which will be adopted

Geertz, C., "Religion as a cultural system" in *The interpretation of cultures*, Basic Books, New York, 1973, pp 87–125.

Smart, N., *The world's religions*, Cambridge U.P., 1989. [An example of the general approach adopted in this book, applied to all of the major religious traditions of the world.]

Smith, W.C., *The meaning and end of religion*, 2nd ed., SPCK, 1978. [A classic examination of change and development in different religious traditions.]

b) Introductory studies of the Christian faith

Carmody, D.L., and J.T., *Christianity: an introduction*, 3rd ed., Wadsworth, Belmont (California), 1995. [An accessible general introduction to the Christian faith.]

Mackenzie, P., *The Christians: their practices and beliefs*, SPCK, 1988. [One of the few publications which explicitly attempts to apply the phenomenological approach of Friedrich Heiler to the Christian faith.]

Nineham, D., *Christianity mediaeval and modern: a study in religious change*, SCM, 1993. [A work which graphically illustrates the extent to which Christian understanding has changed between the medieval and modern periods.]

c) Introductory studies of the Muslim faith

Esposito, J.L., *Islam – the straight path*, 2nd ed., Oxford U.P., 1991. [An accessible general introduction to the Muslim faith.]

Nasr, S.H., *Ideals and realities of Islam*, 2nd ed., George Allen and Unwin, 1975. [A Muslim account of the main themes of Islamic faith and practice.]

Schimmel, A., *Deciphering the signs of God: a phenomenological approach to Islam*, Edinburgh U.P., 1994. [Based on the 1992 Gifford lectures in Edinburgh, this work applies Heiler's phenomenological approach to Islam.]

d) A useful anthology of Jewish, Christian and Muslim sources

Peters, F.E., *Judaism, Christianity and Islam: the classical texts and their interpretation*, 3 Vols, Princeton U.P., 1990.

Chapter 1: Origins

a) Christian origins

Bornkamm, G., *Jesus of Nazareth*, 2nd ed., Hodder and Stoughton, 1973.
Rowland, C., *Christian origins*, SPCK, 1985.
Sanders, E.P., *The historical figure of Jesus*, Allen Lane, 1993.
—— *Paul*, Oxford U.P., 1991.
Theissen, G., *In the footsteps of the Galilean*, SCM, 1987.

b) The establishment of the Muslim community

Cook, M.A., *Muhammad*, Oxford U.P., 1983.
Gabrieli, F., *Muhammad and the conquests of Islam*, Weidenfeld and Nicolson, 1968.
Lings, M., *Muhammad: his life based on the earliest sources*, Unwin, 1983.
Rodinson, M., *Mohammed*, Penguin, 1971.
Watt, W.M., *Muhammad: prophet and statesman*, Oxford U.P., 1961.

Chapter 2: Scriptures

a) Introductory works on the Bible

Coggins, R., *Introducing the Old Testament*, Oxford U.P., 1990.
Court, J.M. and K.M., *The New Testament world*, Cambridge U.P., 1990.
Dunn, J.D.G., *Unity and diversity in the New Testament*, 2nd ed., SCM, 1990.
Rogerson, J., and Davies, P., *The Old Testament world*, Cambridge U.P., 1989.

b) Introductory works on the Qur'ān

Cragg, K., *Readings in the Qur'ān*, Collins, 1988.
Rahman, F., *Major themes in the Qur'ān*, Bibliotheca Islamica, Chicago, 1980.
Sherif, F., *A guide to the contents of the Qur'ān*, Ithaca Press, 1985.
Watt, W.M., *Introduction to the Qur'ān*, Edinburgh U.P., 1970.

c) Comparative works

Bruce, F.F., and Rupp, E.G., (eds.), *Holy book and holy tradition*, Manchester U.P., 1968.

Denny, F.M., and Taylor, R.L., (eds.) *Holy book in comparative perspective*, University of South Carolina Press, 1985.
Muslim-Christian Research Group, *The challenge of the scriptures*, Orbis, Maryknoll, 1989.

Chapter 3: the development of religious thought

a) Early Christian thought

Brox, M., *A history of the early church*, SPCK, 1994.
Chadwick, H., *The early church*, Penguin, 1967.
—— *Christianity and the classical tradition*, Oxford U.P., 1966.
Hall, S.G., *Doctrine and practice in the early church*, SPCK, 1991.
Young, F., *From Nicaea to Chalcedon*, SCM, 1983.
—— *The making of the creeds*, SCM, 1991.

b) Early Muslim thought

Fakhry, M., *A history of Islamic philosophy*, 2nd ed., Longmans, 1983.
Goldziher, I., *Introduction to Islamic theology and law*, Princeton U.P., 1981.
Macdonald, D.B., *The development of Muslim theology, jurisprudence and constitutional theory*, Russell and Russell, New York, 1903.
Rosenthal, F., *The classical heritage in Islam*, Routledge and Kegan Paul, 1975.
Watt, W.M., *Islamic philosophy and theology*, 2nd ed., Edinburgh U.P., 1985.
—— *The formative period of Islamic thought*, Edinburgh U.P., 1973.

Chapter 4: Law and ethics

a) Islamic Law

Burton, J., *An introduction to the Hadith*, Edinburgh U.P., 1994.
Coulson, N., *A history of Islamic law*, Edinburgh U.P., 1964.
Fakhry, M., *Ethical theories in Islam*, Brill, Leiden, 1991.
Kamali, M.H., *Principles of Islamic jurisprudence*, 2nd ed., Islamic Texts Society, Cambridge, 1991.
Siddiqi, M.Z., *Ḥadīth literature: its origin, development and special features*, Islamic Texts Society, Cambridge, 1993.

b) Christian Ethics

Baelz, P., *Ethics and belief*, Sheldon Press, 1977.
Gill, R., *A textbook of Christian ethics*, T and T Clark, 1985.
Ramsey, P., *Basic Christian ethics*, SCM, 1950.
Waddams, H., *A new introduction to moral theology*, 3rd ed., SCM, 1972.
Wogaman, J.P., *Christian ethics: a historical introduction*, SPCK, 1993.

c) The position of women

al-Hibri, A., (ed.), *Women and Islam*, Pergamon Press, 1982.
Hampson, D., *Theology and feminism*, Blackwell, 1990.
Loades, A., (ed.), *Feminist theology: a reader*, SPCK, 1990.
Mernissi, F., *Women and Islam: an historical and theological enquiry*, Blackwell, 1991.

Chapter 5: Worship and spirituality

a) Christian worship and spirituality

Dupré, L., et al., (eds.), *Christian spirituality*, Vol III (Post-Reformation and modern), SCM, 1990.
Jones, C., Wainwright, G., and Yarnold, E., (eds.), *The study of liturgy*, 2nd ed., SPCK, 1992.
—— *The study of spirituality*, SPCK, 1986.
Louth, A., *The origins of the Christian mystical tradition*, Oxford U.P., 1983.
McGinn, B., and Meyendorff, J., (eds.), *Christian spirituality*, Vol I (Origins to twelfth century), SCM, 1989.
Raitt, J., and Meyendorff, J., (eds.), *Christian spirituality*, Vol II (High Middle Ages and Reformation), SCM, 1989.

b) Muslim worship and spirituality

al-Ghazali, *Inner dimensions of Islamic worship*, Islamic Foundation, Leicester, 1983.
—— *The ninety-nine beautiful names of God*, Islamic Texts Society, Cambridge, 1992.
Nasr, S.H., (ed.), *Islamic spirituality*, Vol I (Foundations), SCM, 1989, and Vol II (Manifestations), SCM, 1991.
Schimmel, A., *Mystical dimensions of Islam*, University of North Carolina Press, 1975.
von Grunebaum, G.E., *Muhammadan Festivals*, Curzon Press, 1976.

Chapter 6: Unity and diversity

a) The Islamic community

Deftary, F., *The Isma'ilis: their history and doctrines*, Cambridge U.P., 1990.
Halm, H., *Shiism*, Edinburgh U.P., 1991.
Metcalf, B., *Islamic revival in British India: Deoband 1860–1900*, Princeton U.P., 1982.
Momen, M., *An introduction to Shi'i Islam*, Yale U.P., 1985.
Richard, Y., *Shi'ite Islam*, Blackwell, 1995.
Sachedina, A.A., *Islamic messianism: the idea of the Mahdi in Twelver Shi'ism*, State University of New York Press, 1981.

b) The Christian community

Atiya, A.S., *A history of Eastern Christianity*, Methuen, 1968. [Covers the non-Chalcedonian Orthodox churches.]
Chadwick, O., *The Reformation*, 3rd ed., Penguin, 1975.
Davies, R.E., *Methodism*, Penguin, 1963.
Hollenwegger, W., *The Pentecostals*, SCM, 1972.
Runciman, S., *The Eastern Schism*, Oxford U.P., 1955.
Ware, K., *The Orthodox Church*, Penguin, 1963. [Covers the Chalcedonian Orthodox churches.]

c) Ecumenism

Enayat, H., *Modern Islamic political thought*, Macmillan, 1982.
Rouse, R., and Neill, S.C., (eds.), *A history of the Ecumenical Movement 1517–1948*, SPCK, 1954.

Chapter 7: Spread and history

a) The spread of Islam in history

Hodgson, M.G.S., *The venture of Islam*, 3 Vols, University of Chicago Press, 1974.
Holt, P.M., Lambton, A.K.S., and Lewis, B., (eds.), *The Cambridge history of Islam*, 2 Vols, Cambridge U.P., 1970.
Hourani, A.H., *A history of the Arab peoples*, Faber, 1991.
Lapidus, I.M., *A history of Islamic societies*, Cambridge U.P., 1988.
Robinson, F., *Atlas of the Islamic world since 1500*, Phaidon, 1982.

b) The spread of Christianity in history

Chadwick. H., and Evans, G.R., *Atlas of the Christian church*, Macmillan, 1987.
Johnson, P., *A history of Christianity*, Weidenfeld and Nicolson, 1976.
Latourette, K.S., *A history of Christianity*, Eyre and Spottiswoode, 1954.
McManners, J., (ed.), *The Oxford history of Christianity*, Oxford U.P., 1993.
Neill, S.C., *A history of Christian missions*, Penguin, 1964.
Yates, T., *Christian mission in the twentieth century*, Cambridge U.P., 1994.

c) The treatment of subject peoples and minorities

Parkes, J., *The conflict of the church and the synagogue*, Meridian Books, New York, 1961.
Tritton, A.S., *The caliphs and their non-Muslim subjects*, Cass, 1970.

Chapter 8: Modern developments

a) Modern Islamic thought

Ahmad, A., *Islamic modernism in India and Pakistan, 1857–1964*, Oxford U.P., 1967.

Arkoun, M., *Rethinking Islam: common questions, uncommon answers*, Westview Press, Colorado, 1994.
Cragg, K., *Counsels in contemporary Islam*, Edinburgh U.P., 1965.
Esposito, J.L., *The Islamic threat – myth or reality?*, Oxford U.P., 1992.
—— (ed.), *Voices of resurgent Islam*, Oxford U.P., 1983.
Hourani, A.H., *Arabic thought in the liberal age*, Cambridge U.P., 1983.
Mortimer, E., *Faith and power: the politics of Islam*, Faber, 1982.
Nasr, S.H., *Traditional Islam in the modern world*, Kegan Paul International, 1987.
Rahman, F., *Islam and modernity: transformation of an intellectual tradition*, University of Chicago Press, 1982.
Rahnema, A., (ed.), *Pioneers of Islamic revival*, Zed, 1994.
Rippin, A., *Muslims: their religious beliefs and practices*, Vol II (the contemporary period), Routledge, 1993.
Smith, W.C., *Islam in modern history*, Princeton U.P., 1957.
Voll, J.O., *Islam: continuity and change in the modern world*, Longmans, 1982.

b) Modern Christian thought

Barr, J., *Fundamentalism*, 2nd ed., SCM, 1981.
—— *Escaping from fundamentalism*, SCM, 1984.
Chadwick, O., *The Christian church in the Cold War*, Penguin, 1993.
Ford, D., (ed.), *The modern theologians: an introduction to Christian theology in the twentieth century*, 2 Vols, Blackwell, 1989.
Heron, A., *A century of Protestant theology*, Lutterworth, 1980.
Macquarrie, J., *Twentieth century religious thought*, 4th ed., SCM, 1988.
Peacocke, A., *Theology for a scientific age*, 2nd ed., SCM, 1993.
Smart, N., Clayton, J., Sherry, P., and Katz, S.T., (eds.) *Nineteenth century religious thought in the West*, 3 Vols, Cambridge U.P., 1985.
Tinsley., E.J., (ed.), *Modern Theology*, Epworth, 1973.
Vidler, A., *The church in an age of revolution*, Penguin, 1961.

[For comparative studies on "fundamentalism", see note 9 of Chapter Eight above.]

Conclusion

a) Conversion between the two traditions

Hefner, R.W., (ed.), *Conversion to Christianity: historical and anthropological perspectives on a great transformation*, University of California Press, 1993.
Levtzion, N., (ed.), *Conversion to Islam*, Holmes and Meier, New York, 1979.
Poston, L., *Islamic da'wah in the West: Muslim missionary activity and the dynamics of conversion to Islam*, Oxford U.P., 1992.
Syrjänen, S., *In search of meaning and identity: conversion to Christianity in Pakistani Muslim culture*, Finnish Society for Missiology and Ecumenics, Helsinki, 1984.

b) How to picture the relationship between the two traditions

i) Christian perspectives

Adams, C.J., "Islam and Christianity: the opposition of similarities" in Savory, R.M., and Agius, D.A., (eds.), *Logos Islamikos: studia Islamica in honorem Georgii Michaelis Wickens*, Pontifical Institute of Medieval Studies, Toronto, 1984, pp 287–306.

Cragg, A.K., "Being Christian and being Muslim" in *Religion*, 10 (1980), pp 196–207.

Hodgson, M.G.S., "A comparison of Islam and Christianity as framework for religious life" in *Diogenes*, Spring 1960, pp 49–74.

Paret, R., "Islam and Christianity" in *Islamic Studies*, 3 (1964), pp 83–95.

Smith, W.C., "Some similarities and some differences between Christianity and Islam" in *On understanding Islam*, Mouton, The Hague, pp 233–246.

Watt, W.M., *Islam and Christianity today*, Routledge and Kegan Paul, 1983.

ii) Muslim perspectives

Anees, M.A., Abedin, S.Z., and Sardar, Z., *Christian-Muslim relations – yesterday, today, tomorrow*, Grey Seal, 1991.

Askari, H., "The dialogical relationship between Christianity and Islam" in *Spiritual quest: an inter-religious dimension*, Seven Mirrors, Leeds, 1991, pp 80–88.

Ayoub, M.M., "Islam and Christianity between tolerance and acceptance" in *Islam and Christian-Muslim relations*, 2 (1991), pp 171–181.

Ghrab, S., "Islam and Christianity: from opposition to dialogue" in *Islamochristiana*, 13 (1987), pp 99–111.

Talbi, M., "Islam and dialogue: some reflections on a current topic" in Rousseau, R.W., (ed.), *Christianity and Islam: the struggling dialogue*, Ridge Row Press, Pennsylvania, 1985, pp 53–75.

Vahiduddin, S., "Islam and diversity of religion" in *Islam and Christian-Muslim relations*, 1 (1990), pp 3–11.

INDEX

The main entry for individual topics is given in bold.

'Abbāsid dynasty 59–60, 68, 69, 117, 128
'Abd al-Jabbār 63, 66
'Abd al-Malik 37
'Abd al-Nāṣir, Gamāl 3
'Abd al-Rāziq, 'Alī 153
'Abduh, Muḥammad 160
Abedin, S.Z. 144, 183
Aberdeen 162
Abortion 151, 163, 164
Abraham 88, 94
Abū Bakr 27, 37, 56, 126, 156
Abū Zaid, Muḥammad 165
Acts, Book of 35, 53, 132, 136
Adam 89
Adams, C.C. 160
Adams, C.J. 183
Adultery 21
Aelius Gallus 24
Afghanistan 12, 129, 148, 156, 157
Africa 111, 118, 125, 128, 129, 131, 137, 143
Agha Khan 122
Agius, D.A. 183
Agra 7
Ahl-i-Ḥadīth 106–107
Ahmad, A. 166, 181
Ahmad, Barakat 12
Ahmad, F. 164
Aḥmad, Ghulām 109
Aḥmad ibn Ḥanbal 59, 60, 61
Aḥmadiyya 6–7, 109, 116
Ahmed, Akbar S. 12, 144
'Ā'isha 76
Akhtar, Shabbir 7, 13
al-Afghānī, Jamāl al-dīn 118, 151, 153
al-Ash'arī 58, 65
al-Assad, Hafiz 122
Alawīs 108–109, 122
al-Bannā', Ḥasan 107
al-Bukhārī 69
Alcohol 79, 143
al-Darāzī 108
Alexander the Great 50
Alexandria 42, 51, 63, 100, 110
Algeria 157
al-Ghazālī 61, 62, 164, 180
al-Ḥākim 108
al-Ḥallāj 91, 100, 166
al-Hibri, A. 180
al-Ḥusain 105, 121
'Alī 56–57, 64, 103, 108, 121
al-Khūlī, Amīn 165
Allāh [See also Monotheism, Islamic] 25, 26
Allāt 24, 25
al-Mahdī 107
al-Ma'mūn 60
Almohad dynasty 145
Almond, H.J. 101
Almoravid dynasty 145
Almsgiving [See Giving]
al-Nāshi', 'Alī 65
al-Samāwī, Muḥammad al-Tijānī 174
al-Shāfi'ī 70
al-'Uzzā 24, 25

Ambrose 73, 74
American Revolution [See also Declaration of Independence] 150
Amos 36
Anawati, G.C. 122
Andalucia 138, 144
Anderson, G.W. 45
Anees, M.A. 183
Anglican Christians 14, 30, 79, 81, 82, 115, 150, 163, 164, 174
Anthony 123
Antinomianism 72, 169
Antioch 30, 63, 110
Antoun, R.T. 101, 164
Apocalyptic 19, 28, 31, 35, 36
Apocrypha/Deutero-canonical books 35, 45, 99, 123
Apollinarius 52
Apostasy 126, 161, 162
Appleby, R.S. 164
Approach adopted in this book **9–11**
Arabia 24–25, 27, 28, 29, 67, 89, 106, 126, 128, 139–140
Arabic language 34, 37, 43, 87
Arabic literature 155, 162
Arab world 129, 130, 131
Arafat, Walid 12
Aramaic language 42
Arberry, A.J. 46, 47, 100
Aristotle 54, 73
Arius 52
Arkoun, Muhammad 166, 182
Armenia 112, 134
Arminians 65
Asia 111, 118, 134, 135, 137, 143
Asia Minor 129, 130, 131, 143
'Āṣim 38
Askari, H. 47, 183
Assassins 122
Athanasius 39
Athens 55, 65, 132
Atiya, A.S. 181
Attributes of God 58–59, 119
Augustine of Canterbury 134
Augustine of Hippo 59, 64, 80–81, 141
Australia 82
Authority [See also Leadership] 112–113, 114, 119, 123
Autobiography, spiritual [See Experience, personal]
Averroes [See Ibn Rushd]
Avicenna [See Ibn Sīnā]
Avignon 117, 123
Ayatollah [Shī'ī leader] 104
Ayoub, M.M. 101, 121, 183

Ba'ath party 96
Babylon 84
Babylonia 39
Baelz, P. 179
Baghdad 65, 68, 76, 101, 117, 129, 166
Bahā'īs 6–7, 109, 116
Bahā'ullāh 109
Balkans 129, 131, 134, 143
Bangladesh 129
Baptism 19, 102, 115, 126, 133
Baptists 115
Barelvi movement 107
Barr, James 41, 46, 165, 182
Barth, Karl 160
Barthold, V.V. 143
Barton, John 46
Bayfield, Tony 80
Ben Asher 39
Ben Sirach [See Ecclesiasticus]
Benedict 113
Benedictine order 113
Bennett, Clinton 143
Bethge, Eberhard 96, 101
Bethlehem 19
Bhutto, Benazir 77, 82
Bible [See also Old Testament, New Testament, titles of individual books] 28, **33–44**, 45, 83, 86, 112, 162
  Authorised Version of 46
  Canon of 38–39, 42, 45, 123
  Cartoon version of 47
  Comparison with Qur'ān 29, 40, 43–44
  Compilation and editing **36–40**, 45, 46
  Computerisation of text 42
  Contents and form **33–36**
  Dictated by God? 41, 46, 154, 170
  "External validation of" 41, 46–47

Hebrew script of 38–39
Infallibility of 41, 154, 158
Interpretation of 75, 77, 115, 141, 149, 155
Languages of 35, 42, 45, 47, 50
Later developments in understanding **40–43**
Literary genres of 36
Manuscripts of 40, 46
Methods of study of 43, 90, 147, 155, 157–158, 159, 160, 162, 163
Oral transmission of 38, 39
Order/arrangement of 36, 39
Role in Christian faith 44, 155
Translation of 42–43, 47, 99
Genesis 5:24 51
Exodus 20:1–17 71
Deuteronomy 5:1–21 71
1 Samuel 16:7 80
Isaiah 44:6 99
Joel 2:13 80
Tobit 1:3 99
Tobit 4:10–11, 16 99
Tobit 12:8–9 99
Matthew 5–7 [See Sermon on the Mount]
Matthew 5:21–22 21
Matthew 5:27–28 21
Matthew 5:44 141
Matthew 11:28 168
Matthew 15:19–20 73
Matthew 21:12–13 84
Matthew 22:15–22 21
Matthew 26:47–67 21
Mark 14:43–65 21
Luke 2:41–52 19
Luke 4:16–21 84
Luke 13:10–17 20
Luke 14:1–6 20
Luke 14:23 141
Luke 19:45–46 84
Luke 22:47–71 21
John 8:1–11 21
John 18:1–24 21
Acts 2:1–13 53, 86
Acts 2:42 99
Acts 3:1 99
Acts 9:1–19 23
Acts 11:26 30
Acts 14:1 99
Acts 15 23
Acts 17:16–34 143
Acts 22:6–15 23
Acts 25:1–12 80
Acts 26:12–18 23
Romans 9–11 65
1 Corinthians 10:16 86
1 Corinthians 11:3 75
1 Corinthians 11:10 75
1 Corinthians 13:13 73
1 Corinthians 14:34 75
Galatians 3:28 75
Galatians 5:22–23 73
Ephesians 5:21–24 75
Ephesians 6:10–20 102
1 Timothy 2:9–12 75
Revelation 14:6 42–43
Biggar, N. 164
Black Sea 134
Boethius 55
Bohemia 112
Bohora community 122
Bonaparte, Napoleon 148
Bonhoeffer, Dietrich 95–98, 101
Boniface 134
Bornkamm, G. 178
Bosnia 4, 12, 77, 138, 141–142, 144
Bosworth, C.E. 143
Bowker, John 14, 98, 101, 121, 123
Bradford 119
Britain, Muslims in 3–4, 118–119, 124, 131
British Library 46
Britton, John Bayard 163
Brockington, John 14
Brox, M. 64, 179
Bruce, F.F. 46, 178
Brunner, Emil 160
Bucaille, Maurice 41–42, 47
Buddhism 91, 166
Bulliet, R.W. 144
Burton, John 46, 179
Bush, George 165, 166
Byzantine Empire 111, 112, 126, 129, 133, 134, 138

Cahen, Claude 143
Cairo 7, 117, 162, 164, 175

Calendar, Christian xi, 12–13, 19, 30, 66, 89, 144
Calendar, Muslim xi, 12–13, 26, 30, 66, 89, 122–123, 144
Caliph 64, 68, 70, 78–79, 117, 122, 125, 126, 129
Caliphs, rightly-guided 156, 158
Calvin, John 114, 164
Calvinists 65, 114, 170
Cambridge 162, 163
Canon law 74, 81
Canterbury 39
Caplan, L. 164
Carmody, D.L. and J.T. 177
Catherine of Genoa 91
Catholic Encylcopaedia 100
Central Asia 127, 128, 129, 131, 143
Central Institute of Islamic Research 162
Chadwick, Henry 64, 179, 181
Chadwick, Owen 81, 143, 181, 182
Change 13, 63, 161
Charlemagne 126, 133
Chicago 166
China 111, 127, 134, 135
Ching, Julia 14
Christian community, boundaries of 49, 53, 62, 64–65, 78, 116, 155, 158
Christian origins **17–23**, 27–29, 71, 156
Christian Scientists 116
Christian Socialism 150
Christian thought, early [See also Christology, Theology] **49–56**
Christian Union 93
Christians [See also Anglican Christians, Evangelical Christians, Monophysite church, Nestorian church, Orthodox Christians, Pentecostal Christians, Protestant Christians, Roman Catholic Christians] 23, 30
in Arabia 24–25, 139–140
in the Middle East 3, 156
Christmas 86
Christology [See also Jesus, status of] 6, 44, 50-53, 62, 63, 65, 110, 111–112, 119, 170
Church and society [See also Religion and the state] 150
Church buildings 85, 86–87, 150
Church Fathers 76
Church of the Latter Day Saints [See Mormons]
Cistercian order 113
Clayton, J. 182
Clement of Alexandria 55
Clovis 134
Codex Sinaiticus 40, 46
Coffee 79
Coggins, R. 178
Coliseum 132
Columbus, Christopher 135
Communal emphasis [See Individual, importance of]
Comparative approach 10
Computerisation 42
Congregationalists 114
Conquistadors 126, 135
Constantine 46, 55, 110, 133, 138, 143
Constantinople 110, 111, 129, 134
Constitution of Medina 78
Contraception 151, 163, 175
Conversion, intra-Christian 174
Conversion, intra-Muslim 174
Conversion to Christianity 12, 23, 30, 63, 91, 110, 125, 131, 133, 134, 138, 140-141, 143, **167–169**
Conversion to Islam 5, 8, 42, 63, 68, 88, 125, 127, 128, 129–130, 131, 139–141, 143, 144, **167–169**
Cook, Michael 7–8, 13, 28, 30, 31, 178
Copts 3, 112
Cordoba 117
Corinth 72, 80
Corruption [See Change]
Coulson, N. 179
Council of Chalcedon 52, 63, 111, 112
Council of Churches of Britain and Ireland 117
Council of Constantinople 52
Council of Ephesus 52, 111
Council of European Churches 117
Council of Jamnia 38, 42, 123
Council of Jerusalem 23
Council of Mosques in Bradford 119
Council of Nicaea 52
Counter-Reformation 114
Court, J.M. and K.M. 178

Covenant 51
Cragg, Kenneth 14, 178, 182, 183
Creeds, Christian 49, 53, 62, 64, 78, 87
Creed, Muslim 88, 98
Critical scholarship 7–8, 9–10, 13, 28–29, 43, 45, 147, 155, 157–158, 159, 160, 162, 163
Cromwell, Oliver 100
Crone, Patricia 7–8, 13, 28, 31, 79
Crusades 134, 135, 141
Cupitt, Don 163
Cyril 134

da Gama, Vasco 135
Damascus 68
Daniel 45
Daniel, Norman 144
Danner, Victor 47
Darwin, Charles 149
Da'ūdīs 122
David 18
Davies, P. 178
Davies, R.E. 181
Dawkins, Richard 149
D'Costa, Gavin 165
Dead Sea Scrolls 20, 40
Decius 132
Declaration of Independence, American 147
Deftary, F. 122, 180
Delhi 163
Denny, F.M. 78, 166, 179
de Nobili, Robert 135
Deoband seminary 107, 122
Dependence 159, 166
Descartes, R. 147
Deutero-canonical books 35
Development [See Change]
Diocletian 132
Disciples of Jesus 19–20, 22, 39, 132, 156
Discipline 93–94, 168
Dissent [See Tolerance, Unity and diversity]
Dobbelaere, Karel 174
Doctrine, Christian 49–53, 62
Dominic 114
Dominican order 113–114
Domitian 132
Donatists 141
Double standards, examples of **2–9**, 11, 13–14, 82
Dress of religious leaders, Christian and Muslim 66
Druzes 3, 108
Duchess of Kent 174
Dunn, J.D.G. 46, 63, 178
Dupré, L. 180
Duran, Khalid 144

Easter 86
Eastern Christians [See Orthodox Christians]
Ecclesiastes, Book of 36
Ecclesiasticus/Ben Sirach 38, 51
Ecumenism **117–119**, 123
Edwards, John 12
Egypt 45, 56, 84, 111, 122, 123, 127, 128, 139, 140, 148, 156, 160, 161, 162, 163
Elijah 36
Eliot, T.S. 14
Elisha 36
Elizabeth I 76
Enayat, H. 123, 181
England 112, 115, 134
English language 11
Enlightenment, the 137, 147
Enoch 51
Epistles 35, 39, 72, 85, 156
Erasmus 112
Esposito, J.L. 166, 177, 182
Essenes 18, 20
Esther 40
Ethics, Christian **71–74**, 77, 150-151, 162
Ethics, Muslim 26, 71
Ethiopia 111, 112
Europe, Eastern 134, 150
Europe, Western 137, 141, 142, 149
Eusebius of Caesarea 143
Eutyches 52, 111
Evangelical Christians 2, 115–116, 117, 118, 136, 170
Evans, G.R. 181
Exodus 84
Experience, personal 93, 94, 98, 101, 159, 160

Extremist groups [See also "Fundamentalism", Reform movements] 54, 102, 108
Ezra 38

Fakhry, M. 65, 80, 179
Family [See Relationships between the sexes, Women, position of]
Fanaticism 102
Fasting [See also Ṣawm] 13, 88
Fātiḥa [Opening chapter of Qur'ān] 34
Fāṭimid dynasty 108, 117, 122
Feminism [See also Women] 77
Ferdinand III 144
Ferdinand and Isabella 144
Festivals, Christian 12–13, 86
Festivals, Muslim 12–13, 89, 100
Florida 163
Flügel, G. 46
Force, use of in conversion 125, 126, 129, 133, 134–135, **139–141**
Ford, David 81, 182
Four Languages Heresy 47
Fox, Matthew 174
France 141
Francis of Assisi 114
Franciscan order 113–114
Franks 134
Free will [See Predestination]
Freedom [See also Discipline] 168
Freeman, Anthony 163
French Revolution 147, 150
Friday 89, 90, 99
Fu'ād, King of Egypt 38
Fueck, J. 31
Fuller, Reginald 96
"Fundamentalism" 102, **154–159**, 163, 164–166

Gabrieli, Francesco 30, 143, 178
Gaddafi, Colonel 12
Galerius 132
Galileo 161
Geertz, Clifford 14, 177
Genesis, Book of 36, 149
Geneva 39, 166
Genghis Khan 127
Gerbert, later Pope Sylvester II 61
Germany 6, 96, 113, 115, 134, 159
Ghaznavid dynasty 129, 143
Ghrab, S. 183
Gibb, H.A.R. 160
Gibbelini, R. 143
Gill, Robin 165, 179
Giving [of money] [See also Zakāt] 86, 93
Globalisation 148
Gnostics 54
God [See Monotheism]
Goddard, H.P. 47, 64, 81
Goitein, S.D. 79
Goldziher, I. 179
Gospel accounts, Four 28, 35, 39, 42, 85, 149–150
Gospel of Barnabas 8, 13
Goths 134
Granada 130
Great Schism 111
Greek language 42, 110, 132
Greek philosophy
Christian attitudes to 54–56, 62, 65, 73, 138, 145, 170
Muslim attitudes to 60-62, 65, 69, 71, 100, 127, 138, 145, 170, 172
translation into Arabic 61, 65
translation into Latin 62, 100
Gregory I, Pope 46, 73, 134
Grotius, Hugo 144
Guillaume, Alfred 31
Guinness, Howard 92–95, 101
Gulf Crisis 3, 157
Gulf War [Iran and Iraq] 4
Gunn, David 163

Haddad, Y.Y. 166
Ḥadīth [Tradition] 42, 44, 69–70, 76, 79, 89, 106, 151, 152
Ḥafṣ 38
Ḥajj [Pilgrimage] [See Pilgrimage, Muslim]
Hall, S.G. 64, 179
Halm, H. 180
Hampson, Daphne 81, 180
Ḥanīfs [Arab monotheists] 24–25
Ḥasan al-Baṣrī 58
Ḥasan-i Ṣabbāḥ 122
Hasan, Mushirul 163
Hassan, Rifaat 82

Hastings, Adrian 144
Hawke, Bob 82
Hawkes Bay incident 12
Hebblethwaite, Brian 13
Hebrew scriptures [See Old Testament]
Hebrews, Letter to the 35
Hefner, R.W. 173–174, 182
Hegland, M.E. 101, 164
Heiler, Friedrich 177, 178
Hellenistic culture 50, 54
Herod the Great 84
Heron, A. 182
Hick, John 7, 13
Hijra 26, 30, 67
Hinds, Martin 79
Hinduism 91, 173
Ḥirā, Mount 25
Historical approach 10
Histories/Former Prophets 35, 45
History and relationship to myth 7–8, 22, 30, 149–150, 159
History, views of 148, 156
Ḥizballāh 165
Hodgson, M.G.S. 181, 183
Hollenwegger, Walter 123, 181
Holt, P.M. 143, 181
Holy Spirit 53, 54, 62, 64, 86, 93, 116
Hooker, M.B. 143
Hooker, Morna 81
Hosea 36
Hourani, A.H. 123, 166, 181, 182
Hourani, G.F. 80
Hughes, Gerard 100
Human nature 172, 175
Humphreys, R.S. 31
Hus, Jan 112
Ḥusain, Ṭāhā 162, 165
Hussain, Saddam 12
Huxley, Thomas 149
Hyderabad 144

Ibadan 102
Ibn ‘Abbād 100
Ibn ‘Abbās 68
Ibn ‘Abd al-Wahhāb, Aḥmad 106
Ibn ‘Arabī 100
Ibn ‘Aṭā’ Allāh 100
Ibn Hishām 28
Ibn Isḥāq 28
Ibn Mujāhid 37
Ibn Rushd 62, 65, 161
Ibn Sīnā 61
Ibn Taimiyya 165
Ibrāhīm ibn Adham 100
‘Īd al-fiṭr [Feast of the breaking of the fast] 89
‘Īd al-aḍhā [Feast of the sacrifice] 89
Idealism concerning origins 156, 158
Ideals and realities 8–9, 82, 103, 116–117, 119, 120, 141, 168, 173
Idris 51
Ijmā‘ [Consensus] 69, 70, 79, 158
Ijtihād [Independent reasoning] 151
Ikhwān al-muslimūn [Muslim Brethren] 107, 161, 166
Ilyās, Muḥammad 107
Imam [Shī‘ī leader] 104, 105, 107, 108, 118
Īmān [Faith] 88
Imitation of Christ 73
Imperialism, British and European 106, 120, 135–137, 138, 148, 151, 152–153, 156–157
Inalcik, Halil 143
India 6, 43, 44, 100, 104, 106, 107, 109, 120, 122, 125, 129, 130, 131, 134, 135, 138, 144, 148, 152, 160, 161
Individual, importance of 67, 70, 74, 94–95, 98
Indonesia 109, 130, 131
Indus Valley 127
Industrial Revolution 148, 150
Inquisition [See also Miḥna] 8, 12, 134–135, 161
Intention 73, 81, 98
Inter-Varsity Fellowship 92
Iran [also Persia] 4, 6, 104, 109, 111, 122, 127, 131, 134, 139, 141, 157, 165
Iraq 4, 6, 96, 104, 111, 126, 127
Irenaeus 39
Isaiah 35
Iṣlāḥ [Reformulation] 151–152, 160
Islam [as system] 95, 98
Islam and the West 144, 152–153, 156–157

Islamic Foundation 92, 101
Islamic Revolution 157
Ismā'īl 107
Ismā'īlī Muslims 107–108, 122
Isnād [Chain of transmission] 69
Israel, in Bible 51
Israel, modern nation of 41, 108

Jabriyya 58, 65
Ja'far al-Ṣādiq 118
Jamā'at-i islāmī [Islamic Group] 107, 161, 166
Jamali, Muḥammad Fadhel 96–98, 101
James I 46
Jansen, G.J. 164
Japan 12
Jarasevic, Nermina 77
Jeddah 12
Jehovah's Witnesses 6
Jerba 108
Jeremiah 36
Jerome 43, 47
Jerusalem 19, 22, 24, 38, 50, 55, 65, 83–84, 86, 89, 110, 126, 134
Jesuits 1, 11, 114, 175
Jesus [See also Disciples, Christology] 8, **17–23**, 27–29, 36, 39, 46, 86, 95, 98, 104, 132
  Arrest and trial 21–22, 80
  Ascension 51
  Background 17–19
  Baptism 19
  Birth 19, 30, 51, 86
  Crucifixion and death 22, 30, 50, 85, 86, 150
  Early life 19
  Language of 42
  Messiah? 19, 22, 50
  Miracles 19, 159
  Opposition 20-21
  Originality of 29
  Prophet 71–72
  Redemption through 110
  Resurrection 22, 30, 51, 86, 150
  Sources for 28–29, 31, 35, 149–150
  Status of [See also Christology] 44, 155, 170, 172–173
  Suffering of 97–98
  Teaching [See also Kingdom of God] 17, 19–21, 27, 28, 73, 81, 84
Jesus movement [See also Christian movement] 22–23, 30, 50, 84
Jews [also Judaism] 3, 5, 8, 12, 17–19, 22, 23, 24, 25, 27, 29, 34, 36, 38–39, 42, 45, 49, 50, 51, 54, 58, 68, 69, 71–72, 79, 80, 83–84, 86, 132, 133, 139, 141, 144, 154, 164, 173
Jihād [Struggle] 102
Jinn [Spirits] 83
Jizya [Tribute] 140
Joel 80
John, Gospel according to 53, 79
John of Damascus 73, 112, 123
John of the Cross 91, 100
John the Baptist 19
Johnson, J.T. 102
Johnson, P. 181
Jones, A.H.M. 143
Jones, C. 99, 180
Jonestown 5, 12
Jordan, River 19
Julian of Norwich 91
Jundishapur 55
Justin Martyr 55
Justinian 55
Just War 102

Ka'ba 25, 26, 99
Kabul 12
Kamali, M.H. 179
Kaplan, L. 164–165
Kaptein, N.J.G. 100
Karachi 6, 162
Karadzic, Radovan 12
Katib Celebi 79
Katz, S.D. 182
Kelly, J.N.D. 63, 64
Kelsay, J. 102
Kennedy, J.F. 82
Khadīja 76
Khadīja al-Shahjaniya 76
Khadīja bint al-Baqqāl 76
Khalafallāh, Muḥammad 165
Khān, Sayyid Aḥmad 152, 153, 160
Khawārij 57, 64, 108, 122, 156
Khoja community 122

Khomeini, Ayatollah 157, 164
Kiev 134
King, Ursula 81
Kingdom of God 19, 20, 29, 143
Kings, Books of 36
Kister, M.J. 12
Knappert, Jan 99
Knox, John 165
Kritzeck, James 79
Küng, Hans 14, 80, 81, 163
Kuwait 4

Lambton, A.K.S. 143, 181
Lamentations, Book of 36
Langton, Stephen 39
Lapidus, I.M. 181
Las Casas, Bartholemew 135
Latin America 126
Latin language 110, 150
Latourette, K.S. 181
Law [See Sharī'a, Torah]
Lawrence, B.B. 164, 165
Lazarus-Yafeh, Hava 31, 100
Laylat al-isrā' wa'l-mi'rāj [Night of the journey/ascent of Muḥammad] 89
Leadership of Christian community [See also Papacy, Patriarchs] 53–54, 74–75, 76, 77, 110, 114
Leadership of Muslim community [See also Caliph] 56–57, 75–76, 77, 103, 104, 107, 108
Lebanon 104, 105, 108, 165
Leeds 99, 144
Leicester 92, 100
Leonard, Graham 174
Letters from prison **95–98**
Levels of faith 9
Levtzion, R. 144, 182
Levy, Reuben 81
Lewis, Bernard 31, 64, 143, 181
Lewis, I.M. 143
Lewis, Philip 124
Liberalism 141–142, **159–161**, 163, 166
Lindbeck, George 14
Lindsey, Hal 47
Lings, Martin 30, 178
Little, D.P. 166
Loades, Ann 81, 180
Logos 44, 47, 51, 52
London 162
Los Angeles 92
Louth, Andrew 100, 180
Lull, Ramon 91
Luther, Martin 114, 164
Lutherans 96, 114

Maccabees 18
Macdonald, D.B. 179
Macedonia 77
Mackenzie, P. 177
Macquarrie, J. 182
Mahdī [Guided One] 104, 121
Maḥfūz, Naguib 163
Makdisi, G. 65
Malacca 130
Malaysia 130
Manāt 24, 25
Marty, M.E. 164
Martyrdom 101, 105, 106, 132
Marx, Karl 2
Mary 44
Masoretes 39
Maurice, F.D. 161–162
Mawdūdī, Abu'l-A'lā 107, 161, 166
Mawlid al-nabī [Birthday of Muḥammad] 89, 100
McGuinn, B. 180
McLellan, David 11
McManners, J. 181
Mecca 12, 13, 25–26, 27, 34, 37, 68, 88, 89, 90, 99, 126, 153
Medina [See also Yathrib] 12, 37, 67, 69, 126, 153
Medina, F. de B. de 100, 144
Mehmet II 129
Mernissi, Fatima 81, 82, 180
Messiah, concept of 18–19, 21–22, 28, 30, 104, 121
Metcalf, B.D. 122, 180
Methodists 115
Methodius 134
Meyendorff, J. 180
Michel, Tom 175
Middle East [See also Arab world]
Christians in 3, 138, 139–142
Events in as fulfilment of prophecy 41, 46–47

Miḥna [Inquisition] 60
Mihrāb [Niche] 90
Milan 74
Minbar [Pulpit] 90
Ministry of the Faithful 85, 87
Ministry of the Word 85
Minorities, Christian 2–4, 138, **139–142**, 145
Minorities, Muslim 2–4, 118–119, **139–142**, 144, 145
Mishnah 71
Miskawayh 71
Mission, Christian [See also Spread of Christianity] 2, 12, 23, 117, 135–137
Mission, Muslim [See also Spread of Islam] 2
Mitchell, R.P. 166
Modernism, Christian 160
Modernism, Islamic 66, 152, 160, 161
Modernity **147–149**, 156, 163, 170-171
Moghul Empire 120, 129
Moltmann, Jorgen 101
Mombasa 128
Momen, M. 121, 180
Monasticism, Christian 91, 113, 123
Mongol Empire 127
Monophysite church 111, 112
Monotheism, Christian [See also Trinity] 1–2, 17, 27–28, 50, 53, 64, 65, 99, 103, 170, 172, 174
Monotheism, Islamic 24–25, 26, 27, 27–28, 29, 59, 60, 64, 65, 88, 103, 126, 171, 172, 174
Montanists 54
Montefiore, Hugh 30
Moral Theology [See Ethics, Christian]
Morality [See Ethics, Sharīʻa, Torah]
Moravian movement 115
Mormon church 6, 116
Morocco 13, 109
Mortimer, E. 182
Moscow 134
Moses 21, 36
Mosque buildings 90
Muḥammad 5, 12, 17, **24–27**, 27–29, 36–37, 41, 56, 57, 59, 62, 67, 68, 76, 79, 88, 89, 100, 103, 152, 158, 162, 163, 170
Background 24–25
Birth 24
Call to prophethood 25–26
Death 27, 126, 127
Early life 25
Example of 69, 70, 77, 89, 94, 153
Hijra [Migration from Mecca] 26, 30, 67
Leader of community in Yathrib 26–27
Opposition 26
Originality of 29
Sources for 28–29, 31
Status of 44, 47, 107, 171, 172–173
Teaching 26, 27, 28, 33, 36–37
Muḥarram 105
Mujaddid [Renewer of Islam] 151, 164
Mujahidin 156, 157
Mullah [Shīʻī leader] 104
Murad, Khurram 92–95, 101
Muratorian Fragment 39
Murjiʻa 58
Mūsā 107
Muslim [Collector of Ḥadīth] 69
Muslims [See also Shīʻī Muslims, Sufi Muslims, Sunnī Muslims] 26
Muslim-Christian Research Group 45, 165, 179
Muslim community, boundaries of 57–58, 78, 108–109, 155, 158
Muslim community, establishment of **24–27**, 27–29, 156
Muslim Students' Association 92, 93
Muslim thought, early [See also Theology] **56–62**
Muslim Institute [London] 11
Muslim World League 118
Mustaʻlīs 122
Muʻtazila 59, 60
Mutual ignorance of Christians and Muslims **1–2**, 10, 11, 33, 45
Mysticism **90-92**
Mystics, Christian 76, 81, 90-92, 98, 100
Mystics, Muslim [See Sufi Muslims]
Myth and relationship to history 7–8, 22, 30, 149–150, 159

Najrān 24
Namier, Lewis 123
Nasr, S.H. 174, 177, 180, 182
Nasr, S.V.R. 166
Nathan, Isaac 39
Natural disasters, interpretation of 5–6
Nazir-Ali, Michael 143
Nebuchadnezzar 84
Nehemiah 38
Neill, Stephen 143, 181
Nero 132
Nestorian church 55, 111, 112, 134
Nestorius 52, 63, 111
New religious movements [in modern West] 6
New Testament 34, 35, 39, 40, 42, 43, 53, 54, 72, 73, 76, 77, 79, 84, 86, 115, 149–150, 159, 172–173
Nicene Creed 64
Nicholson, R.A. 100
Nielsen, J.S. 124
Nigeria 12, 102
Nile Valley 128
Nineham, Dennis 14, 177
Niyya [See Intention]
Nizārīs 122
North Africa 55, 122, 127, 128, 132, 138, 141
Northern Ireland 4, 8, 165
Nuclear weapons 151, 164
Nusairīs 108

Old Testament/Hebrew scriptures 34, 35, 36, 38–39, 40, 41, 43, 46, 51, 53, 71, 84, 99, 123, 141, 159, 162
Oman 108
Optimism 148–149, 160, 164, 172
Opus Dei 165
Organisation of the Islamic Conference 118
Original sin 172
Origins [See Christian origins, Muslim community, establishment of]
Orientalism 11, 158
Originality of messages of Jesus and Muḥammad 29
Orthodox Christians 3, 4, 12, 45, 65, 81, 85, 87, **109–112**, 117, 118, 119, 123
Orthodoxy and orthopraxy 78, 87
Ottoman Turks 111, 129, 138, 143
Oxford 149

Pachomius 123
Pacifism 115
Pakistan 5, 6, 77, 82, 104, 127, 129, 130, 162, 166, 167, 173
Palacios, M.A. 100
Palestine 17–19, 20, 21, 22, 23, 27–28, 39, 84, 86, 127, 132, 138, 139
Papacy 112, 113, 114, 115, 117, 123, 160, 164, 174
Paret, R. 183
Paris 39
Parkes, J. 181
Passover 84, 86
Patriarchs of Christian Church 54, 110
Paul 22–23, 30, 35, 36, 39, 42, 46, 58, 65, 72, 73, 75, 80, 102, 125, 132, 156
Peacocke, Arthur 149, 182
Pentateuch [See Torah]
Pentecost 86
Pentecostal Christians 116, 123, 170
Persecution 22, 54, 132, 137, 143
Persia [See Iran]
Persians 63, 66, 100, 156
Person/book relationship 44
Pessimism 148–149, 164, 172
Peters, F.E. 31, 178
Pfander, Karl 7
Pharisees 18, 20, 21, 22, 71, 72
Phenomenology 9, 10, 45
Philip II 137
Philippines 109, 130, 137, 141
Philo 51
Philosophy [See Greek philosophy]
Pickthall, M.M. 47
Pietist movement 115, 136
Pilate, Pontius 22, 80
Pilgrimage [Christian] 86
Pilgrimage [Muslim] 12, 88, 89, 99, 106
Pisa 117
Plassey, battle of 148
Plato 54
Polygamy 75–76, 143, 152

Polytheism 24–25, 27–28, 64, 99
Portugese explorers 135
Poston, L. 167, 173, 174, 182
Powell, Averil 13, 143
Predestination 18, 58, 59, 65, 119, 135
Pre-Islamic poetry 162
Presbyterians 114
Prophecy 26, 29, 34, 36, 41, 46–47
"Prophecy Today" [Christian magazine] 12
Prophets, Former/Histories 35, 38, 45
Prophets, Later/Latter 35, 38, 45
Protestant Christians [See also Baptists, Calvinists, Congregationalists, Lutherans, Methodists, Presbyterians, Radical Reformation, Reformation] 3, 39, 43, 45, 81, 85, 87, 92, 105, 112–113, 114–115, 117, 118, 119, 121, 122, 135, 150, 151, 154, 155, 160, 165, 173, 174
Proverbs, Arabic 100
Proverbs, Book of 36
Psalms, Book of 36, 83
Pye, Michael 14

Qadariyya 59, 65
Qāḍī [Judge] 68, 70
Qādisiyya, battle of 127
Qiyās [Analogy] 69, 70, 79
Quakers 122
Quraish tribe 56
Qur'ān 8, 26, 28, 29, **33–44**, 45, 51, 58, 60, 69, 70, 78, 89, 90, 106, 121, 139, 151, 152, 158, 162, 163, 174
  Arabic script of 37
  Cartoon version of 47
  Commentary on 37, 157–158
  Comparison with Bible 29, 40, 43–44
  Computerisation of text 42
  Compilation and editing **36–40**, 45–46
  Contents and form **33–36**
  Created or uncreated? 41, 59–60, 65, 119, 154–155, 157
  Dictated by God? 41, 47, 154, 162, 170
  Division into chapters and verses 37, 46
  "External validation of" 41–42
  Interpretation of 41, 43, 59, 76, 77, 106, 152, 155
  Later developments in understanding **40-43**
  Legal material 67–68
  Manuscripts of 40, 46
  Methods of study of 43, 90, 147, 155, 157–158, 162, 163
  Oral transmission of 36–37
  Order/arrangement of 34–35
  Role in Islam 44, 155, 172–173
  Royal Egyptian edition of 38
  Science and 41–42, 47
  Translation of 43, 99
  Variant readings of 37, 38
  1:6 69
  2:228 75
  2:255 59
  2:256 139
  2:282 76
  3:64 139
  4:3 75–76
  4:11 76
  4:34 75
  4:58 70
  4:171 2
  5:71–72 2
  5:90 79
  6:151–153 80
  12:2 43
  17:22–39 80
  24:30-31 76
  33:21 70
  33:33 70
  33:35 75
  33:59 76
  37:35 88
  40:21 59
  43:3–4 59
  45:18 69
  48:29 88
  49:13 11
  50:16 171
  51:56 83
Quṭb, Sayyid 161, 166

Rabbinic Judaism 80
Rābi'a al-'Adawiya 76
Radical Reformation 114–115

Rahbar, Daud 174
Rahman, Fazlur 162, 166, 178, 182
Rahnema, A. 166, 182
Raitt, J. 180
Ramaḍān 13, 88, 89, 90
Ramet, S.P. 82
Ramsey, P. 179
Ra'y [Individual opinion] 70
Reconquista [Spain] 5, 130, 134, 138, 141
Red Sea 128
Reform movements 106–107, 112–113, 119–120, 128, 151–152, 156
Reformation [Protestant] 43, 64–65, 112–113, 114–115, 120, 123, 135, 164
Relationship between the two traditions **167–173**
Relationships between the sexes 93, 94, 95, 151
Religion and the state [See also Church and society] 20-21, 27, 54, 55, 58, 59, 64, 70-71, 74, 81, 110, 111, 114, 115, 118, 133, 135–136, 147, 150, 153–154, 156–157, 158–159, 169, 170
Religious thought [See Christian thought, early, Greek philosophy, Muslim thought, early]
Renaissance, 12th century 55
Repentance 19, 26, 34
Republican Brothers 154
Resurrection 18, 22, 30
Revelation, Book of 35, 42–43, 99
Revelation, concepts of 44, 45, 160
Revolution in name of religion [See also "Fundamentalism"] 156, 158
Ricci, Matthew 135
Richard, Y. 180
Riesebrodt, M. 165
Rippin, Andrew 79, 82, 99, 165, 182
Robbins, T. 12
Robinson, Francis 122, 181
Rodinson, Maxime 30, 178
Rogerson, J. 178
Roman Catholic Christians 3, 4, 45, 81, 85, 87, **109–114**, 117, 118, 119, 120, 121, 123, 135, 150, 151, 158, 160, 163, 165, 173, 174, 175
Roman Empire 17–18, 20-21, 22, 23, 24, 27–28, 49, 54, 55, 62, 72, 79, 80, 85, 91, 109, 111, 115, 125, 132, 133, 134
Romans 63, 66
Rome 23, 58, 86, 110, 112, 117, 123, 132, 134
Ronda 100
Rosenthal, Franz 65, 179
Rouse, R. 181
Rowland, C. 178
Rūmī, Jalāl al-dīn 91, 100
Runciman, S. 181
Rupp, E.G. 46, 178
Rushdie, Salman 8, 44, 119, 163
Russia 134, 156
Russian Revolution 150
Ruth 45
Ruthven, Malise 47

Sabbath 20, 84, 85
Ṣabr [Patience] 94
Sachedina, A.A. 121, 180
Sacrifice, Christian and Muslim concepts of [See also Martyrdom] **92–95**, 98, 110
Sadducees 18, 20, 21
Safaga 12
Safavid dynasty 104
Sahara desert 128
Sahas, Daniel 123
Said, Edward 11
Ṣalāt [Prayer] 88, 89, 90, 94, 99
Salmon, P. 31
Salvation 160, 168
Samuel 80
Samuel, Books of 35
Sanders, E.P. 29, 31, 63, 80, 178
Sanhedrin 21
Sarajevo 12, 77
Sardar, Z. 144, 183
Sassanian Persian Empire 126
"Satanic Verses" 8, 13, 165
Sa'udi Arabia 7, 12, 82, 118, 148, 157
Savory, R.M. 183
Ṣawm [Fasting] [See also Fasting] 88
Saxony 126, 133
Scandinavia 114
Schimmel, A. 47, 178, 180

Schleiermacher, Friedrich 159
Schools of Law, Muslim 106, 118, 121
Schubel, V.J. 121
Science and religion 147–148, 149, 151, 152, 160
  Relationship to Qur'ān 41–42, 47
Scotland 114, 165
Scriptures [See also Bible, Qur'ān] 17, 29, **33–44**, 90, 147, 154, 155, 170
Sea of Faith movement 163
Second Vatican Council 117, 150, 160
Secularisation 137, 147
Seljuk Turks 129
Senegal 109
Septuagint 42, 45, 50, 51, 123
Serjeant, R.B. 78
Sermon on the Mount 73, 82
Servetus, Michael 166
Shāh Walīullāh 43
Shahāda [Declaration of faith] 88
Sharī'a [Islamic Law] [See also Schools of Law] 18, **67–71**, 74, 78, 79, 80, 106, 118, 127, 151, 153, 157, 169
Sheikh, Bilquis 174
Shepard, William 165
Sherif, F. 178
Sherry, P. 182
Shī'a [See Shī'ī Muslims]
Shiels, W.J. 12
Shī'ī Muslims [See also Ismā'īlī Muslims, Zaidī Muslims] 6, 57, 58, 64, 79, 89, 99, **103–108**, 109, 114, 118, 119, 121, 122, 123, 165, 173, 174
Sicily 100
Ṣiddīq, Yūsuf 47
Siddiqi, M.Z. 179
Siddiqui, Kalim 11
Simeon 100
Sins, Seven 73
Sīra [Biography of Muḥammad] 28
Sivan, E. 165
Slavs 134
Slomp, Jan 13
Smart, Ninian 14, 177, 182
Smith, Wilfred Cantwell 14, 45, 100, 177, 182, 183
Smith, William Robertson 161–162
Society of Friends [See Quakers]
Socrates 54
Solomon 83
Somalia 128
Sources for Christian origins 28–29, 30, 31
Sources for establishment of Muslim community 28–29, 30, 31
South Africa 4, 8, 141
South America 116
South-East Asia 125, 130, 131, 143
South Korea 137
Southern, R.W. 61, 65, 144
Spain 5, 12, 62, 91, 100, 127, 130, 134, 138, 141, 144–145
Spanish explorers 130, 135
Spectrum of opinion in both traditions **169–173**, 174
Spirituality, Christian and Muslim [See also Warfare, spiritual] **90-98**, 144
Spread of Christianity 125–126, **131–138**
Spread of Islam 27, 30, 67, 91, 102, **125–131**
Statistics of Christians and Muslims 1, 136
Stephanus, Robert 39
Stern, S.M. 66
Student Christian Movement 102, 166
Subject peoples [See also Minorities] **139–142**
Submission to God 26, 29
Sudan 4, 128, 154
Suez campaign [1956/1376] 3
Suffering, understanding of 96–98, 101, 105–106
Sufi Muslims 18, 76, 90-92, 100, 102, 106, 107, 114, 123, 125, 127, 128, 130, 166, 172
Sugirtharajah, R. 143
Sulaimānīs 122
Sunday 85–86, 133
Sunna [Custom] 67, 69, 103, 158
Sunnī Muslims 6, 69, 79, 89, 99, **103–108**, 109, 118, 119, 121, 123, 154, 157, 158, 173, 174

Swartz, M. 31
Synagogue, Jewish 17, 50, 83, 84, 99, 132
Syria 78, 108, 111, 122, 126, 127, 138, 139, 140
Syriac language 43, 112
Syrjänen, S. 167, 173, 174, 182

Tablīghī jamā'at 107
Ṭāhā, Maḥmūd 154, 164
Tajdīd [Renewal] 151, 164
Takfir wa'l-hijra group 122
Talbi, M. 183
Ṭarīqa [Sufi groups] 106
Tarsus 23
Tawḥīd [See Monotheism, Islamic]
Taylor, R.L. 179
Ta'ziya [Passion play] 105, 121
Telford 82
Temple, Jewish 17, 18, 19, 20, 24, 50, 83, 84, 99
Ten Commandments 71, 72
Tertullian 55, 65, 132
Teutonic Knights 134
Thailand 166
Thatcher, Margaret 82
Theissen, G. 30, 178
Theodosius 74
Theology [See also Christian thought, early, Muslim thought, early] 78, 79, 110, 119, 127
  Schools of, Christian 112
  Schools of, Muslim 106
Thessalonica 74
Thompson, Ahmad 12
Tillich, Paul 7
Timbuktu 128
Tinsley, E.J. 182
Tiridates 133
Tolerance 6, 8, 54, 132, **139–142**, 144–145, **161–163**
Torah [Jewish Law] 18, 20, 21, 22, 35, 36, 38, 51, 71–72, 73, 162
Tribalism 24, 25, 26, 27, 67
Trimingham, J.S. 143
Trinity 53, 59, 60, 63–64, 116, 166
Tritton, A.S. 181
Tunisia 96, 108
Turkey 130, 138, 148, 154, 164
Turks [See also Ottoman Turks, Seljuk Turks] 128, 129, 131, 143
Tyndale, William 47

Uganda 128
'Ulama' [Sunnī religious scholars] 60, 104
'Umar ibn al-Khaṭṭāb 27, 30, 37, 56, 125, 126
'Umar ibn Sa'd 105
Umayyad clan/dynasty 56, 57, 58, 60, 68, 105, 117
Umma [Community] [See Unity and diversity]
Unitarian church 6, 116
United Nations 144
United States of America 12, 116, 131, 137, 144, 148, 154, 164, 165, 166
Unity and diversity 5–6, 120, 122–123
  In Christian church 52, 103, **109–117**, 123, 135, 155–156, 169–173
  In Muslim community **103–109**, 116–117, 155–156, 169–173
Universalism, claims of 23, 30-31, 42–43, 50, 80, 131
Universities and Colleges Christian Fellowship 93, 100
University [as Islamic institution] 65–66
Urvoy, D. 66
'Uthmān 27, 37, 46, 56

Vahiduddin, S. 183
Van Der Leeuw, G. 169, 174
Vander Werff, L.L. 143
Vermes, Geza 29, 31
Vidler, A. 182
Vienna 138
Virtues, Seven 73
Vladimir 134, 143
Voll, J.O. 182
von Grunebaum, G.E. 121, 180

Waco 5–6
Waddams, H. 179
Wahhābī movement 106, 107
Wainwright, G. 99, 180
Wansbrough, John 8

Ware, K. 143, 181
Warfare, spiritual 102
Wars of Religion 6, 113, 135, 144
Watt, William Montgomery 13, 30, 46, 65, 121, 175, 178, 179, 183
Wesley, John 115
West, Muslims in the [See also Islam and the West, Imperialism, Western] 3–4, 92, 118–119, 131, 142, 166, 167
Whitefield, George 115
Widengren, G. 46
Wilberforce, Samuel 149
Wiles, Maurice 46
Wisdom 51
Wisdom of Solomon 51
Wogaman, J.P. 179
Women, position of [See also Relationships between the sexes] 20, 21, **74–78**, 81, 82, 150, 156, 157, 168, 170, 174
World Council of Churches 117, 123
Worship, Christian **83–87**, 89, 98, 99, 110, 112, 150
Worship, Jewish 83–84, 85, 89, 99
Worship, Muslim [See also Pilgrimage, Muslim] 1, **87–90**, 98, 99, 109, 121
Writings 35, 36, 38, 45, 51
Wycliffe, John 112

Ximenes, Cardinal 112

Yarmūk, battle of 127
Yarnold, E. 99, 180
Yates, T. 181
Yathrib [See also Medina] 24, 26–27, 34, 67, 68, 69, 126
Yazīd 57, 105
Yemen 79, 108, 122, 179
Young, Frances 63, 64, 81
Young Men's Muslim Association 101
Young, W.G. 143
Yugoslavia [See also Bosnia] 77, 82

Zaehner, R.C. 26, 30
Zaidī Muslims 108
Zakāt [Almsgiving] 88
Zanzibar 128
Zealots 18, 20, 21
Zirker, H. 165
Zoroastrianism 91, 139